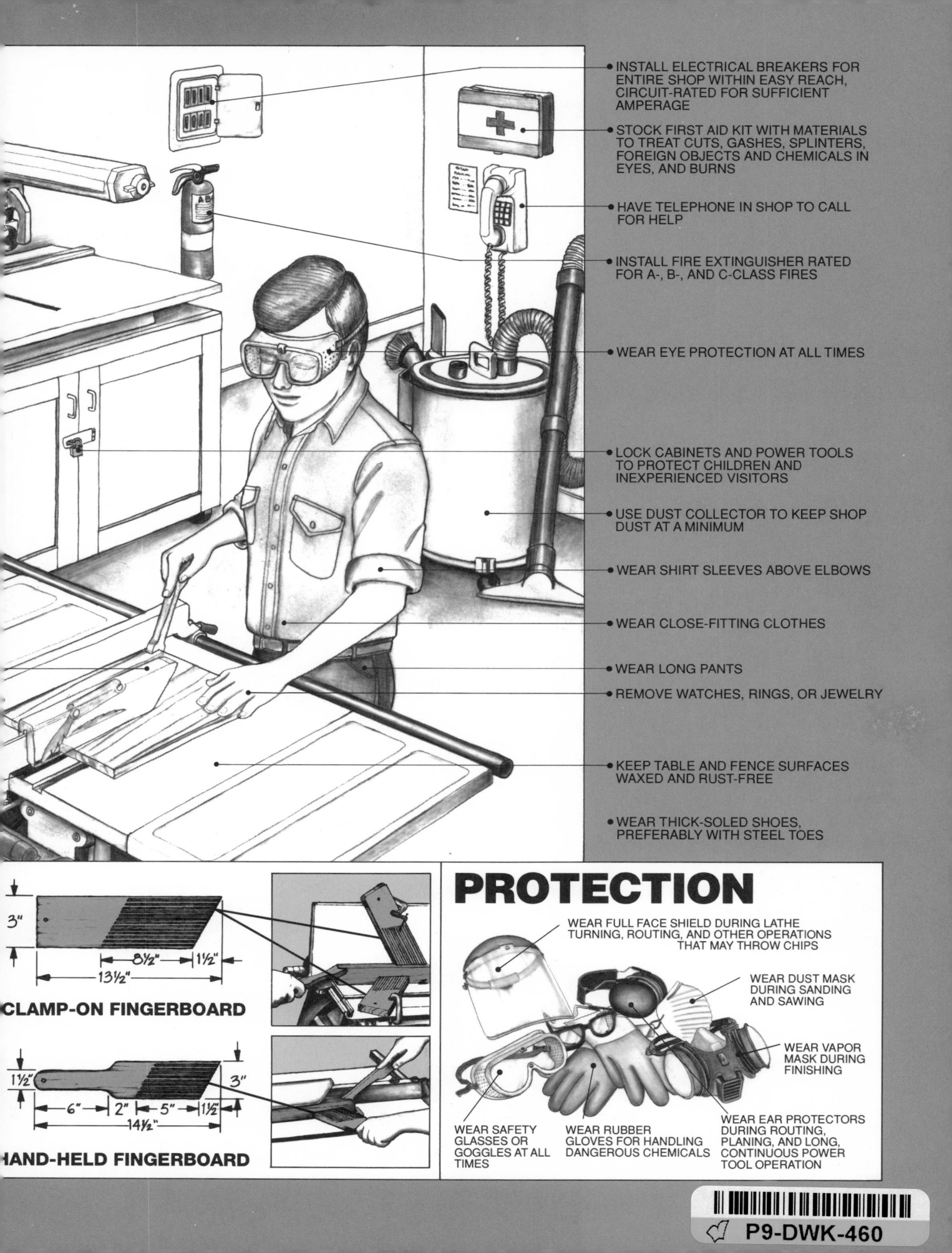

INSTALL ELECTRICAL BREAKERS FOR ENTIRE SHOP WITHIN EASY REACH, CIRCUIT-RATED FOR SUFFICIENT AMPERAGE

STOCK FIRST AID KIT WITH MATERIALS TO TREAT CUTS, GASHES, SPLINTERS, FOREIGN OBJECTS AND CHEMICALS IN EYES, AND BURNS

HAVE TELEPHONE IN SHOP TO CALL FOR HELP

INSTALL FIRE EXTINGUISHER RATED FOR A-, B-, AND C-CLASS FIRES

WEAR EYE PROTECTION AT ALL TIMES

LOCK CABINETS AND POWER TOOLS TO PROTECT CHILDREN AND INEXPERIENCED VISITORS

USE DUST COLLECTOR TO KEEP SHOP DUST AT A MINIMUM

WEAR SHIRT SLEEVES ABOVE ELBOWS

WEAR CLOSE-FITTING CLOTHES

WEAR LONG PANTS

REMOVE WATCHES, RINGS, OR JEWELRY

KEEP TABLE AND FENCE SURFACES WAXED AND RUST-FREE

WEAR THICK-SOLED SHOES, PREFERABLY WITH STEEL TOES

3"

8½" — 1½"

13½"

CLAMP-ON FINGERBOARD

1½"

6" — 2" — 5" — 1½"

3"

14½"

HAND-HELD FINGERBOARD

PROTECTION

WEAR FULL FACE SHIELD DURING LATHE TURNING, ROUTING, AND OTHER OPERATIONS THAT MAY THROW CHIPS

WEAR DUST MASK DURING SANDING AND SAWING

WEAR VAPOR MASK DURING FINISHING

WEAR EAR PROTECTORS DURING ROUTING, PLANING, AND LONG, CONTINUOUS POWER TOOL OPERATION

WEAR SAFETY GLASSES OR GOGGLES AT ALL TIMES

WEAR RUBBER GLOVES FOR HANDLING DANGEROUS CHEMICALS

THE WORKSHOP COMPANION®

USING THE TABLE SAW

TECHNIQUES FOR BETTER WOODWORKING

by Nick Engler

Rodale Press
Emmaus, Pennsylvania

Printed in the United States of America on acid-free ∞, recycled paper ♲

If you have any questions or comments concerning this book, please write:
    Rodale Press
    Book Reader Service
    33 East Minor Street
    Emmaus, PA 18098

About the Author: Nick Engler is an experienced woodworker, writer, and teacher. He worked as a luthier for many years, making traditional American musical instruments before he founded *Hands On!* magazine. Today, he is a contributing editor to *Workbench* magazine and has written over 20 books on the wood arts. He teaches woodworking at the University of Cincinnati.

Series Editor: Jeff Day
Editors: Roger Yepsen
            Kenneth Burton
Copy Editor: Sarah Dunn
Graphic Designer: Linda Watts
Graphic Artists: Mary Jane Favorite
                    Chris Walendzak
Photographer: Karen Callahan
Cover Photographer: Mitch Mandel
Proofreader: Hue Park
Typesetting by Computer Typography, Huber Heights, Ohio
Interior and endpaper illustrations by Mary Jane Favorite
Produced by Bookworks, Inc., West Milton, Ohio

Library of Congress Cataloging-in-Publication Data

Engler, Nick.
    Using the table saw/by Nick Engler.
        p.   cm. — (The workshop companion)
    Includes index.
    ISBN 0–87596–127–4   hardcover
    ISBN 0-87596-609-8 paperback
    1. Circular saws.   2. Woodwork.   I. Title   II. Series.
TT186.E544   1991
684'.083—dc20   91–33469
                                            CIP

Special Thanks to:

Brown & Kroger Printing Company
Dayton, Ohio

Delta International Machinery Corp.
Pittsburgh, Pennsylvania

Excalibur Machine & Tool Co.
Lewiston, New York

Garrett Wade Company, Inc.
New York, New York

HTC Products, Inc.
Royal Oaks, Michigan

In-Line Industries
Webster, Massachusetts

JDS Company
Columbia, South Carolina

Powermatic
McMinnville, Tennessee

Ryobi America Corp.
Anderson, South Carolina

Shopsmith, Inc.
Dayton, Ohio

Wertz Hardware
West Milton, Ohio

12   14   16   18   20   19   17   15   13   hardcover
    4   6   8   10   9   7   5   3   paperback

CONTENTS

TECHNIQUES

PROJECTS

TECHNIQUES

1

TABLE SAWS AND ACCESSORIES

Few tools have revolutionized a craft as much as table saws have changed woodworking. These saws saved tedious hand work and — more importantly — made precise copies of wooden parts. Their ability to reproduce parts quickly and accurately not only affected how furniture and other woodenware was built but also transformed woodworking design.

The table saw first appeared around 1800, although historians disagree on who invented it. Some credit a German craftsman, Gervenius; others think that it was developed simultaneously by several different people in Europe and America. The story I find most interesting was told to me by the late Brother Theodore (Ted) Johnson, a Shaker scholar and member of the Sabbathday Lake, Maine, Shaker community.

According to Brother Ted, the idea popped into the head of Sister Tabitha Babbitt as she sat at her spinning wheel at the Watervliet, New York, community. (Sister Tabitha, it seems, was from an inventive family; her brother developed "Babbitt metal," an alloy that is still used in bearings and bushings.) Sister Tabitha happened to be looking out the window at two Shaker brothers as they bucked firewood with a two-man saw. She marveled at how much more efficient her revolving wheel was than their reciprocating saw. Why couldn't the brothers simply mount saw teeth on a wheel?

She asked them, and they decided to try it. They snipped a crude circular saw blade from tin, mounted the tin blade on an arbor, and fastened the arbor to a workbench. Spinning the arbor with a hand crank, they found that a circular motion cut much more efficiently than a traditional straight-line, back-and-forth motion. The brothers soon installed an improved version in a water-powered mill to cut siding and flooring to size — the first recorded circular saw in America. From these humble beginnings evolved the table saw.

Choosing a Table Saw

For almost two centuries, the table saw has remained a simple machine. There are only four crucial components, the same four that comprised the original invention — a table, a circular saw blade, an arbor, and some means of powering the arbor. However, there have been several useful developments along the way. For example, most modern table saws also have a *fence* and a *miter gauge* to guide the wood past the blade, a *blade carriage* to adjust the angle and height of the blade in relation to the table, and a *blade guard* to protect the operator. (SEE FIGURE 1-1.)

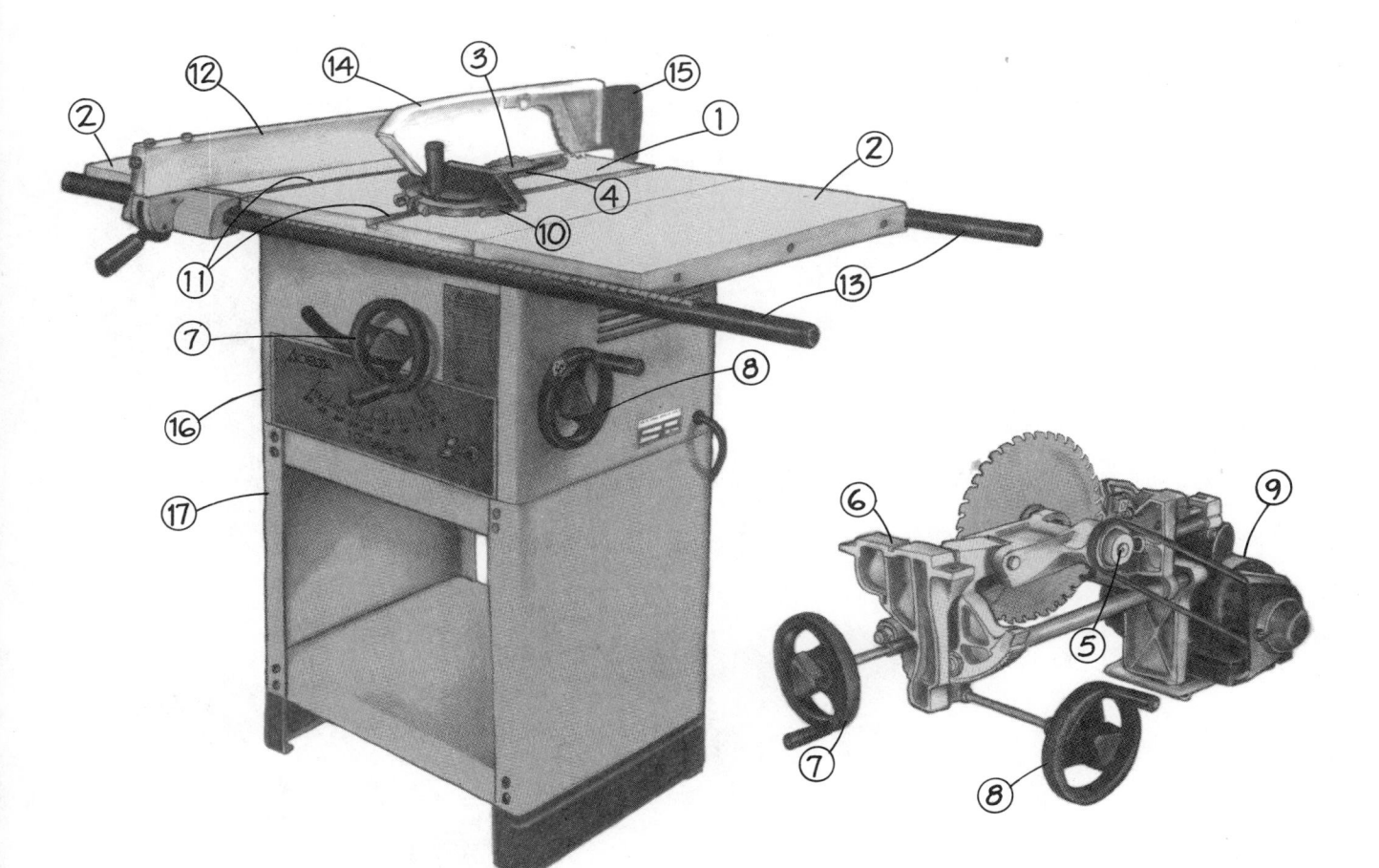

1-1 The most distinguishing feature of the table saw is, of course, the large *table* (1). This table is often further enlarged by *table extensions* (2) on either side. A *circular saw blade* (3) protrudes through a removable *table insert* (4) set flush with the table surface. Removing the insert allows access to the *arbor* (5), the shaft on which the blade is mounted. The arbor is, in turn, mounted in a *blade carriage* (6), a mechanism that changes the blade height and angle.

To raise or lower the blade, turn the *elevation crank* (7), usually located toward the front of the saw. To change the blade angle, turn the *tilt crank* (8), usually located to one side. The blade and arbor are powered by an electric *motor* (9), located beneath or just behind the table. When cutting across the grain, a *miter gauge* (10) guides the wood. The gauge travels in one of two *miter gauge slots* (11) that are ground into the table on either side of the blade. When cut-

ting with the grain, a *rip fence* (12) guides the wood. This fence is mounted on *fence rails* (13) in the front and back of the saw. Whether crosscutting or ripping, a *saw guard* (14) protects you from injury. The guard is often mounted on a *splitter* (15), which keeps the wood from pinching the blade after it's cut. The components underneath the table saw are enclosed in the *saw body* (16), and the entire assembly usually rests on a *stand* (17).

There are several different ways in which the basic components of a modern table saw can be arranged. The configuration of these components determines the *type* of saw.

On a *bench saw,* the motor and the blade carriage are encased in the saw body. (*SEE FIGURE 1-2.*) These are "direct-drive" table saws — the blade is mounted directly on the motor shaft. Bench saws usually have a blade capacity between 8 and 10 inches. The body may be mounted on a stand, or simply clamped to a workbench.

The motor of a *contractor's saw* is mounted behind the table, making it easier to disassemble the saw and transport it from one building site to another. The motor is connected to the arbor by pulleys and one or more V-belts. (*SEE FIGURE 1-3.*) The V-belt helps to isolate motor vibrations so they don't reach the blade. With more room under the table, the blade carriage can be bigger and beefier, and the massive components further absorb vibrations from the saw. As a result, the blade runs smoother and truer. These saws usually mount 9- or 10-inch-diameter blades.

1-2 This bench saw is small and light enough to be picked up and stored in a cabinet or on a shelf. When you want to use it, take it out of storage and clamp it to a workbench.

1-3 Of the three basic types of table saws, the contractor's saw is the most popular — perhaps because it's a good compromise between quality and cost. Some manufacturers use the same saw table and blade carriage in their contractor's saw as they do in their cabinet saw, but skimp on the stand, motor, and drive train to bring down the cost. Because the table and carriage are the most important parts, you still get a good, basic saw for your money.

Hanging the motor off the back of the saw is okay on an open building site where there's lots of room, but it takes up precious space in a shop. A *cabinet saw's* motor is mounted beneath the saw body, encased in the stand. *(SEE FIGURE 1-4.)* This configuration not only saves room, it's also better balanced because the weight of the motor is directly beneath the table. This, together with the mass of the enclosed stand, makes the tool less top-heavy and more stable. Some cabinet saws have a larger blade capacity as well, mounting blades 10 inches or more in diameter.

In addition to the basic types — bench saw, contractor's saw, and cabinet saw — there are several miscellaneous configurations:

■ *Miniature table saws* are downsized versions of bench saws. They mount a blade less than 8 inches in diameter.

■ *Tilting-table saws,* such as the Inca, some multipurpose tools (see page 6), and some older makes, use tilting tables rather than tilting arbors. *(SEE FIGURE 1-5.)*

1-4 Cabinet saws are top-of-the-line models — massive, accurate, and powerful. Although they may look top-heavy, they aren't. Because there is so much weight in the base, they are much more stable than stand-mounted bench saws or contractor's saws.

1-5 Because a tilting-table saw doesn't have its tilting mechanism on the blade carriage, a beefy carriage can be accommodated under even a rather small saw, thus increasing the accuracy. The disadvantages are that the wood tends to creep downhill when the table is tilted, and it's impossible to miter long boards.

■ *Multipurpose tools* such as the Shopsmith, the Kity, and the Robland, usually include a table saw in their list of "tool modes." (*SEE FIGURE 1-6.*) The Shopsmith, for example, serves as a disc sander, lathe, horizontal boring machine, drill press, or table saw.

■ *Sliding-carriage saws* can best be described as upside-down radial arm saws. (*SEE FIGURE 1-7.*) By pull-

ing a handle, you can slide the entire blade carriage and motor assembly back and forth under the table.

■ *Rolling-table saws* have one of the table extensions mounted on rails so it rolls back and forth. (*SEE FIGURE 1-8.*) This enables you to use the entire extension to guide the wood when cutting across the grain.

1-6 **The tables on most multi-**purpose tools are smaller than you'd like, but surprisingly accurate and capable. Some of these tools, particularly the Shopsmith and its look-alikes, have a tilting table rather than a tilting arbor.

1-7 **A sliding-carriage saw gives** you two ways to cut across the grain. Use the miter gauge to guide the work-piece as you would on a standard table saw, or hold the wood on the table and pull the blade through it.

1-8 The left table extension is movable on most rolling-table saws, since most woodworkers are right-handed. To crosscut with the saw, simply place the wood on the movable extension and slide it past the blade.

Each of these configurations, as you can see, has advantages and disadvantages. There is no one optimal arrangement for a table saw; the best saw for you will depend on the size of your shop, the sort of woodworking you like to do, and the tool you feel comfortable with. When purchasing a table saw, carefully match the individual features with your own requirements.

Materials — The materials from which a table saw is made will tell you a lot about its quality. On the better saws, the table and blade carriage are made from cast iron or anodized cast aluminum. Cast iron is considered the best material because it's massive and wears well. Anodizing will make aluminum hard enough to resist wear, but it doesn't add weight. Table saws made from stamped steel or plastic are on the low end of the scale, and those made from untreated cast aluminum are somewhere in the middle.

Blade size — The advertised "size" of a table saw is the largest diameter blade that it will accommodate. This, in turn, determines its cut-off capacity — the thickest board it will saw through. The larger the blade, the larger the cut-off capacity. *(SEE FIGURE 1-9.)* It's useful to have a cut-off capacity of at least 2½ inches — this allows you to cut one-by (4/4) and two-by (8/4) stock in one pass, and four-by (16/4) stock in two passes. However, there's no sense in buying a saw with a blade that's too large. Large blades require lots of power, and you may not have the necessary wiring in your workshop. Saws with 9- and 10-inch blades have adequate cut-off capacity and can be powered with ordinary 110-volt motors, and there is a better selection of 10-inch blades than any other size.

1-9 Larger blades offer a larger cut-off capacity. In addition, larger blades have room for more teeth per inch. With more teeth, each tooth does less work. The blade stays sharper and lasts longer.

Arbor size — Most table saws have ⅝-inch arbors, so there is a larger variety of blades with ⅝-inch arbor holes than any other size. Some small bench saws have ½-inch arbors, and some large cabinet saws have ¾-inch arbors; you may have to order blades for these tools through the mail. Other manufacturers, such as Shopsmith, use special-size arbors; if you buy these tools, you must also buy their blades or pay extra to have standard blades rebored. In addition to considering the arbor's diameter, you should also give some thought to its length. If you want to mount a dado cutter or molding head on the arbor, it should be able to accommodate a ¾-inch-thick accessory. **Note:** If you have other saws in your shop, such as a radial arm saw or a chop saw, it will be more convenient and economical if all the saw arbors are the same size — all your tools will be able to share blades.

Table — Most woodworkers consider that the bigger the table on a table saw, the better. Bigger tables offer more support for the workpiece. However, bigger is not necessarily better if you have a small shop or do fine work. Pick a comfortable size rather than automatically going for the biggest. Also check to see that the table is perfectly flat. *(See Figure 1-10.)* If the table is even the slightest bit out of true, either don't buy the saw or demand another table.

Blade carriage — Since this part of the saw will see the most stress, it should be made from massive, well-machined components. Avoid saws with carriages made from stamped steel or plastic components; these often flex under a load. This, in turn, can play havoc with the accuracy of your cuts.

Horsepower — The power you need is determined by the type of woodworking you do and the diameter of the blade on the saw. Needless to say, the lighter the work and the smaller the blade, the less power you need. If you own a 10-inch saw and the jobs you do vary between light and heavy, the saw should have a motor rated for *at least* 1½ continuous horsepower. The general rule of thumb is that bench saws should have ¾ to 1½ horsepower, contractor's saws, 1½ to 3 horsepower, and cabinet saws, 3 to 5 horsepower. **Note:** These figures are for *continuous* horsepower, or power under load — you'll find them stamped on the side of the motor. Pay no attention to advertising claims of peak horsepower, usually worded in this manner: "...*develops* up to 2 horsepower." Any motor can *temporarily* develop fantastic amounts of peak horsepower — but this power cannot be sustained under load.

Type of motor — In addition to the horsepower of the motor, you should also be concerned about the type of motor, especially when buying a bench saw. Many direct-drive saws have series or *universal* motors, similar to those in hand-held power tools. Universal motors are okay for jobs that can be accomplished quickly, but they will not stand up to continuous use. A table saw should have an *induction* motor.

Drive — As mentioned before, belt drive is better than direct drive because a V-belt helps to isolate motor vibrations from the running saw blade. Furthermore, short V-belts are better than long ones — long belts flop as they run, setting up a vibration that could be worse than the motor's. The smoothest-running saws are driven by *several* short V-belts. **Note:** A few new saws use a flexible cable to drive the arbor. While appearing to be a good idea, flex drive has problems. When the cable is flexed, the blade starts and stops with a jerk. Under continuous use, the cable heats up alarmingly, indicating that much power is lost to friction.

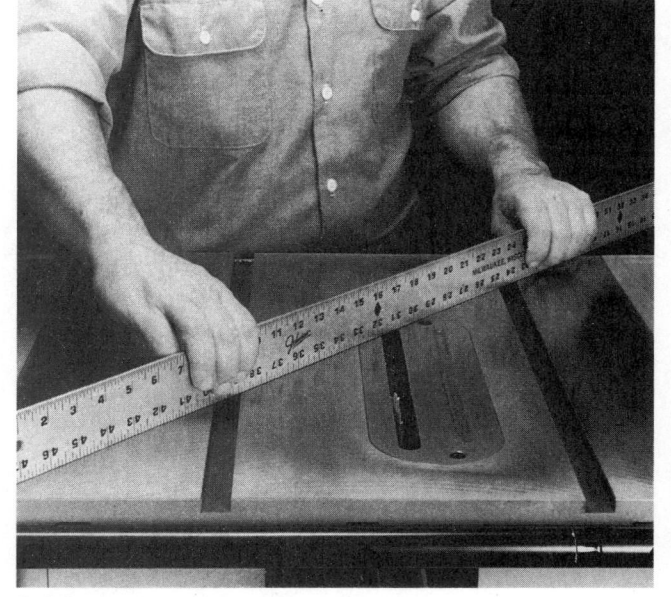

1-10 To determine if the table on a table saw is perfectly flat, lay a level or a straightedge diagonally across the table from right front to left rear, then left front to right rear. If you can see daylight *anywhere between the table and the straightedge, the table has been improperly cast or machined.* **Note:** This is the first thing you should check if you order a saw through the mail. If the table isn't flat, don't accept the shipment.

Fence — The rip fence is the Achilles' heel of every table saw, even high-quality cabinet saws. New saws often do not come with a fence that can be easily aligned and adjusted. The best standard fences seem to be those that are mounted on tubular rails. However, no matter which saw you choose, you may want to replace your factory fence with something better. Refer to "Table Saw Accessories" later in this chapter.

Miter gauge — The most important part of the miter gauge is the bar or guide. This should be solid, machined tool steel. Avoid gauges made from stamped steel; they won't stand up to constant use. Many woodworkers prefer T-shaped slots and bars — the slot holds the miter gauge bar flat on the table at all times. *(SEE FIGURE 1-11.)* However, these are only available on high-priced table saws.

Body and stand — It doesn't matter what materials the saw body and stand are made from as long as they are rock-steady. It's also helpful to have a means of sawdust collection built into the stand. This feature shouldn't be a deciding factor, however. As long as the saw body is open at the bottom, you can easily build your own.

Remember that these recommendations are *advice,* not gospel. Depending on your woodworking circumstances, it may not even be good advice. My first table saw was none of the things that I am recommending to you — it was inexpensively made and underpowered. It was what I could afford, not what I wanted. Yet I used it professionally for seven years to make musical instruments. This just goes to show that there are factors that affect the quality of your sawing more than the saw itself — accurate alignment and adjustment, careful layout, proper sawing technique, and (most important of all) a good saw blade.

1-11 T-shaped miter gauge bars and T-slots offer both advantages and disadvantages. The gauge remains even with the surface of the table, even when extended slightly out from the table. However, it's more difficult to mount and dismount the miter gauge. It's also harder to keep the T-slots clean.

CHOOSING A SAW BLADE

The saw blade is critical to the ease and accuracy of your sawing. A top-quality blade mounted on a medium-quality table saw will cut infinitely better than a mediocre blade mounted on the best saw money can buy. The reason is obvious — it's the blade, not the saw, that does the actual cutting.

To choose a good blade, you need to understand a little about how it works. Every blade has several obvious parts — the plate, teeth, gullets, expansion slots, and arbor hole. *(SEE FIGURE 1-12.)* Of these, the *teeth* define how a saw blade cuts.

Each saw tooth is ground, sharpened, and often bent at a specific angle depending on the job it has to do. If you draw a radial line out from the center of the blade through a tooth, you'll find the tooth is ground at a slight angle to the line. This is the *hook* angle. The greater the hook angle, the more stock a tooth will remove in a single pass. Teeth may also be bent or *set* toward one side of the blade or another so that the *kerf* left by the saw will be slightly wider than the saw plate. This prevents the saw from rubbing in the cut. On some saws, the teeth are not set; instead, the plate is *hollow-ground* slightly thinner than the teeth. Or, on carbide-tipped saws, the teeth are *wider* than the plate. Both arrangements — a hollow-ground plate and wide teeth — serve the same purpose as the set; they prevent the plate from rubbing in the cut.

In addition to hook and set, the cutting edge of every tooth has a *profile*. The edge can be flat or square, beveled right or left, or shaped in other ways to suit its job. *(SEE FIGURE 1-13.)* Often, the teeth on a single blade will have two or more different profiles alternating in a pattern called a *grind*. The profile determines how each *tooth* cuts, while the grind determines how the *blade* cuts.

Finally, saw teeth can be made from several different materials. If made from *high-speed steel,* they are usually ground from the same blank as the plate. Some manufacturers have begun to offer *bi-metal* saw blades in which the plate and the teeth are different grades of steel, but *carbide-tipped* saw blades are more common. Carbide is made up of fine grains of tungsten-carbon bound together with cobalt, making an extremely hard, brittle alloy. This material is too brittle (and too expensive) to use for the plate, so individual carbide teeth are brazed to a steel plate. Also owing to its brittleness, you cannot hone carbide as sharp as steel. However, it takes an adequate cutting edge and holds this edge much longer than steel, particularly when cutting hardwood.

For Your Information

The prevalent myth is that carbide-tipped blades are better than all-steel. Depending on the type of woodworking you do, this is not necessarily true. Carbide-tipped blades are more *durable* than steel. They are also more expensive to purchase and to sharpen, which partially offsets the advantage of their durability. And because you can hone a finer edge in tool steel, a properly sharpened steel blade will give you a *cleaner cut*. I use carbide-tipped blades for every day cutting, but switch to a steel hollow-ground planer blade or a steel plywood blade for super-smooth cuts in solid wood or plywood.

The various aspects of the saw teeth — hook, set, and profile — can be arranged to make different cuts or to cut different materials. There are three basic types of blades, each designed to make certain cuts:

■ *Rip blades* have a large hook angle (20 to 25 degrees) and, since it's much easier to cut with the grain, they remove a lot of stock with each pass. Compared to other blades, they have fewer teeth and larger gullets to make room for the big chips. The tooth profiles are usually all flat. This pattern is called a flat or flat-top grind (FTG).

1-12 The *sawteeth* (1) are mounted on the circular *plate* (2) of the saw blade. Between the teeth are valleys or *gullets* (3), which help to clear sawdust and wood chips. There may also be *expansion slots* (4) between some teeth. As the blade heats up and expands during a cut, these slots keep it from distorting or warping. Finally, every saw blade has an *arbor hole* (5) to mount it on a table saw arbor.

■ *Crosscut blades* or cut-off blades have a much smaller hook angle (5 to 10 degrees) to remove just a little stock, since it's much harder to cut crossgrain. Because the chips are smaller, the gullets can be smaller too, and this makes room for more teeth. The profiles of the teeth alternate right bevel and left bevel in a grind called "alternate top bevel" (ATB). An ATB grind allows each tooth to slice the wood at a slight angle to the grain, making the cut easier and smoother. **Note:** Some crosscut blades have a "steep alternate top bevel" grind (SATB). The steeper bevel makes extremely smooth cuts.

■ *Combination blades* will perform both rip cuts and crosscuts, and their design is a compromise between the first two types of blades. The teeth are usually arranged in sets of five. The gullets between the five teeth in a set are the same size as on a crosscut blade; those between the sets are larger, like the gullets on rip blades. The profiles of the teeth alternate in a five-tooth grind called "alternate top bevel and flat" (ATBF) or "alternate top bevel and raker" (ATBR) — right bevel, left bevel, right bevel, left bevel, flat (or raker). The large gullets are placed in front of the flat-profile raker teeth. **Note:** There are also chisel-tooth combination blades (sometimes advertised as rip/combination blades) which, like rip blades, have few teeth and large gullets. They do not produce smooth crosscuts and are used mostly for carpentry.

In addition to rip, crosscut, and combination blades, there are several common types intended for specific jobs:

■ *Plywood blades* are designed to make smooth cuts in plywood without lifting or chipping the veneer. They usually have 80 or more teeth, each with a small hook so it removes just a little stock. Steel plywood blades have a SATB grind with almost no set. The rims are often ground much thinner than the plate, which further limits the amount of stock each tooth will remove. Carbide-tipped plywood blades may use the SATB grind, or the profile of the teeth may alternate between triple-chip and flat. **Note:** The carbide triple-chip grind (TCG) also works well for cutting particleboard.

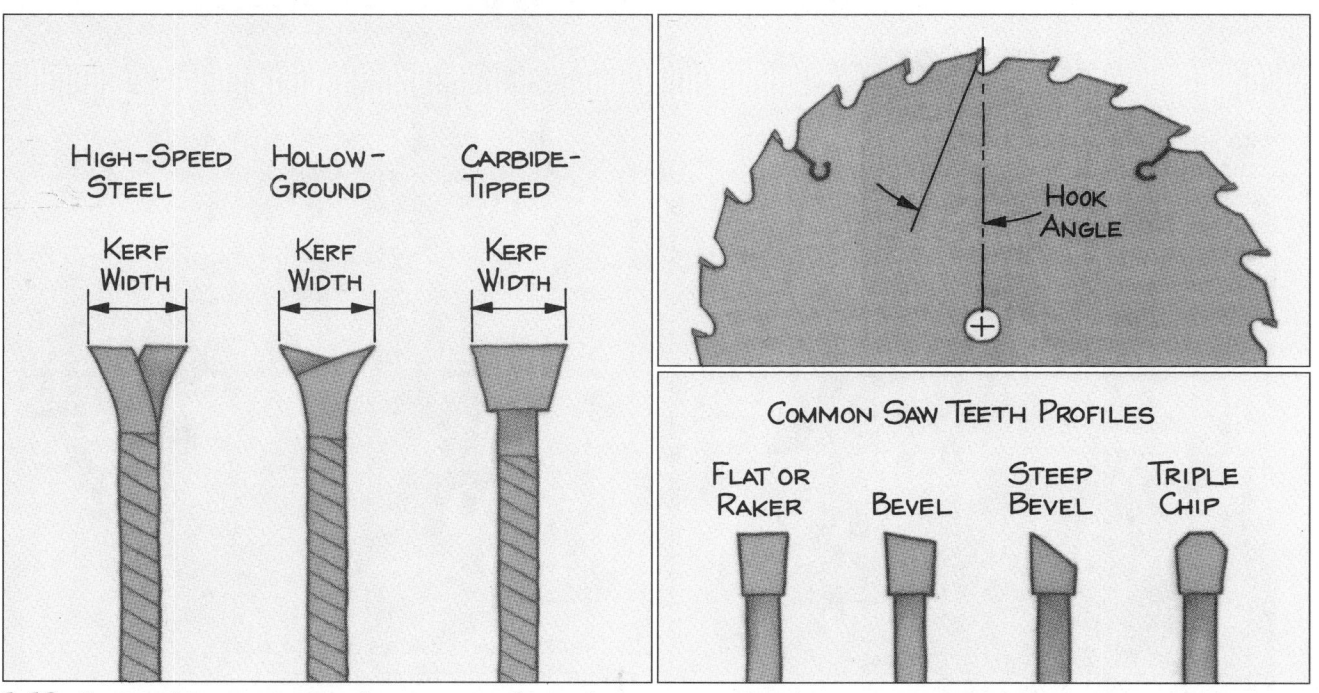

1-13 Sawteeth are ground and sharpened at a specific *hook* angle and arranged so the saw cut or *kerf* will be wider than the plate. If the blade is made from high-speed steel, the teeth are usually *set* to one side or the other. On some fine-cutting saws the teeth are not set; the plate is *hollow-ground* instead. On carbide-tipped blades, the teeth are ground slightly wider than the plate. All of these arrangements prevent the plate from rubbing in the cut. Finally, the cutting edge of each tooth is ground to a specific shape or *profile* that controls how it cuts. There are four common profiles — *flat, bevel, steep bevel,* and *triple-chip*. **Note:** Sometimes a flat-profile tooth is called a *raker.*

■ *Hollow-ground planer blades* are usually steel combination blades with the same hook and profile pattern of other combination blades. The teeth, however, have no set; instead, the plate is thinned out so it will clear the sides of the kerf. This arrangement produces extremely fine cuts and is useful for making joints, raised panels, or any other operation for which a smooth surface is important. **Note:** A hollow-ground blade requires more "projection" than other blades. Adjust the blade height so the deepest gullets will rise above the top surface of the work. Otherwise, the chips won't clear properly and the blade will burn the wood as it cuts.

■ *Thin-kerf blades* are usually carbide-tipped and are available in the same styles as ordinary blades — rip, crosscut, and combination. However, the plate and teeth of a thin-kerf blade are approximately two-thirds as wide as an ordinary blade. Because the blade removes less stock, the table saw does less work and makes a smoother, quicker cut. Thin-kerf blades are more prone to vibration than ordinary blades and may require *blade stabilizers*. (*SEE FIGURE 1-14.*)

Knowing this, what sorts of blades should you choose? The answer depends on the sorts of woodworking you do. However, most craftsmen can get along nicely with just four blades:

■ A *combination blade* for general work. You'll probably keep this on your saw 90 percent of the time. And since you're likely to use this blade more than any other, it should be carbide-tipped.

■ A *rip blade* for cutting stock to width. Often, at the beginning of a project, you'll find yourself doing a lot of ripping lumber to size. A ripping blade will make this chore go faster.

■ A *hollow-ground planer blade* for smooth cuts. This blade will come in handy for making close-fitting butt and miter joints.

■ A *plywood blade* to prevent chipping and tearing when cutting plywood. If you do much work with particleboard and other composites, this blade should be carbide-tipped.

1-14 Thin-kerf blades often require *blade stabilizers* — thick, massive washers mounted on either side of the blade to dampen the vibrations. Purchase machined-steel stabilizers rather than those made from cast aluminum. The steel washers have more mass and tend to be better balanced.

FOR YOUR INFORMATION

Several blade manufacturers now offer blades with an "anti-kickback" design. In addition to the ordinary forward-facing teeth, an anti-kickback blade has backward-facing teeth or "limiters" that limit the depth of cut. This greatly reduces the chance that the blade will kick the work back at you, but it does not completely eliminate the risk.

COMMON TABLE SAW BLADES

TYPE	HOOK AND SPACING	GRIND	USES
RIP	20–25°, wide gullets **High-Speed Steel** **Carbide-Tipped**	Flat	Cutting parallel to the wood grain; ripping to width
CROSSCUT OR CUT-OFF	5–10°, narrow gullets **High-Speed Steel** **Carbide-Tipped**	Alternate top bevel	Cutting across the wood grain; cutting to length
COMBINATION	5–25°, narrow gullets alternating with wide gullets **High-Speed Steel** **Carbide-Tipped**	Alternate top bevel and flat	Ripping and crosscutting most woods and wood products
PLYWOOD	5–10°, narrow gullets **High-Speed Steel** **Carbide-Tipped**	Steep alternate top bevel (steel) or triple chip (carbide)	Cutting plywood; with carbide teeth will also cut composites
HOLLOW-GROUND PLANER	5–25°, narrow gullets alternating with wide gullets **High-Speed Steel Only**	Alternate top bevel and flat	Joinery; moldings; any operation requiring a smooth cut
THIN-KERF (Crosscut blade shown)	Depends on type; can be configured for rip, crosscut, or combination **Rip** **Crosscut** **Combination** **Carbide-Tipped Only**	Depends on type	Ripping or crosscutting hardwood

It goes without saying that all the blades you choose should be high quality. But don't fall for the advertising line that the more teeth a blade has (particularly carbide teeth), the better it must be. Too many teeth may actually hurt the performance of the blade. When there are lots of teeth and small gullets, chips won't clear as quickly. The teeth may cut up the same chip several times before it's finally thrown free. Consequently, the teeth do more work than necessary and dull quickly.

When choosing a rip blade, 24 teeth is plenty for a 10-inch blade. Some 10-tooth ripping blades cut extremely fast and clean. Crosscut and combination saws should have between 24 and 60 teeth, depending on the size of the blade and the kind of work you do: The smaller the blade and the rougher the work, the fewer teeth you want. Only plywood and composite blades benefit from lots of teeth; 10-inch blades should have 80 or more.

TABLE SAW ACCESSORIES

There are dozens of table saw accessories you can mount on your machine to modify or extend its capacity. By carefully choosing from these options, you can soup up your old table saw or customize a new one. The most common additions are a reliable fence, a cut-off system (an improved miter gauge, sliding table, or rolling table), a dado cutter to make simple joints, and a molder to make decorative cuts.

Fences — Perhaps the most necessary option is a replacement fence. (SEE FIGURE 1-15.) Factory fences commonly have two problems: (1) They don't stay parallel to the blade, and (2) they cannot be accurately positioned without lots of measuring. A good replacement fence will solve both problems. Various brands of fences employ different mechanisms for perfect alignment, and they all come with precise scales and hairline indicators.

Beyond these essentials, however, there are many differences between brands. When you choose a replacement fence, consider these important features:

■ *How long are the fence rails?* Most replacement fences extend the ripping capacity — the maximum distance between the blade and fence. To do so, they use longer rails and a larger table extension, increasing the size of the saw. If you're cramped for space in your shop, you may not have room for this accessory. **Note:** Several brands offer different lengths of rails to accommodate woodworkers with limited floor space.

■ *Will the fence dismount easily?* For many operations, you must remove the fence from the saw. This task is easier with some brands than others.

■ *Can the fence be used easily on both sides of the blade?* Like most factory fences, replacement fences slide to the right and to the left side of the blade. But on some, the fence face must be removed and reversed when changing sides.

■ *Can you easily mount jigs on the fence?* Many table saw operations require that you mount shop-made

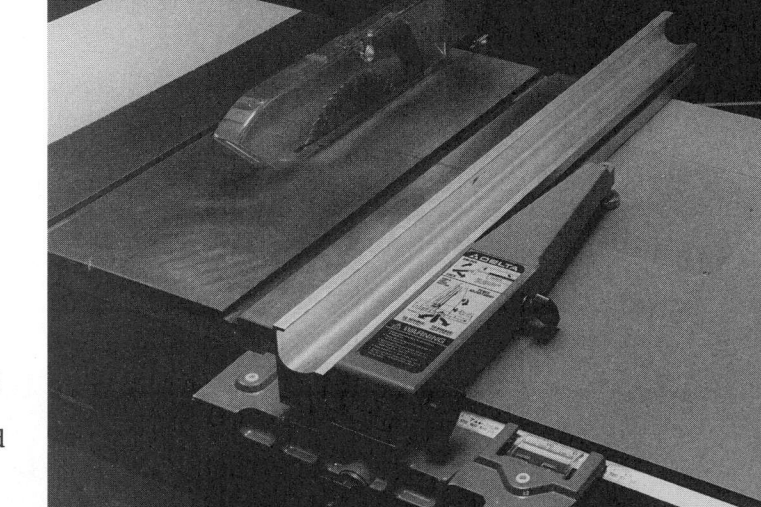

1-15 **The Delta Unifence is typical** of many replacement fences — it makes a table saw more accurate and easier to use. Most of these fences will adapt to all common brands of table saws *except* tilting-table and rolling-table saws.

jigs on the fence. It's easier to drill bolt holes in some replacement fences than others. You may also find a fence that cannot be drilled at all — you must clamp the jig to it.

Miter gauges — Factory miter gauges are often as inadequate as factory fences, but deciding whether to replace them is more complex. How much cut-off work do you perform on your table saw, and how large are the boards that you must cut accurately? If you crosscut lots of large boards, you need a sliding table or rolling table instead of a replacement miter gauge. For small work and an occasional large board, a good miter gauge will serve well. *(SEE FIGURE 1-16.)*

Sliding tables — When you use a miter gauge, whether a factory gauge or a replacement, there is friction between the wood and the saw table as you push the work across the surface. The larger the

board, the greater the friction — and the greater tendency for the board to twist or creep as you cut it. A sliding table works like a miter gauge, but it supports the wood and eliminates the friction. *(SEE FIGURE 1-17.)* Crosscuts — particularly cuts in large boards — are smoother and more accurate when you use a sliding table.

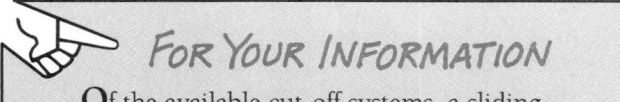

FOR YOUR INFORMATION

Of the available cut-off systems, a sliding table is probably the best compromise between economy and utility. And you can easily make your own. (See the "Sliding Table" on page 94.)

1-16 A good replacement miter gauge should have a long, solid face to support the work, and a large trunnion pin to lock the face securely in position. The Accu-Miter gauge shown also has a built-in extension, stop, and hold-down.

1-17 As a sliding table glides back and forth in the miter gauge slots, it supports the stock and prevents it from rubbing on the saw table. Sliding tables come in several different configurations — the Dubby (shown) is one of the easiest to set up and use.

Rolling tables — Like a sliding table, a rolling table supports the work so you can crosscut large stock accurately and easily. But unlike a sliding table, the supporting surface is flush with the saw table. And instead of sliding back and forth in the miter gauge slots, this accessory rolls back and forth on bearings and rails. (*SEE FIGURE 1-18.*) **Note:** To attach a rolling table to your saw, you must shorten the fence rails so they don't extend past the left side of the saw. This limits how far you can position the fence to the left of the blade.

Dado cutters — A dado cutter makes dadoes, grooves, rabbets, and other common joints. It mounts on the arbor like a saw blade, but removes a great deal more stock. Most dado accessories can be adjusted to cut a kerf between 1/4 inch and 13/16 inch wide.

There are several types of dado cutters. The two most common are *wobble dadoes* and *stacked dadoes*. (*SEE FIGURE 1-19.*) A wobble dado is made from a single 1/8-inch-wide blade that moves back and forth as it cuts. The kerf is infinitely adjustable between the minimum and the maximum width, but the setting sometimes slips during hard use. A stacked dado, which is made from several blades of varying thicknesses, is a better choice for heavy work. Less common are *dado washers* and *groovers*. Dado washers convert ordinary saw blades to wobble dadoes, but aren't as reliable. They should be used only for occasional light cuts. Groovers are single heavy-duty blades, up to 1 inch thick. They are expensive, but if you cut the same widths of dadoes and grooves over and over again, they can save you set-up time.

1-18 A rolling table, such as this Powermatic, replaces the left table extension with a surface that rolls front to back. The fence on this accessory can be angled for miter cuts.

1-19 A *wobble dado* (right) is a single blade mounted between two tapered washers. The washers cause the blade to wobble from side to side, cutting a wide kerf. To adjust the width of the kerf, you simply rotate the washers. A *stacked dado* (left) consists of two different blades: trimmers and chippers. These blades are stacked on the arbor with the trimmers on the outside of the chippers. To adjust the width of the kerf, add or subtract chippers.

Molders — A molder is a thick, round metal disc or *head* which holds sets of interchangeable *knives*. (SEE FIGURE 1-20.) Like a dado cutter, this accessory mounts on the saw arbor. It makes shaped cuts — you can use a molder to turn out decorative shapes such as beads, coves, and ogees. Or you can cut complex joinery — glue joints, tongue-and-groove joints, and various coped joints. There is a wide variety of knives available, including blanks from which you can grind your own shapes.

FOR YOUR INFORMATION

Both the dado cutter and the molder require special *table inserts* to properly support the work as it passes across the cutters or knives.

In addition to these major table saw accessories, there are many more that improve the accuracy, capacity, or capability of a saw. Two accessories, however, deserve a mention because they make the machine safer:

■ *Hold-downs* keep the stock flat on the table as you feed it past the blade. (SEE FIGURE 1-21.)

■ *Overhead blade guards* replace the factory-supplied guard-and-splitter systems. (SEE FIGURE 1-22.)

1-21 Fence-mounted hold-downs, such as this Rip-Strate, hold the stock flat on the table and against the fence as it is cut. They also prevent the stock from kicking back. Unfortunately, they often interfere with the blade guard. On many operations, you cannot use both a hold-down and a blade guard.

1-22 Many woodworkers have a love-hate relationship with the factory-supplied blade guard and splitter. They want the protection it offers, but find it difficult to work around. It's hard to set up for a cut with a splitter-mounted guard in place, and time consuming to mount the guard after the set-up is done. If you've experienced this problem, consider refitting your saw with an overhead guard like this Brett-Guard. It swings out of the way and then back into place quickly and easily.

1-20 Most molding heads mount three identical knives. These knives are interchangeable — you can easily remove one set and change it for another. The knives will make both decorative cuts and joints, depending on the shapes you choose.

2

TABLE SAW KNOW-HOW

The table saw is a precision cutting tool. As such, it must be precisely aligned, operated, and maintained if you are to get the best results possible. Small problems can have large consequences. A rip fence that angles slightly toward the blade, a miter gauge slot slightly out of line with the blade, a tendency to feed the work too quickly or too slowly, or a blade whose teeth have become coated with pitch — all of these seemingly insignificant problems can completely ruin a cut.

Before you make any cut, you must be sure that the "working" parts — blade, arbor, carriage, table, fence, and miter gauge — are properly aligned to one another. For example, the face of the rip fence must be parallel to the plate of the rotating blade. If it isn't, the saw will bind and burn the work.

As you make a cut, you must be aware of how the saw operates so you can recognize the signs that it's not working properly. An experienced craftsman not only watches what the saw is doing but

also listens, feels, and smells. The whine of the saw blade, the vibrations that resonate through the wood, the smell of the lumber as it's cut — all of these are clues to how the cut is progressing.

And there are chores you must do periodically to maintain the saw in cutting condition. Blades should be kept clean and sharp; working surfaces should be waxed or lubricated. And every so often you must check for parts that may have drifted out of alignment — and the cycle begins again.

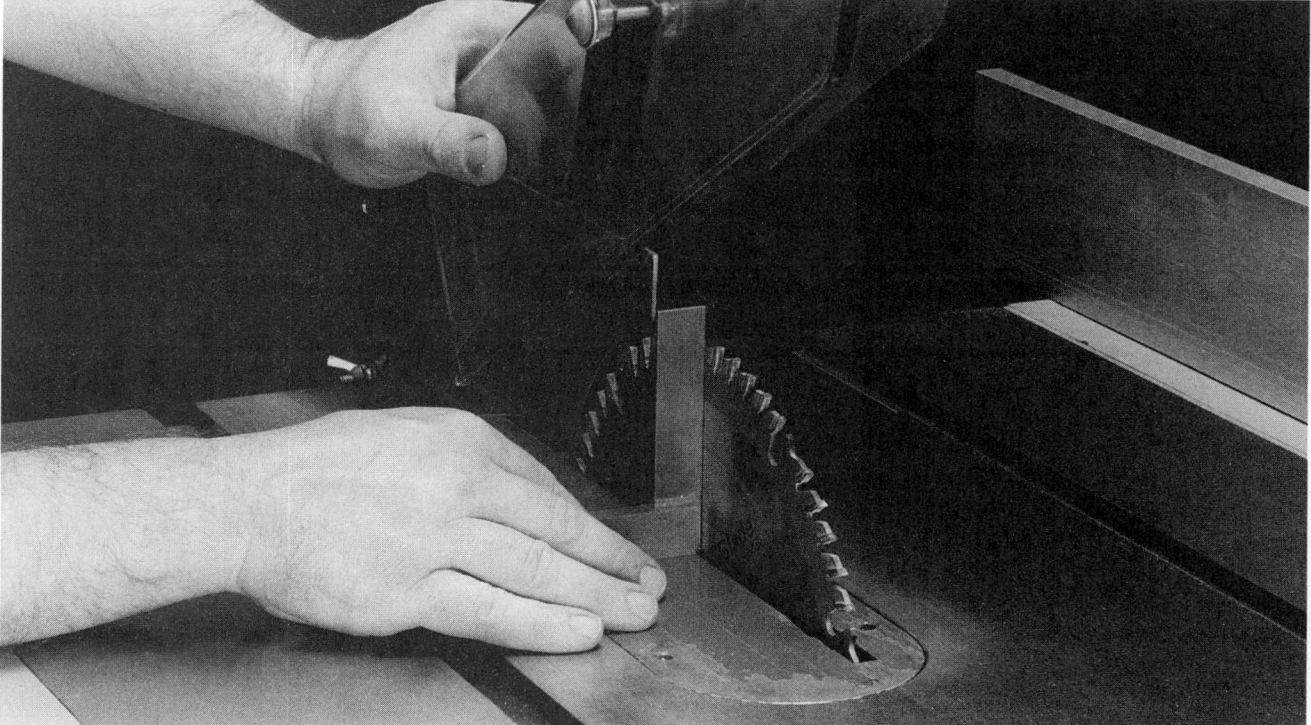

ALIGNMENT AND ADJUSTMENT

New table saws don't come ready to run — the parts must be aligned. And like any machine with moving parts, a table saw needs an occasional realignment. As the machine runs, many of its working parts are pulled or pushed this way and that. The entire machine constantly vibrates — each sawtooth hits the wood like a small hammer and the shock resonates throughout the mechanical system. After a time, owing to stress and vibration, the parts will creep out of alignment and must be realigned.

There are many parts to check and adjust on a table saw, and each table saw will be slightly different, depending on its construction. For instructions on how to perform a complete tune-up, check your owner's manual. There are, however, three important alignments that affect the tool's accuracy and ease of operation more than any others. These should be checked often:

■ The blade must be parallel to the miter gauge slots.

■ The rip fence must be parallel to the blade.

■ The splitter must be parallel to and in line with the blade.

FOR BEST RESULTS

Tuning up a table saw requires two measuring tools — a true straightedge and an accurate combination square. To check that a straightedge is straight, use one edge to draw a line along its full length. Flip the straightedge face for face and draw a second line on top of the first, *using the same edge*. Superimposed, the two lines should appear as one. If they diverge at any point, your straightedge is crooked. To check that a square is square, place the arm against the edge of a board and use one edge of the rule to draw a line. Flip the square face for face and draw a second line on top of the first, *using the same edge*. Again, the two lines should appear as one. If they diverge, your square isn't square.

ALIGNING THE BLADE

Before you can align any part of the table saw, you must select a base reference — a line or plane from which you can measure the position of every other part. The reference most often used is the miter gauge slots, since their positions cannot be changed.

Use a combination square to measure the distance between a slot and a sawtooth near the front of the blade. Then rotate the tooth near the rear of the table and measure again. (*SEE FIGURES 2-1 AND 2-2.*) Both

2-1 Unplug the saw when checking that the blade is parallel to the miter gauge slots. Mount a blade on the arbor and mark a tooth — any tooth will do. Rotate the blade so the marked tooth is near the front of the saw. Place the arm of a combination square against the side of a miter gauge slot and slide the rule sideways until it just touches the marked tooth.

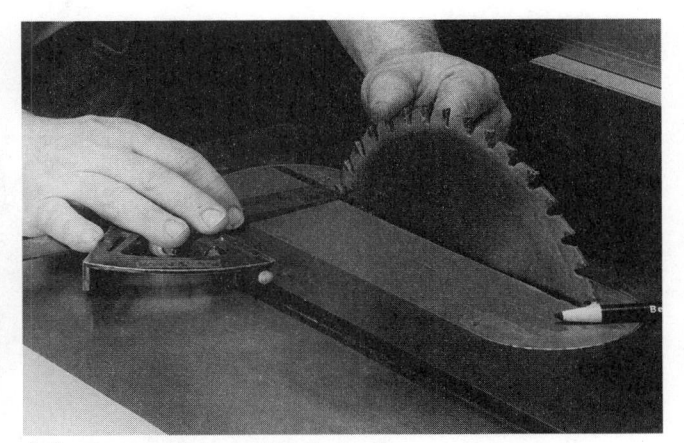

2-2 Rotate the saw blade so the marked tooth is near the back of the saw. Move the combination square and measure the distance from the slot to the tooth again. If both measurements are precisely the same, the blade is parallel to the slot.

measurements must be precisely the same for the blade to be parallel to the slot. If they differ, loosen the bolts that hold the blade carriage to the table and adjust the position of the carriage. *(SEE FIGURE 2-3.)*

ALIGNING THE RIP FENCE

Position the fence near a miter gauge slot and lock it in place. Use the combination square to measure the distance between the slot and the fence face near the front and back of the saw. *(SEE FIGURE 2-4.)* If the measurements differ, adjust the fence to be parallel to the slot. When both the fence and the blade are parallel to the miter gauge slot, they will also be parallel to one another.

ALIGNING THE SPLITTER

Lay a straightedge against the saw blade and the splitter to check the alignment. *(SEE FIGURE 2-5.)* If the straightedge does not lie flat against both parts, the splitter is misaligned. Using a hand screw, bend the splitter into position. *(SEE FIGURE 2-6.)*

Some procedures may differ from those shown here, depending on the construction of your table saw. However, the importance of checking and adjusting the blade, fence, and splitter remains, no matter what type or brand of saw you own. Carefully read the section on alignment and adjustment in your owner's manual and follow its recommendations *before* using the saw.

2-3 If the blade is not parallel to the slot, reach under the saw and loosen the bolts that hold the blade carriage to the table. Don't loosen them completely — just so they're finger-tight. Remove the table insert. Using a dowel and a mallet, lightly tap on the side of the carriage near the front or back, shifting its position slightly. Check the alignment and, if necessary, tap again. When the blade is properly aligned, tighten the bolts. **Note:** On some saws, you must shift the table instead of the carriage. Refer to your owner's manual for complete instructions.

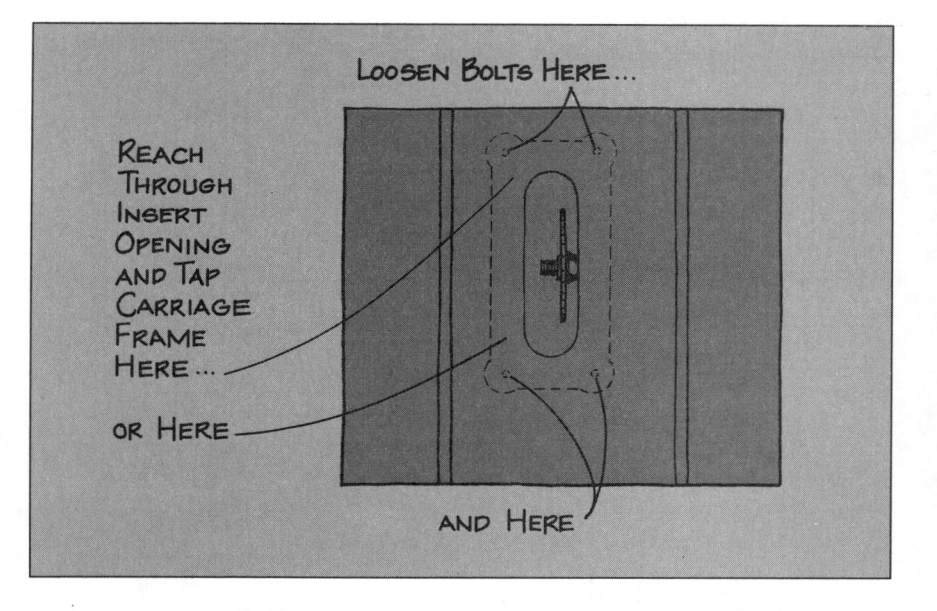

2-4 Once you know the blade is parallel to the miter gauge slots, check if the fence is parallel to the blade. To do this, position the fence near a slot. Place a combination square so its arm rests against the side of the slot, near the front of the saw. Slide the rule sideways until it just touches the rip fence. Repeat near the back of the saw. If the two measurements are the same, the rip fence is parallel to the blade. If not, the fence must be aligned. This is usually a simple procedure, but it differs with the make of each fence. Check the owner's manual.

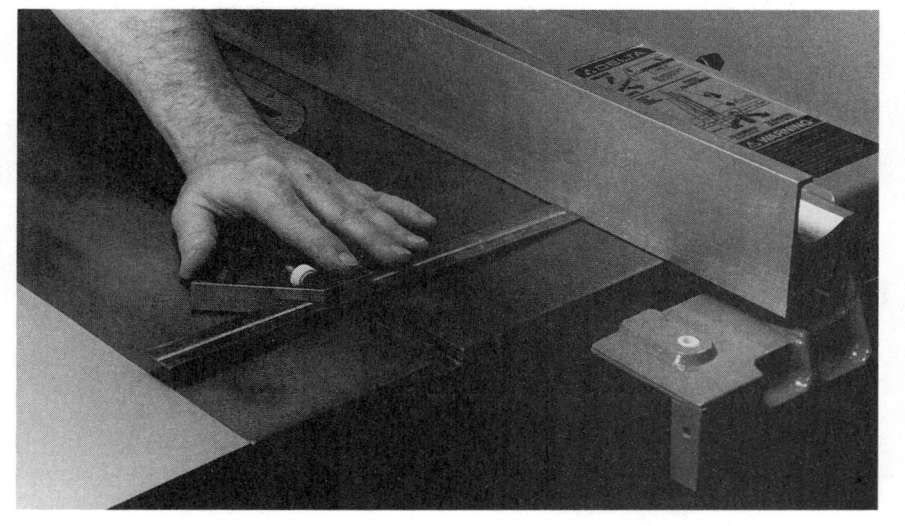

2-5 To check if the splitter is aligned with the blade, unplug the saw and raise the blade as high as it will go. Place a straightedge next to the blade and rotate the blade until the straightedge rests flat against the plate but *not* the teeth. If the splitter is properly aligned with the blade, the straightedge will also rest flat against the splitter.

2-6 If the splitter is not aligned with the blade, bend it into position. Most splitters are made from a light-gauge steel which can be easily bent by hand. To keep the splitter from kinking as you bend it, fasten it in a hand screw. The clamp will also provide a comfortable way to hold on to the splitter.

MAKING A CUT

Making a cut on a table saw is one of the simplest operations in woodworking. Crosscuts, rips, and miters are all considered basic cuts. Despite this, a good deal of preparation and skill are needed if these simple tasks are to be accomplished safely and accurately.

There are four steps to making a table saw cut, no matter how you slice up the board:

- Lay out the cut on the board, if necessary.
- Adjust the saw blade and other accessories for that specific cut.
- Align the board with the blade.
- Pass the wood over the saw.

MARKING THE CUT

A single table saw cut must be measured and marked *precisely,* and a series of cuts must be measured and marked *consistently.* For precision, use a quality measuring device. Make the mark with a *scratch awl*

or *marking knife.* Pencils dull quickly and, as they do, the lines broaden and appear fuzzy. This can interfere with the accuracy of your cut. The lines left by an awl or a knife remain narrow and crisp.

For consistency, *use the same measuring device* for each cut, if you can. Although scales are standardized, the same measurement made with different measuring tools may vary slightly. When you must use more than one measuring tool, make sure the measurements are consistent from tool to tool.

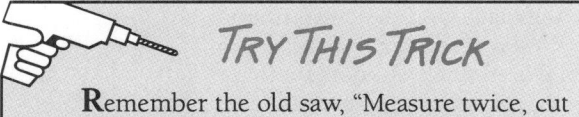

TRY THIS TRICK

Remember the old saw, "Measure twice, cut once"? It describes this age-old technique: Measure the cut, make a mark, then measure the mark. This takes very little effort — just an extra glance at the measuring tool before you remove it from the board.

When you lay out the cut, make your marks on a *visible surface* — one that can be easily seen when you place the board on the table saw. If you must measure and mark a hidden surface, carefully transfer the marks to a visible one. Also, remember to allow for the saw kerf. Every layout line has a *save side* and a *waste side*. (SEE FIGURE 2-7.) The saw kerf should fall entirely on the waste side; the blade must remove no stock from the save side. The edge of the sawteeth should brush the line.

ADJUSTING THE SAW

Once you've laid out the cut on the stock, adjust the saw to make the cut. Most of these adjustments use the plane of the saw blade as a reference. Unfortunately, because most saw blades have a small amount of *run-out* (side-to-side wobble), this reference isn't always as accurate as you'd like. To compensate, mark the run-out on the saw blade so you can work around it. (SEE FIGURE 2-8.)

2-7 When laying out the cut on a board, think ahead to how you will line up the cut marks with the saw blade. If necessary, use a square to transfer the marks to a more visible or more convenient surface. Many woodworkers mark both a face and an edge. They use the mark on the edge to align the stock with the blade, and the mark on the face to monitor the cut as it progresses. In addition to marking the cut, also indicate the *waste side* of the line. This will help you remember on which side of the line to make the saw kerf.

2-8 Before you can use a blade as a reference for measurements and adjustments, you must compensate for the run-out. First, unplug the saw. Then, using a combination square as shown in *FIGURE 2-1* on page 19, find and mark the "near" and "far" teeth — the tooth that comes closest to the rule when you rotate the blade, and the one farthest away. With a permanent marker, draw a dotted line from near tooth to far tooth, through the center of the blade. Then draw a solid line, perpendicular to the first, that also passes through the center of the blade. When making measurements, use this solid line.

Once you've marked the run-out, raise the saw blade as high as it will go. (This will make it easier to measure accurately.) If you're using the rip fence, secure it the proper distance from the blade. (*SEE FIGURE 2-9.*) If you're using the miter gauge, adjust it to the proper angle from the blade. (*SEE FIGURE 2-10.*) Set the saw blade to the proper tilt, then adjust the height of the blade. (*SEE FIGURES 2-11 AND 2-12.*)

FOR BEST RESULTS

A set of *metal* drafting triangles helps to set the miter gauge angle and the blade tilt. The various corners are cut to precise 30-, 45-, 60-, and 90-degree angles. Don't purchase plastic triangles — in a workshop, they are easily nicked and scratched and soon lose their accuracy.

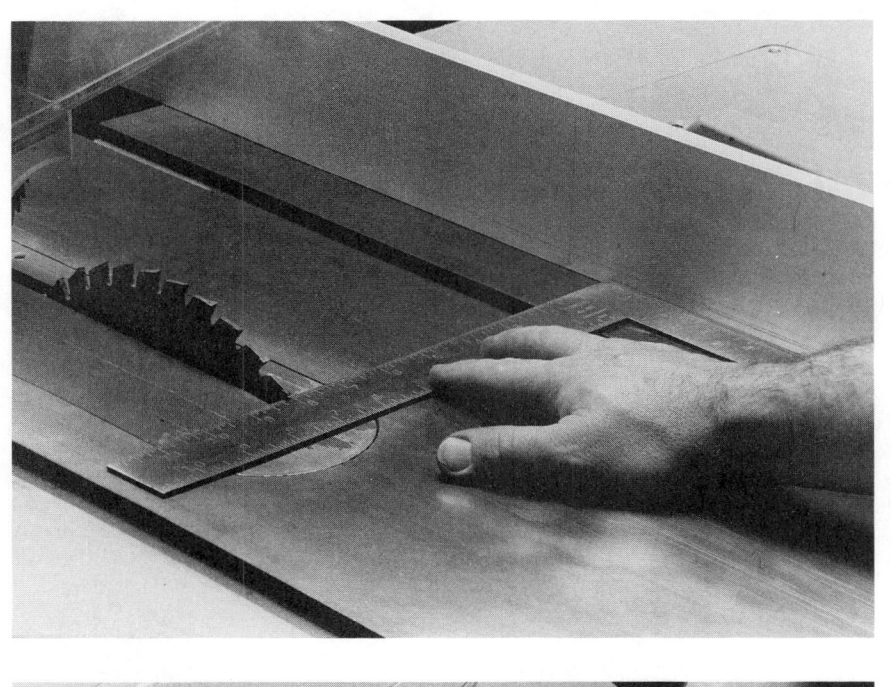

2-9 To position the rip fence accurately, first select a tooth at one end of the solid line on the blade. If the sawteeth are set, choose a tooth that's set *toward the rip fence*. Rotate the blade by hand until this tooth is near the front of the machine. Adjust the position of the fence, measuring from the inside edge of the tooth (closest to the fence) to the inside face of the fence. Secure the fence to the rails, then double-check the setup by rotating the tooth to the back of the saw and measuring again. **Note:** A framing square is perhaps the easiest and most accurate measuring tool for this adjustment.

2-10 To set the angle of the miter gauge accurately, rotate the saw blade by hand until the solid line is horizontal. Loosen the miter gauge quadrant and place one edge of a square or drafting triangle against the miter gauge face. Slide the measuring tool sideways until another edge touches the saw blade plate. (It mustn't contact the saw teeth.) Turn the quadrant until the tool rests flat against the face *and* the plate, then secure the quadrant.

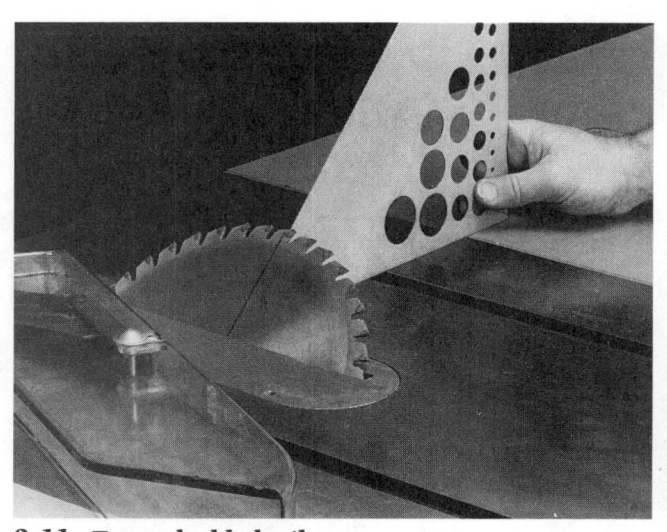

2-11 To set the blade tilt, rotate the blade until the solid line is vertical. Rest one side of a square or drafting triangle on the table next to the blade. Tilt the blade until the plate lies flat against the other side. The measuring tool must *not* touch the sawteeth.

Note: The adjustment procedures shown work well for most types of saw blades, but not for *hollow-ground planer blades*. Because a hollow-ground blade plate is slightly concave, you cannot accurately set the miter gauge angle or blade tilt with a square or drafting triangle. You have to set them as close as you can using the scales on the miter gauge and the saw. Furthermore, a hollow-ground planer blade requires more projection than other blades. The bottoms of the deepest gullets must clear the stock, or the blade will burn the wood as it cuts.

If necessary, fine-tune these adjustments by making test cuts in scrap stock. Carefully measure the size and angles of the scrap after it's cut, and readjust the saw as needed. (*SEE FIGURES 2-13 THROUGH 2-17.*)

2-12 To set the blade height, use the workpiece or a scrap of wood the same thickness as the workpiece as a gauge. There is some controversy about how high the teeth should project above the wood. Most woodworkers agree that for the best possible cut, the bottoms of the gullets between the teeth should clear the wood. This will help to throw the sawdust and chips away from the blade. However, for the safest possible cut, adjust the blade height so the tops of the teeth just barely rise above the wood. You must feed the wood more slowly to get a good cut with the blade at this height, but if your hand should slip during the operation, there is less chance that the blade will cut you deeply.

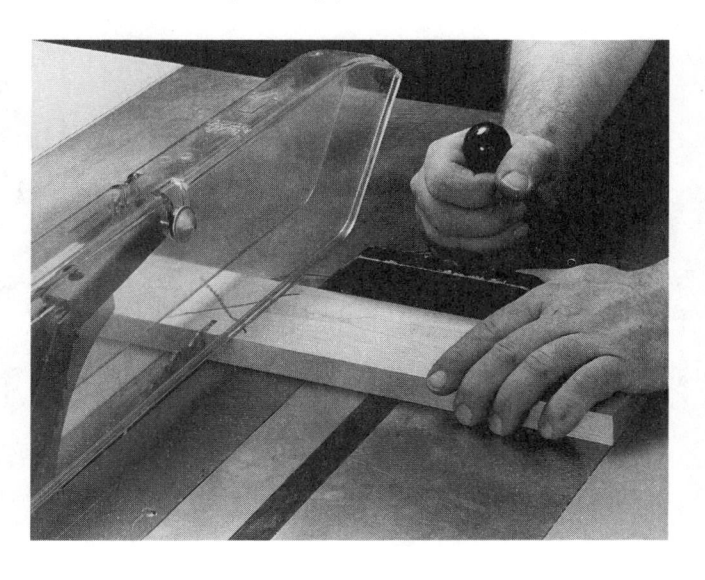

2-13 To test the miter gauge angle, select a scrap about ³/₄ inch thick, 1¹/₂ to 3 inches wide, and at least 18 inches long. Mark an X on the face of the scrap near the middle. Rest the scrap on a face and cut through the mark.

2-14 Flip one part of the scrap face for face and put the cut ends together. Measure the angle between the two parts — it should be precisely *twice* the angle you want to cut. In the example shown, the gauge was set to 90 degrees and the angle between the scraps measures 180 degrees, as shown by the straightedge.

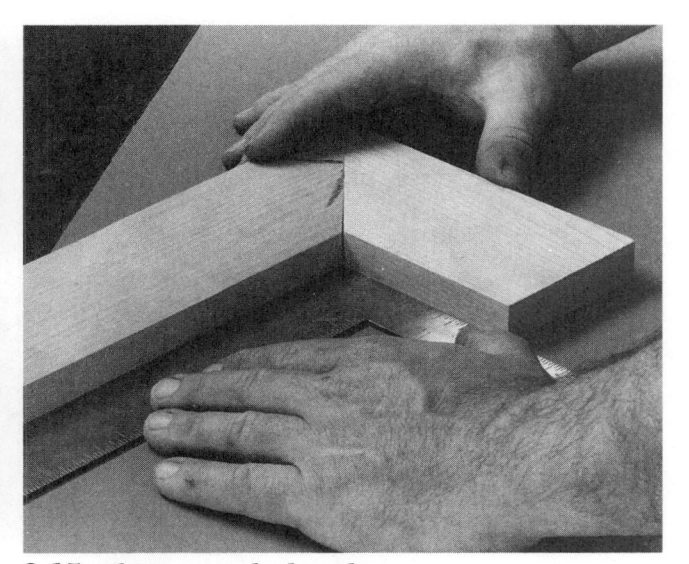

2-15 This test method works well for any angle. Here, the cut was made at 45 degrees and the measured angle is 90 degrees. The advantage of this technique is that any error in the setup is doubled, making it easier to detect.

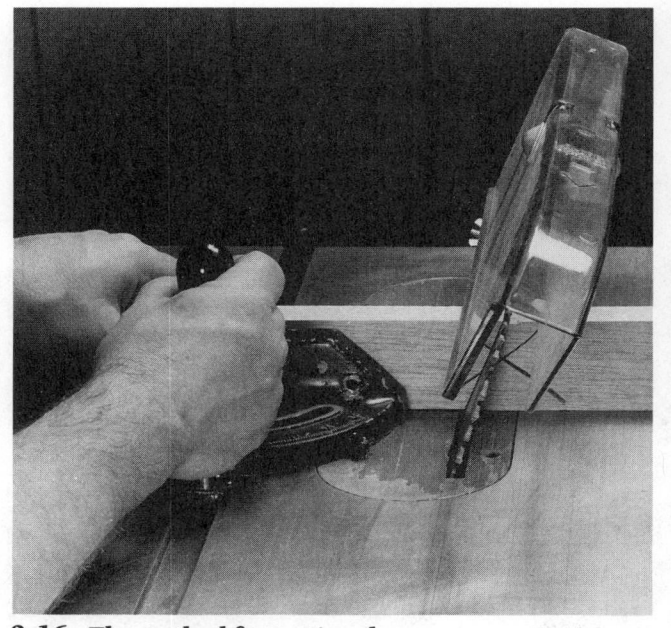

2-16 The method for testing the blade tilt is similar. Select a scrap and mark an X on one face. However, rest the scrap on its edge as you cut through the mark.

2-17 Again, flip one part of the board face for face and put the cut ends together. Measure the angle between the scraps. It should be twice the blade tilt *subtracted from 180 degrees.* For example, the cut shown was made with the blade tilted at 22½ degrees from vertical. The inside angle between the two scraps measures 135 degrees: 180 - (2 x 22½) = 135

ALIGNING THE BOARD WITH THE BLADE

For some cuts, positioning the board on the saw requires little thought. When ripping, simply butt the edge of the board against the fence. If the rip fence is set properly, the board will be properly positioned.

> ### TRY THIS TRICK
>
> To double-check the position of the rip fence, turn the saw on and advance the stock until it just "kisses" the blade (you can hear when this happens). Quickly stop feeding and turn the saw off. Measure the distance between the guiding edge of the board and the tiny mark left by the saw.

The procedure is more complex if you use the miter gauge. You must place the board in the gauge and align the sawteeth with the layout line. (*See Figure 2-18.*) While not particularly difficult, this can be awkward. The layout line usually faces away from you, so you must hold the blade guard up and out of the way while you lean over the saw. To make the chore more comfortable, install a *Kerf Indicator* on your saw table. (*See Figures 2-19 and 2-20.*)

2-18 To position a board in the miter gauge, rotate the blade until the solid line is horizontal. Place the board against the miter gauge face and slide it right or left, aligning the layout line with the sawteeth. The edges of the teeth *nearest the save side* must be even with the line. If the sawteeth are set, use a tooth that's set toward the save side to align the board.

2-19 To make it easier to position boards on the table saw, you may want to install a *Kerf Indicator*. Stick a thin piece of colored film or tape on the saw table several inches in front of the blade. (You can purchase colored "filament tape" at an art supply store.) Place the miter gauge in the left slot, make sure the face is square to the blade, and clamp a wood scrap to the face. Saw the scrap and slide it back over the tape. Cut the tape with a razor blade or utility knife, using the sawed edge of the scrap as a guide. Repeat this procedure with the miter gauge in the right slot, then peel up the thin strip of tape between the two cuts. The gap between the two pieces of tape left on the saw indicates the precise width and position of the saw kerf.

2-20 To use the indicator to position a board in the miter gauge, simply line up the layout line with one of the cut edges of the tape. Remember, the saw kerf should fall on the waste side of the line. **Note:** This tape indicator is only accurate for the specific saw blade and blade tilt you used when you installed it. If you change blades or tilt, you must reinstall the indicator.

CUTTING THE WOOD

As you make a saw cut, your overriding concern should be the dangers posed by a running saw blade. If you let some part of your body venture close to the blade — into the "danger zone" — you may not be able to retrieve it safely should something go wrong. It's commonly believed that this danger zone extends about 2 inches in all directions from the blade, an area that is roughly marked by the blade insert. That's why many manufacturers paint the insert red.

The blade insert, however, does not indicate the entire zone. The sawteeth of a 10-inch saw blade typically travel at about 120 miles per hour, and they will fling (or "kick back") a board with great force. For this reason, the danger zone extends about 2 feet behind the blade, and all the way forward to the wall of your shop. (*SEE FIGURES 2-21 AND 2-22.*)

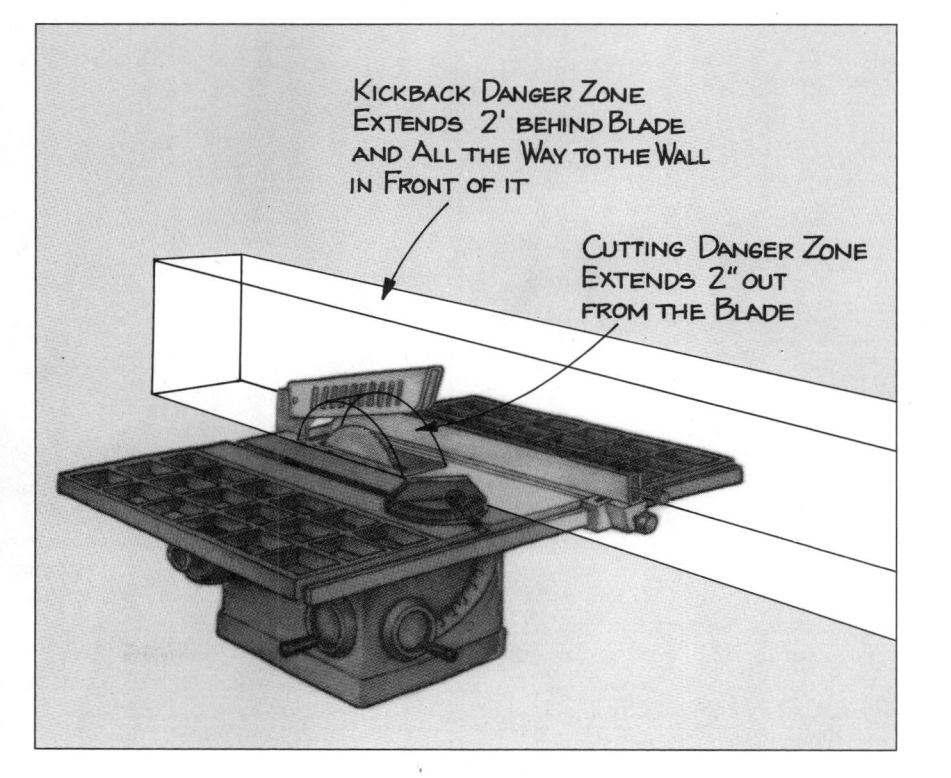

KICKBACK DANGER ZONE EXTENDS 2' BEHIND BLADE AND ALL THE WAY TO THE WALL IN FRONT OF IT

CUTTING DANGER ZONE EXTENDS 2" OUT FROM THE BLADE

2-21 Over half of all serious workshop accidents happen on the table saw. This is partly due to the nature of the tool — the action of the saw will draw your hand into the blade should you get too close. The blade may also kick wood at you if you stand in front or in back of it. Most table saw accidents can be prevented simply by remembering — and respecting — the danger zone that surrounds the tool.

Be mindful of the entire danger zone when you get ready to make a cut. If you've never made this sort of cut before, carefully think it through — know where you're going to stand, how you're going to hold your hands, and what you will do if something goes wrong.

Stand to one side of the blade or the other, wherever you can reach the saw switch quickly and easily. Carefully position your hands so as not to cross over the invisible barrier marked by the blade insert. If necessary, use a push stick or a featherboard to help make a cut. These devices keep your fingers out of the danger zone *and* help to prevent kickback. (*SEE FIGURE 2-23.*) See "Push Sticks" on the facing page and "Adjustable Featherboard" on page 30 for suggestions on how to make these safety devices.

TRY THIS TRICK

Keep your push sticks *close at hand* — a safety tool does little good if you can't get to it when you need it. To keep a push stick within easy reach, mount it on the front of your table saw or the side of your rip fence with Velcro.

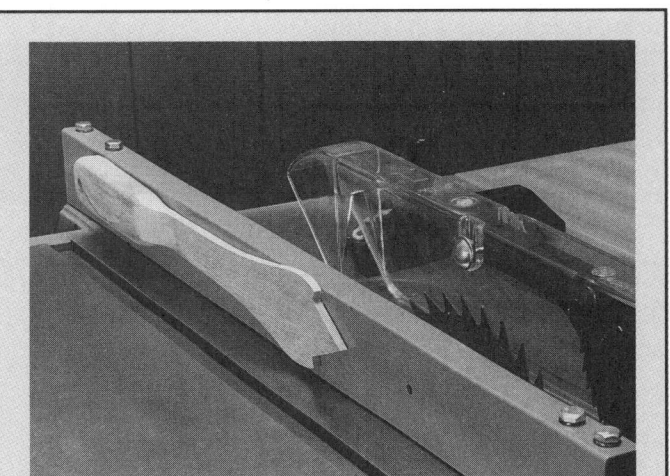

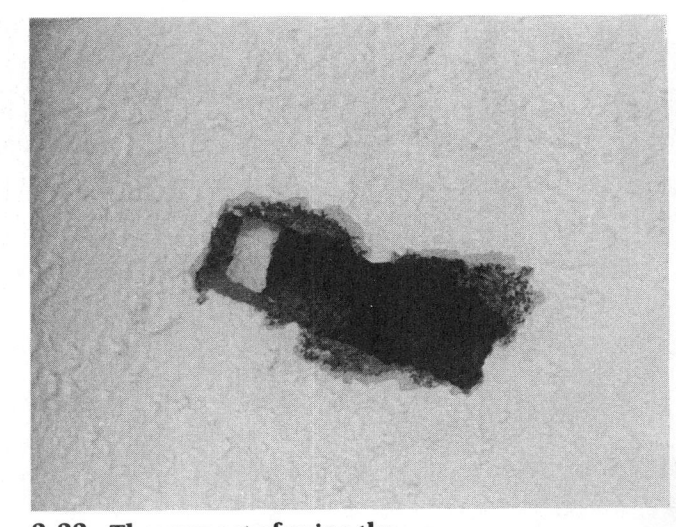

2-22 The very act of using the table saw is a vivid reminder of one of its dangers — any tool that cuts wood can cut you. The danger of kickback is not as evident, but it's just as serious. The hole in this concrete block wall was made by a board that was thrown by a table saw blade *fifteen feet away!*

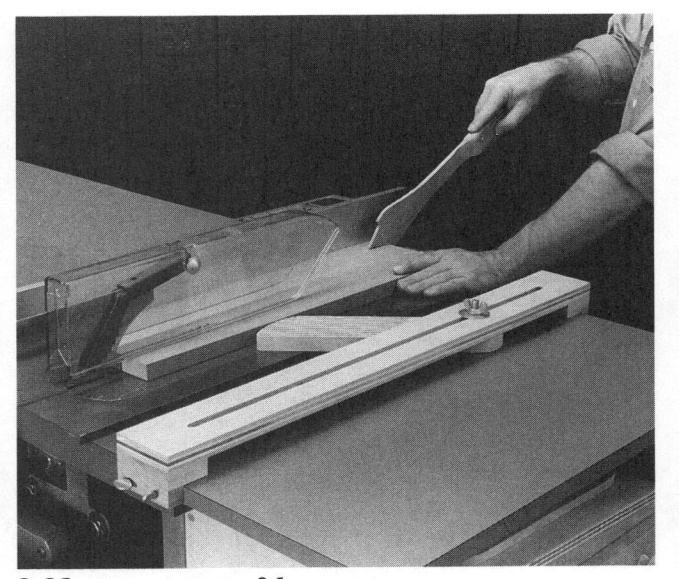

2-23 You cannot safely operate a table saw without push sticks and featherboards; keep several of them on hand. Use push sticks to guide or feed the wood, and featherboards to hold the wood against the rip fence or the saw table.

PUSH STICKS

There are many designs for push sticks, from unadorned boards with a notch in one end to elaborate shapes with handsaw handles. Most experienced craftsmen gravitate toward the simpler designs for two reasons: You can easily make a lot of them — one or more for every power tool that needs them — and you don't feel so bad when they get chewed up. (Push sticks, after all, are *supposed* to get chewed up — it's either the sticks or your fingers.) Here are three simple designs for you to consider.

The advantage of the *Push Board,* besides its extreme simplicity, is that it holds the work flat on the table as you push it past the blade. To make it, simply cut notches in both edges of a scrap board.

The *Reversible Push Stick* has a thin shaft so you can easily reach between the saw blade and the fence to maneuver narrow stock. Yet it will also work with large boards. The design is reversible — you can use it with the bulge of the handle facing left or right so you will never have to pass your hand directly over the saw blade. Cut this design on a band saw or with a coping saw.

The *Featherboard/Push Stick* serves as either a hand-held featherboard or a push stick, depending on how you hold it. Cut the "feathers" by making several long, evenly spaced kerfs on the table saw.

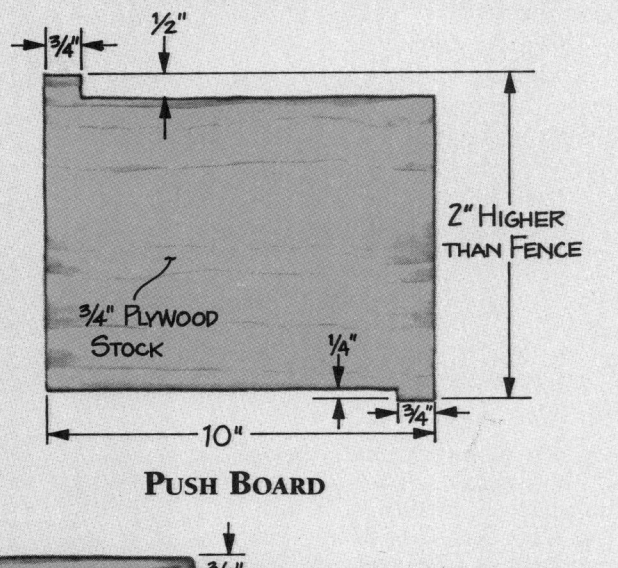

PUSH BOARD

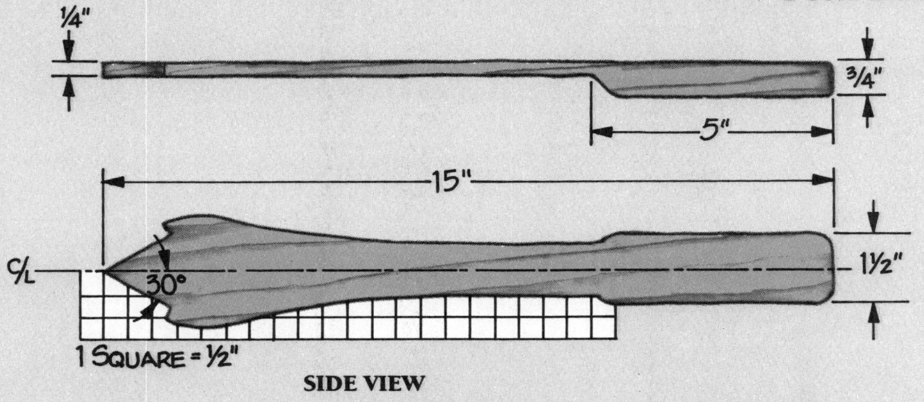

REVERSIBLE PUSH STICK

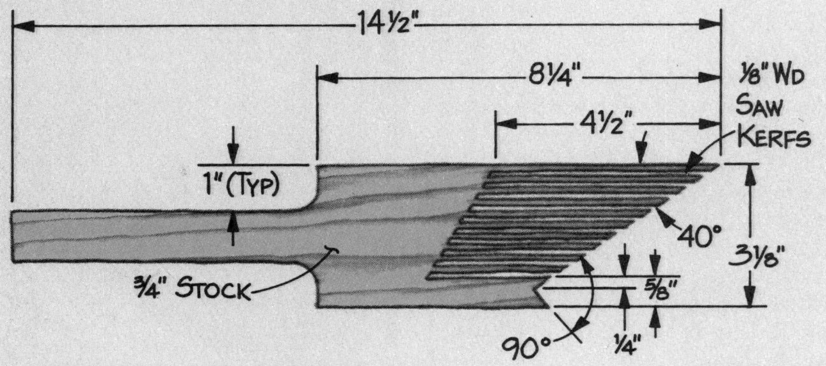

SIDE VIEW

FEATHERBOARD/ PUSH STICK

ADJUSTABLE FEATHERBOARD

Most featherboards are single pieces of wood with flexible "feathers" or fingers cut into one end. They are designed to be clamped to the worktables of various power tools. Unfortunately, this simple design doesn't always work well for the table saw because the table is often too large to clamp the jig near the work.

This adjustable featherboard solves that problem. The mount, not the featherboard, clamps to the table. By moving the mount from side to side and the featherboard back and forth, you can position the featherboard anywhere you need it on the saw.

The procedures for making this jig are straightforward, but there are two important considerations. First, you must adjust the length of the mount to fit your table saw — when assembled, the space between the inside edges of the mount blocks should only be about $1/16$ inch longer than the front-to-back dimension of the saw table. Second, you must glue a disc of 220-grit emery cloth to the top surface of the featherboard, over the pivot hole, to help keep the featherboard at the proper angle.

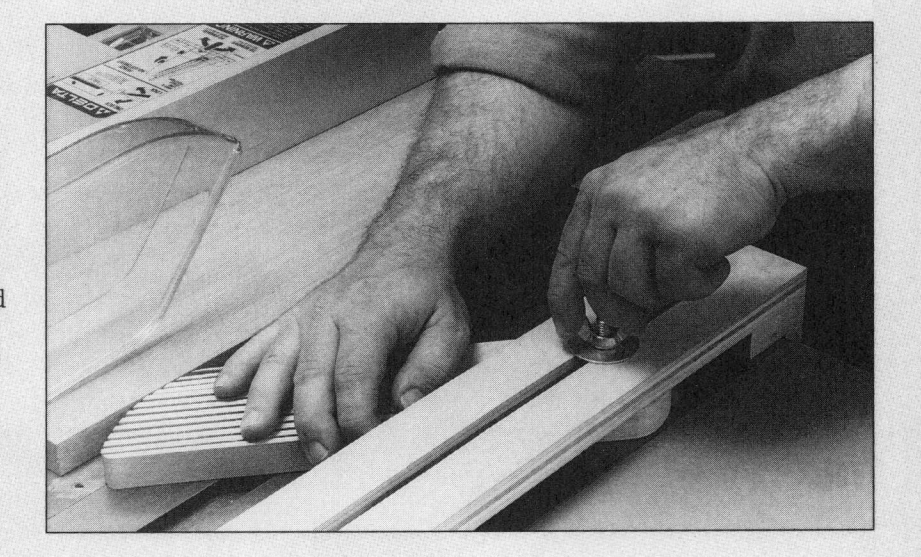

1 **To mount the featherboard** on the saw table, place it so the mount blocks straddle the front and back edges of the table. Turn the thumbscrews *finger-tight* only. They don't have to be any tighter; the sideways pressure from the featherboard locks the assembly in place. And if you do overtighten the screws, the mount will bow in the middle.

2 **Place the piece of wood you** plan to cut on the table saw. Position the featherboard next to the wood and adjust the angle so the feathers are flexed *slightly*. Secure the featherboard by tightening the wing nut. **Note:** the featherboard must press against the board *before* it reaches the saw blade. If there is sideways pressure at the saw blade or behind it, the blade may bind in the cut.

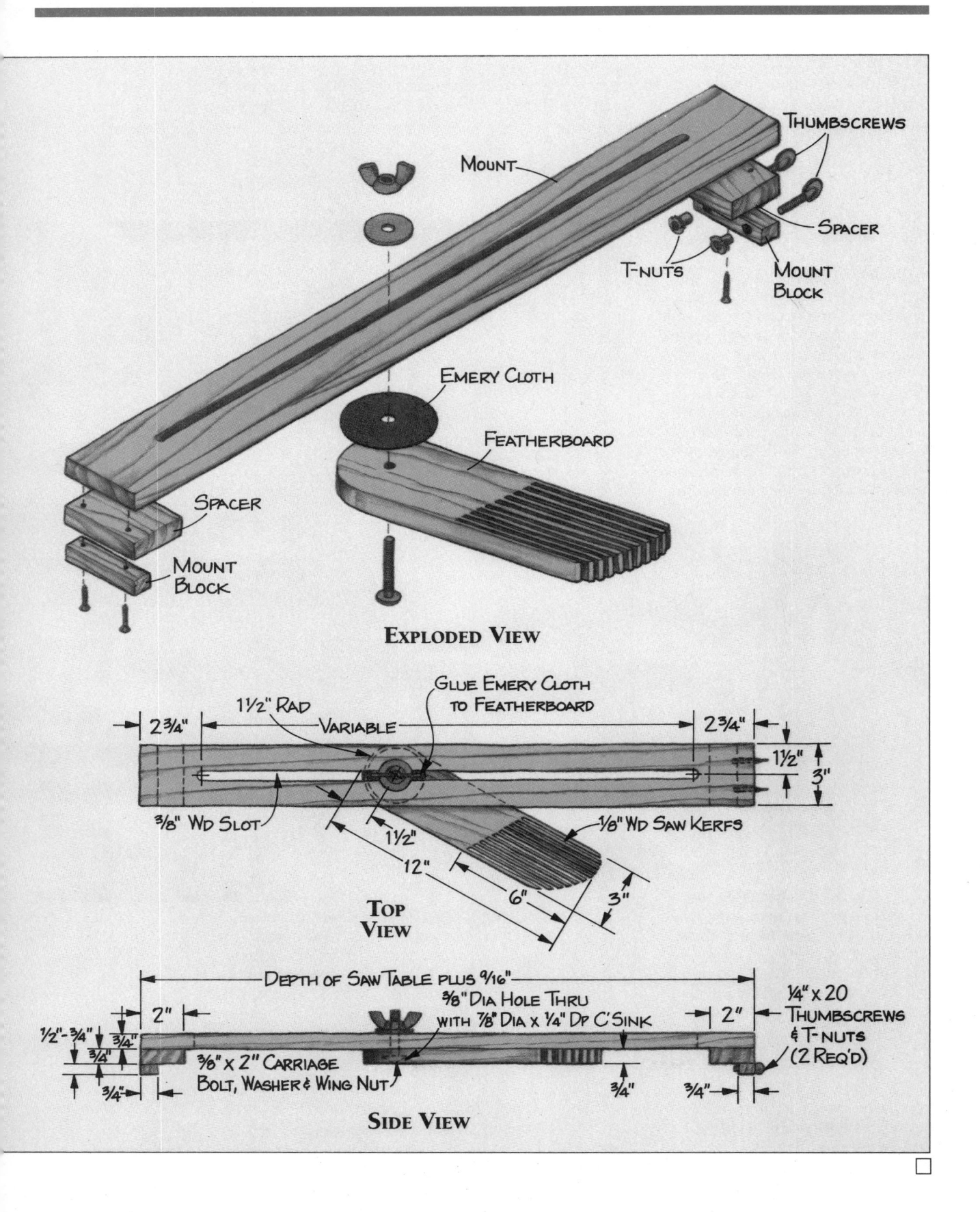

THUMBSCREWS

MOUNT

SPACER

T-NUTS

MOUNT
BLOCK

EMERY CLOTH

FEATHERBOARD

SPACER

MOUNT
BLOCK

EXPLODED VIEW

GLUE EMERY CLOTH
TO FEATHERBOARD

2¾"   1½" RAD   VARIABLE   2¾"

1½"
3"

⅜" WD SLOT

1½"

12"

6"

3"

⅛" WD SAW KERFS

**TOP
VIEW**

DEPTH OF SAW TABLE PLUS 9/16"

⅜" DIA HOLE THRU
WITH ⅞" DIA x ¼" DP C'SINK

¼" x 20
THUMBSCREWS
& T-NUTS
(2 REQ'D)

2"   2"

½"-¾"   ¾"

¾"

⅜" x 2" CARRIAGE
BOLT, WASHER & WING NUT

¾"

¾"   ¾"

SIDE VIEW

There are several special safety considerations if you are cutting extremely small or extremely large stock. Small boards can easily fall down between the blade and the insert, where they will likely be splintered. They may also be lifted off the table as they pass by the rear of the saw blade and flung like arrows. To prevent small pieces from dropping down, make a *Zero-Clearance Table Insert* for your table saw. (SEE FIGURES 2-24 AND 2-25.) To prevent them from lifting up, cover them with or attach them to larger scraps as you cut them. (SEE FIGURE 2-26.)

2-24 To make a *Zero-Clearance Table Insert,* plane a piece of hardwood to the thickness of your regular blade insert. Trace the shape of the insert on the planed stock and saw it on a band saw or with a saber saw, cutting about $1/16$ inch wide of the line. Fasten the metal blade insert to the wooden blank with double-faced carpet tape, and rout the final shape with a flush-trim bit. Adjust the height of the bit so the pilot bearing follows the shape of the metal insert while the cutters trim the wood.

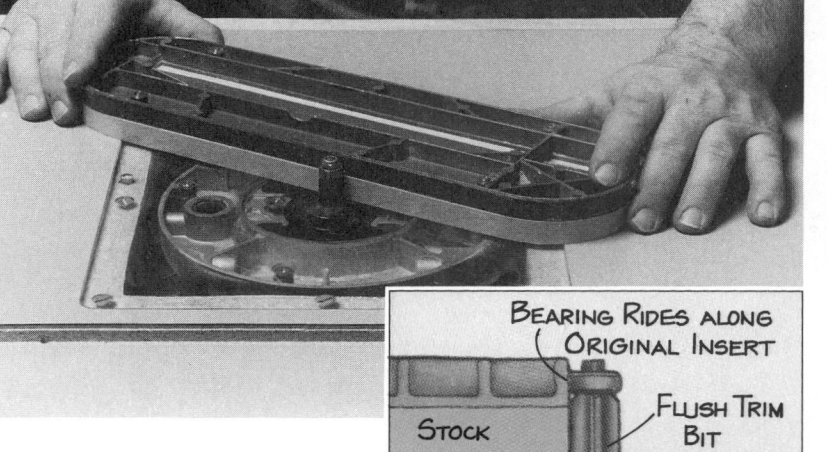

2-25 Check that the table saw blade is set at the proper angle, then lower it beneath the surface of the table. Install the wooden insert in place of the metal one. Position the rip fence beside the insert and clamp a featherboard to the fence. Adjust the featherboard to press down on the insert and keep it from lifting up. Turn on the saw and slowly raise the blade. The blade will cut a narrow kerf in the insert, leaving almost no clearance between the blade plate and the sides of the kerf.

2-26 Use the *Zero-Clearance Table Insert* when cutting small or narrow parts — it will keep them from falling down into the saw. To prevent the saw blade from lifting the parts and possibly flinging them at you, place a scrap over the good stock, sticking the two pieces together with carpet tape. Note that on the operation shown, the blade does not project through the scrap. In this case, the scrap also serves as a blade guard.

The table may not be large enough to properly support large or long boards. They can tip one way or the other as you feed them past the blade. To help support the end of the board that hangs over the edge of the table, use a *roller stand*. (SEE FIGURES 2-27 AND 2-28.) There are many commercial stands available, and you can also make your own. See "Roller Stand" on page 34.

As you make the cut, constantly monitor the blade. Use your senses:

■ *Watch* the cut as it progresses. The saw must follow the layout lines. If you're using a rip fence, the guiding edge of the board must remain against the fence. Also watch that your fingers and other parts of your body don't stray into the danger zone.

■ *Feel* the vibrations that are generated by the saw. If they begin to build up, the motor may be straining or the blade may be fluxing. Feed the wood more slowly. Sudden, violent vibrations may mean the stock is about to kick back. Shut off the saw immediately.

■ *Listen* to the whine of the saw blade and the hum of the motor. Frequently, a change in pitch or a ringing sound is the only clue the machine gives you that something is wrong. If the sound gets lower, the motor may be straining and bogging down. Slow the feed. If there's a ringing sound, particularly when you finish a cut, some part of the saw may be out of alignment.

■ *Smell* the cut as you make it. There should be nothing but a clean, woody scent — the smell of fresh-cut lumber. If there is a burning smell, there could be several things wrong. The saw blade might be dull or clogged with pitch, sawdust could be building up in the gullets and not clearing fast enough, the feed rate might be too slow, or the saw parts could be out of alignment.

Finally, when you finish the cut, push the wood completely past the saw blade. Turn off the saw and let it come to a complete stop before you retrieve the cut pieces.

2-27 To use a roller stand when making a rip cut, position the stand directly behind the saw blade and several feet out from the saw, depending on the length of the board. If you are sawing thin stock and the board droops as it passes the edge of the table, lower the stand so it's slightly below the table surface.

2-28 To use a roller stand when crosscutting a long board, place the stand directly to the side of the saw blade and several feet out from the saw. Note that in both operations — ripping and crosscutting — the rollers travel in the same direction as the board.

ROLLER STAND

A roller stand helps to support boards that are too large or too long to be properly supported by the saw table alone. This particular stand has two interchangeable "heads" — one for crosscuts and the other for rips. The height of the rollers can be adjusted from 28 inches to 40 inches so the jig can be used with any table saw and a wide variety of other stationary power tools. To prevent it from wobbling on uneven floors, the stand rests on three feet. These feet are equipped with levelers to keep the roller heads horizontal and level with the saw table.

Make the rollers from hardwood rolling pins. Slice the narrow rollers on the crosscut head from two pins, and use a single uncut pin for the wide roller on the rip head. Rout the slots in the head supports, then assemble the parts of the stand with simple butt and lap joints. Nail *and* glue each part together. However, be careful not to get any glue on the rollers — these must turn easily.

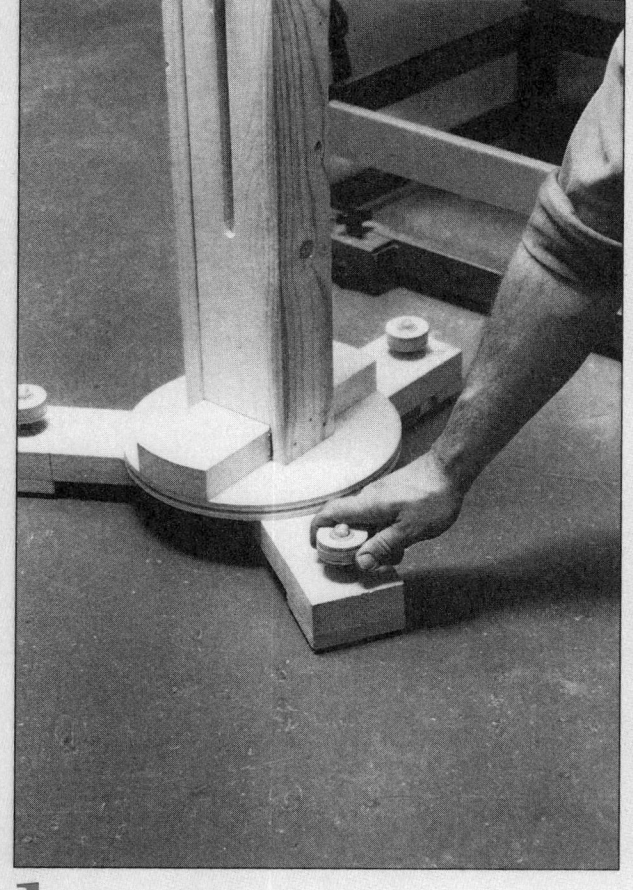

1 **To use the roller stand, first** install the proper head — crosscut or rip. Place the stand several feet out from the saw and adjust the levelers until the head is horizontal.

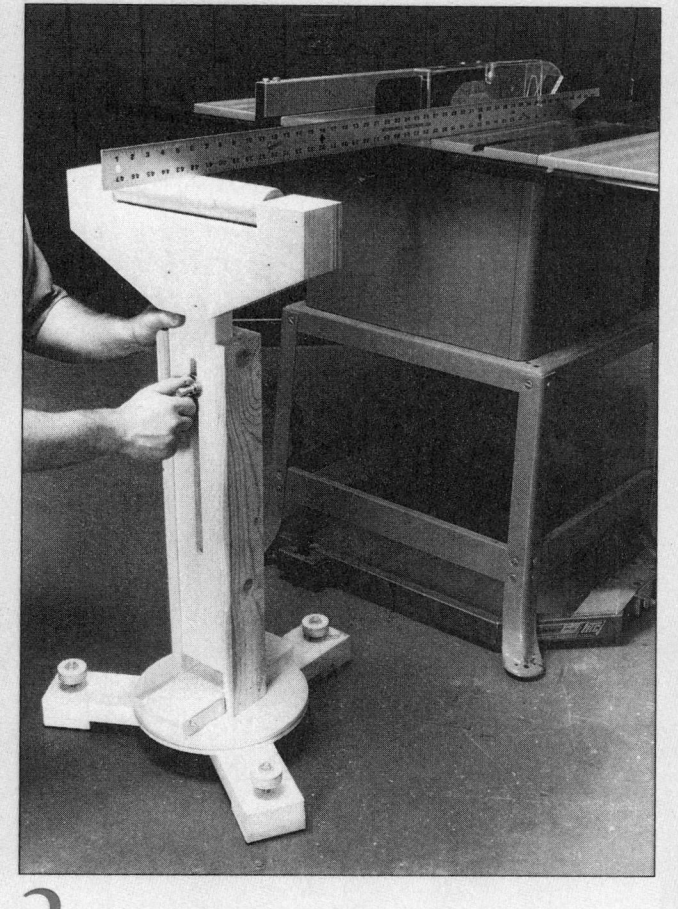

2 **When the head is level,** adjust it to the proper height. Place a straightedge or a straight board across the table and the rollers. Raise or lower the head until the straightedge lies flat on the table.

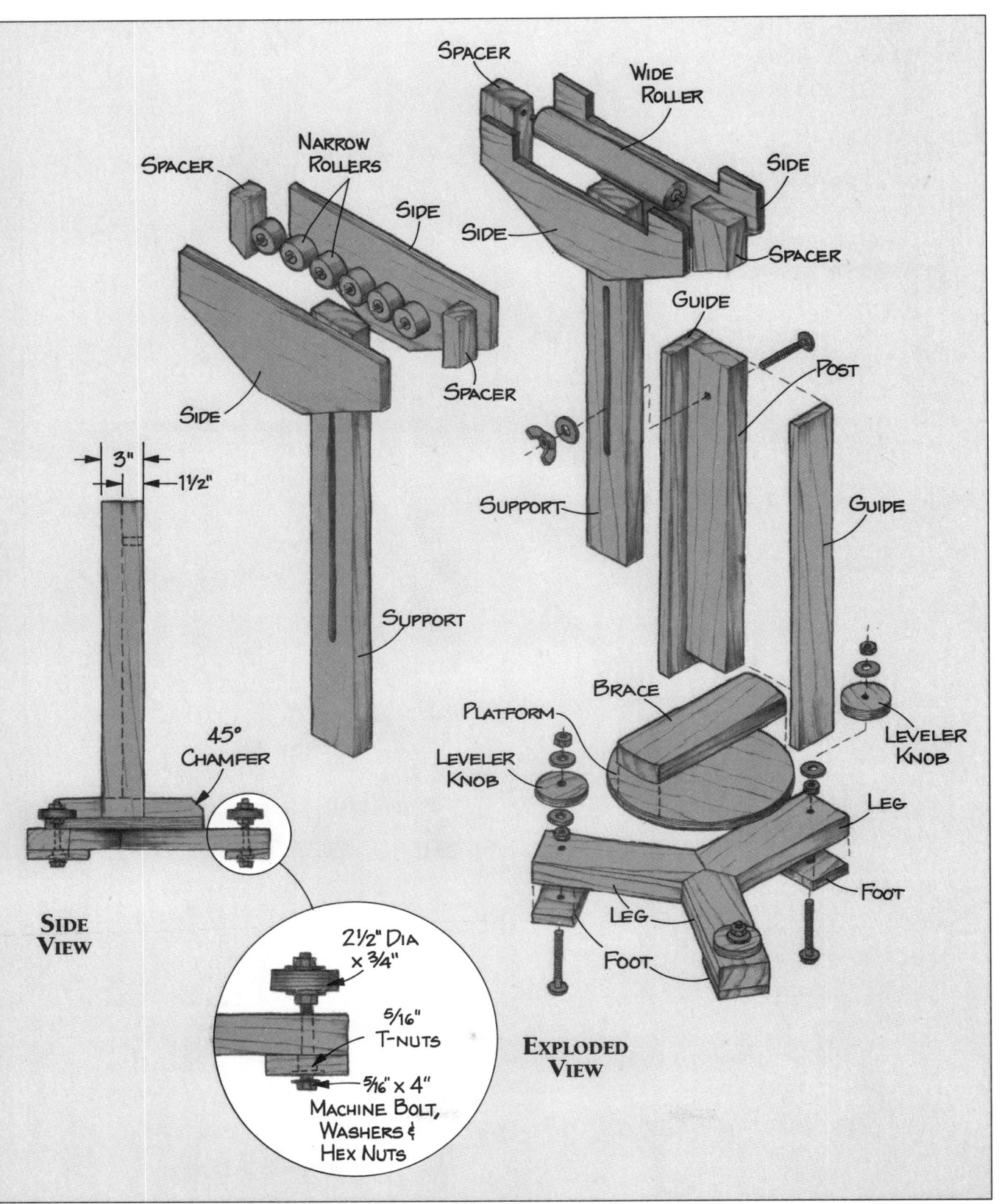

SPACER

NARROW
ROLLERS

SPACER

SIDE

SIDE

SPACER

3"

1½"

SUPPORT

45°
CHAMFER

SIDE
VIEW

SPACER

WIDE
ROLLER

SIDE

SIDE

SPACER

GUIDE

POST

SUPPORT

GUIDE

BRACE

PLATFORM

LEVELER
KNOB

LEVELER
KNOB

LEG

FOOT

LEG

FOOT

EXPLODED
VIEW

2½" DIA
x ¾"

5/16"
T-NUTS

5/16" x 4"
MACHINE BOLT,
WASHERS &
HEX NUTS

(continued) ▷

Roller Stand — continued

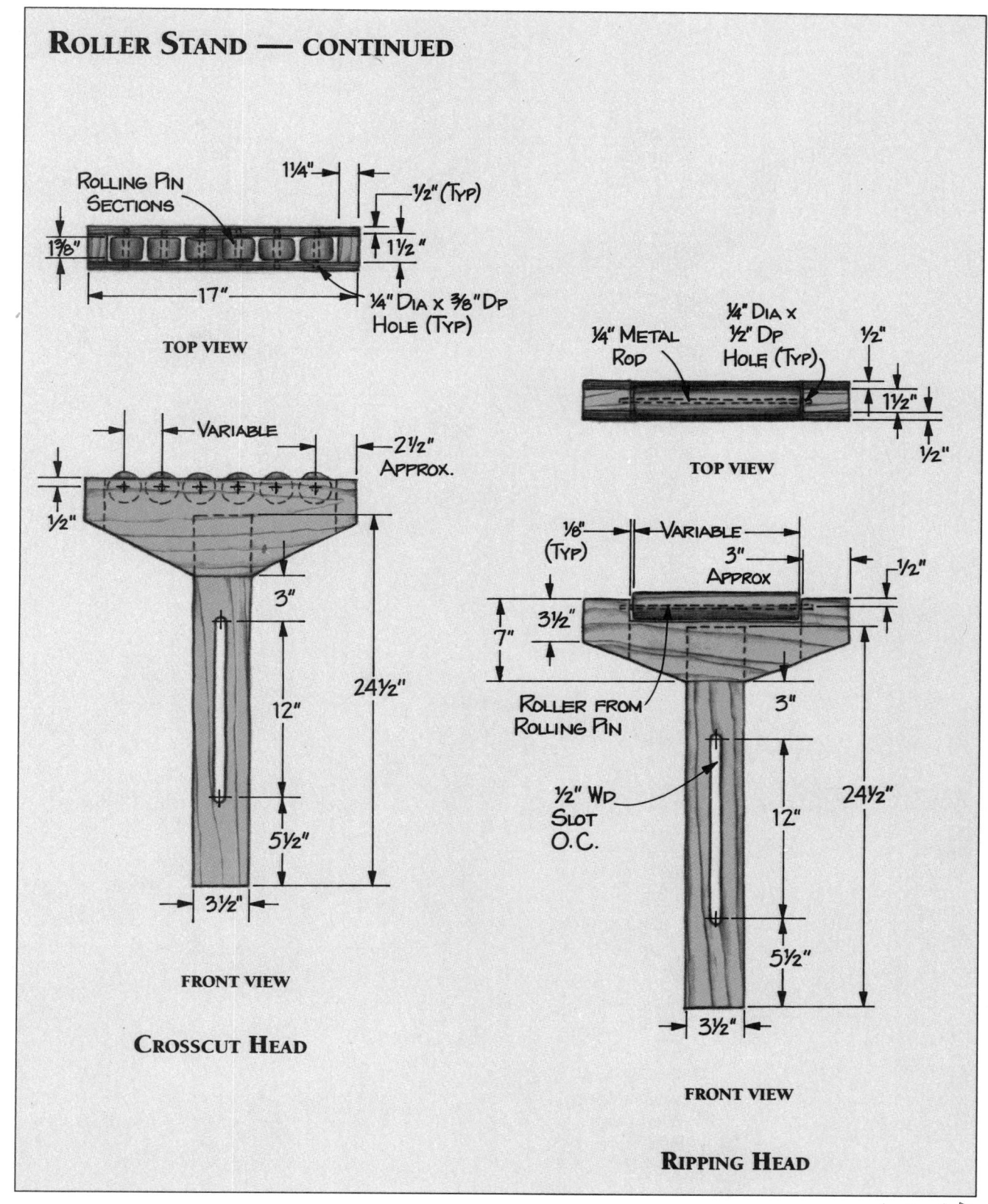

ROLLING PIN SECTIONS

1¼"

½" (Typ)

1⅜"

1½"

17"

¼" Dia x ⅜" Dp Hole (Typ)

TOP VIEW

VARIABLE

2½" Approx.

½"

3"

24½"

12"

5½"

3½"

FRONT VIEW

Crosscut Head

¼" METAL ROD

¼" Dia x ½" Dp Hole (Typ)

½"

1½"

½"

TOP VIEW

⅛" (Typ)

VARIABLE

3" Approx

½"

3½"

7"

ROLLER FROM ROLLING PIN

3"

½" Wd Slot O.C.

12"

24½"

5½"

3½"

FRONT VIEW

Ripping Head

(continued) ▷

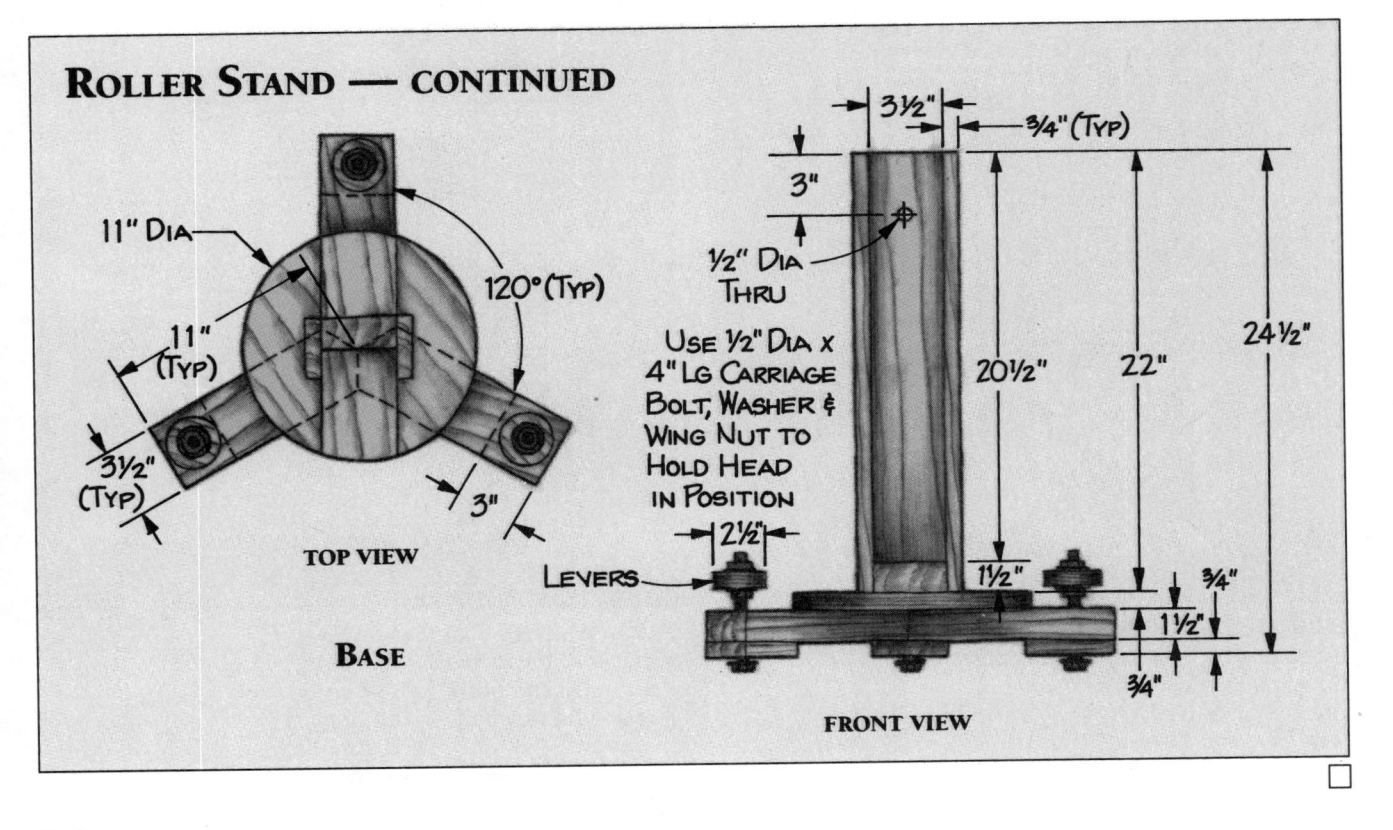

ROLLER STAND — CONTINUED

11" DIA

120° (TYP)

11" (TYP)

3½" (TYP)

3"

TOP VIEW

BASE

3½"

3"

½" DIA THRU

Use ½" DIA x 4" LG CARRIAGE BOLT, WASHER & WING NUT TO HOLD HEAD IN POSITION

¾" (TYP)

20½"

22"

24½"

2½"

1½"

¾"

1½"

¾"

LEVERS

FRONT VIEW

MAINTENANCE

As you make each cut, sawdust collects inside the saw body. The table and fence grow sticky with wood resins, particularly if you work with pine, cedar, teak, rosewood, and other oily woods. Wood pitch builds up on the blade and the sawteeth lose their sharp edge. To maintain the machine in proper cutting order, it must be periodically cleaned and lubricated, and the blades must be sharpened.

CLEANING AND LUBRICATION

Sawdust has an abrasive effect. If allowed to build up inside the table saw, it will cause the blade tilt, blade elevation, bearings, and other mechanisms to wear prematurely. Furthermore, fine sawdust can work its way into the switch and motor, causing these electrical parts to fail. To prevent these problems, provide some sort of sawdust collection for your table saw and clean the inside of the saw regularly.

To clean the saw, unplug it and remove the blade. Vacuum inside the saw body, removing as much sawdust as you can reach. Inspect the blade carriage and other parts for gummy buildup. As you cut wood, the saw blade heats the wood resins and flings them all over the inside of the saw, where they stick. Dissolve

the bigger lumps of resin with turpentine or oven cleaner. Then scrub all the parts with a stiff bristle or brass wire brush. (*SEE FIGURE 2-29.*)

When the parts of the blade carriage are clean, lubricate the blade tilt and blade elevation mechanisms with a light application of graphite or spray silicone. (Do *not* use oil or grease; this will mix with sawdust and gum up the works.) The bearings and bushings in most modern table saws rarely require lubrication because they are permanently sealed or made from a self-lubricating alloy. Your owner's manual will tell you if any additional lubrication is required. **Note:** If you purchase a new saw, clean the grease from the carriage parts.

Once the inside of the saw is cleaned and lubricated, do the same for the outside. Brush or vacuum away the sawdust, then inspect the table, rip fence, fence rails, and miter gauge. Remove any rust, stains, or wood pitch from these surfaces with fine steel wool or Scotch-Brite. Apply a coat of paste wax to these parts and *buff thoroughly.* (*SEE FIGURE 2-30.*) This buffing is *extremely* important! When properly buffed, wax repels sawdust, inhibits rust, and lubricates the surfaces, making it easier to feed the wood across them.

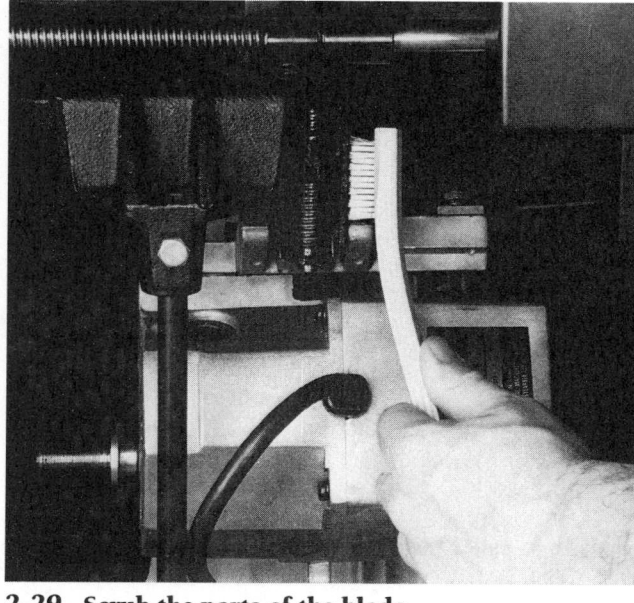

2-29 Scrub the parts of the blade carriage with a stiff brush to remove built-up wood resins and compressed sawdust. Do *not* use a steel wire brush to clean these mechanisms, especially if they are made from cast aluminum or some other soft material.

2-30 Wax *and* buff the working surfaces of the saw table, rip fence, fence rails, and miter gauge to protect and lubricate them. Buffing is important — if not rubbed out, the wax will mix with sawdust and gum up the surfaces.

Note: When buffed, the wax film that covers the metal is only a few molecules thick and *extremely* tenacious. There is little chance it will rub off on the wood and interfere with a finish — especially if you scrape or sand the wood before applying the finish.

FOR YOUR INFORMATION

I can't overemphasize the difference a good wax-and-buff job makes in the operation of a table saw. I was once present in a tool design lab when several engineers measured the force required to push a board across a worktable before and after it was waxed. When buffed, the wax reduced the force required by almost 400 percent!

BLADE CARE

Saw blades, of course, must be kept clean and sharp to cut properly. When a blade ceases to cut well, it's not always an indication that the teeth are losing their cutting edge. Usually, the problem is caused by accu-mulated wood pitch on the teeth. To restore the edge, simply clean the blade.

There are several ways to do this. Woodworkers swear by all sorts of solvents — ammonia, baking soda dissolved in water, turpentine, mineral spirits, even vegetable oil. My own favorite is oven cleaner. The blade doesn't have to be warm, as the directions on the can might lead you to believe. Just spray the cleaner on the teeth, wait a few seconds, and wipe it off with a damp cloth. (*SEE FIGURE 2-31.*) Use a brass wire brush to remove stubborn deposits. After cleaning a saw blade, wax and buff the plate to help the blade run cooler and keep it clean longer.

If cleaning the blade doesn't restore the edge, the blade probably needs to be sharpened. Unfortunately, sharpening a blade — or even touching up the cutting edges — is not something that most woodworkers can do in their own shops. There are many facets to the teeth of most modern saw blades, and special equipment is needed to accurately grind and hone these complex angles. This is especially true of carbide-tipped saws. It's best to find a good professional sharpening service and take your blades to them as necessary.

Many craftsmen swear that their old saw blades cut better than their new ones. This is true, but not because manufacturers made better blades in days gone by. Resharpened blades, no matter what the date of manufacture, often cut better than they did when fresh from the factory. There are two reasons for this. First, the cutting edges that many manufacturers — even well-respected manufacturers — put on their sawteeth leave a lot to be desired. They don't take time for the honing and polishing that a sharpening service provides. Second, resharpening removes a little material from each tooth. As the teeth grow smaller, there is less metal to drag through the wood. The blade cuts quicker and cleaner.

When a blade isn't mounted on a table saw, protect its teeth from nicks and dents by wrapping the rim in a length of polyethylene tubing or garden hose. (SEE FIGURE 2-32.)

In addition to sharpening the sawteeth, there are other ways in which a sharpening service may be able to tune up your saw blades:

■ If the blade *run-out* is so pronounced that it interferes with the operation, have the blade balanced.

■ If the blade *whistles,* the depth of the gullets may be incorrect. Have the gullets checked and, if necessary, reground.

■ If the blade *screams* or *rings,* and realigning the table saw doesn't solve the problem, there may be internal stress in the blade plate. Ask the sharpening service to relieve this stress, if they can.

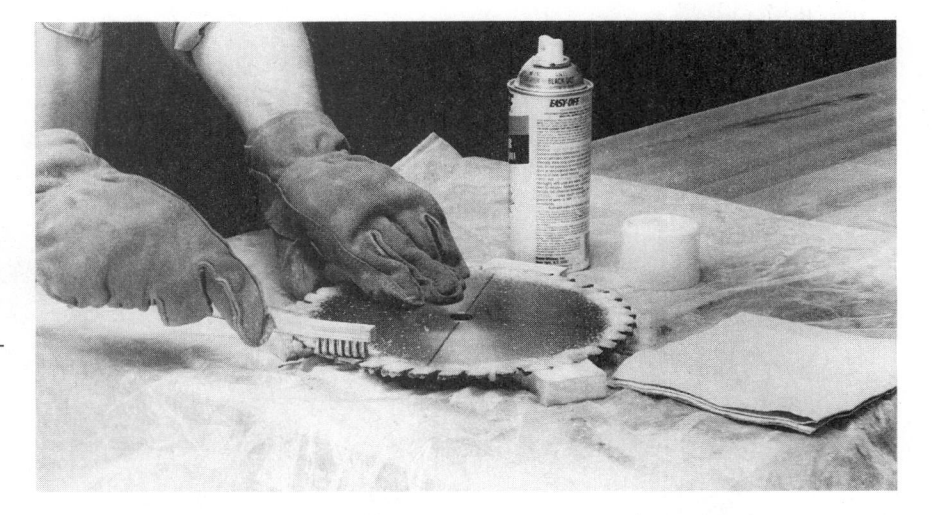

2-31 There are several solvents you can use to clean saw blades, but the easiest to apply is oven cleaner — just spray it on. Remember, the cleaner is caustic. Wear a face shield and old leather work gloves when using it. Don't use rubber gloves — the sawteeth may puncture them.

2-32 To protect a saw blade when it isn't in use, cut a length of old garden hose or polyethylene tubing. (A 10-inch saw blade requires about 33 inches of tubing.) Split the hose or tubing down one side, then wrap it around the blade rim, inserting the teeth in the split.

3
CROSSCUTS, RIPS, AND MITERS

There are three basic saw cuts — crosscuts, rips, and miters. Crosscuts are made perpendicular to the wood grain, rips are parallel to the grain, and miters are cut at angles in between. None of these requires elaborate jigs or complex techniques. However, each type of cut presents special problems which you must deal with to make the cut safely and accurately.

Of the three, crosscuts are perhaps the most troublesome to make on a table saw. To cut across the grain, you must move the board sideways, perpendicular to its length. The longer the board, the more difficult this is to do. To crosscut accurately, you must use equipment and techniques that improve balance and control.

Rips are the least difficult. It's much easier to feed a board parallel to its length than perpendicular. Unfortunately, table saws aren't as deep as they are wide, and so provide less support when ripping. You must still balance the board to maintain accuracy.

Miters are the most frustrating. In addition to presenting the usual problems of balance and control, angled cuts are more difficult to measure and lay out than crosscuts and rips. Not only do you need to employ the proper equipment and techniques, you must test and retest your setup to ensure its precision.

CROSSCUTS

Straight from the factory, a table saw is a poor cut-off tool. Using nothing but the equipment provided, you'll find it difficult to crosscut a long board, and almost impossible to do it accurately. Yet many craftsmen consider their table saws to be the most precise, reliable cut-off tools in their shops — even more so than radial arm saws and other tools designed especially for cut-off work. All the table saw needs is a little fine tuning and a few custom jigs.

The problem is the factory-supplied miter gauge. The typical gauge has a small face, often less than 6 inches wide — too small to properly support even a medium-size board. Consequently, when you feed the board past the blade, it tends to twist or pivot on the gauge. The solution is straightforward — *provide more*

support by enlarging the face of the miter gauge with a *miter gauge extension*. Making an extension is as simple as attaching a board to the gauge. This board must be long enough and rigid enough to keep the wood steady during the cut. (*SEE FIGURES 3-1 AND 3-2.*) You can also build more elaborate, more versatile extensions, if you need them. See the "Miter Gauge Extension and Stop" on page 47.

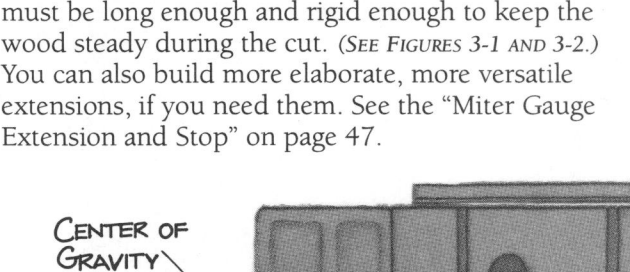

CENTER OF GRAVITY

48" LONG BOARD

24" LONG MITER GAUGE EXTENSION

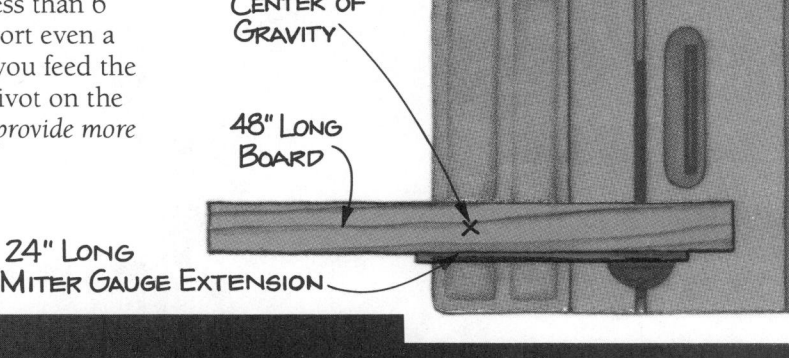

3-1 To provide proper support, a miter gauge extension must reach at least as far as the middle or *center of gravity* of the board — the point at which it will balance. This, in turn, keeps the board from twisting or pivoting as it's cut. For example, this 24-inch-long extension will support boards up to 48 inches long.

3-2 An extension must also be rigid enough to support a fairly large board without flexing. The easiest way to make a rigid extension is to use a thick hardwood board. You can also make a beam-type construction by joining two or more boards at right angles, as shown.

You can also provide additional support and rigidity by ganging two miter gauges. Purchase an extra miter gauge from the saw manufacturer and place one in each slot. Adjust them to the proper angle, then attach a single long extension to both. *(SEE FIGURE 3-3.)* This setup supports the board directly behind the cut, and it's more rigid than a single miter gauge. The "Cut-Off Bar" on the facing page is an adaptation of this idea.

Many craftsmen dispense with the miter gauge completely, replacing it with a *sliding table* or *rolling table* to provide the support needed for accurate crosscuts. *(SEE FIGURE 3-4.)* Of the two, a sliding table is more popular. Rolling tables are much more costly and take up additional floor space.

TRY THIS TRICK

When using a miter gauge extension to cut off large, wide panels, clamp a block of wood to the extension to serve as a hold-down. This will keep the panels from tipping over the back edge of the table saw as you finish the cut.

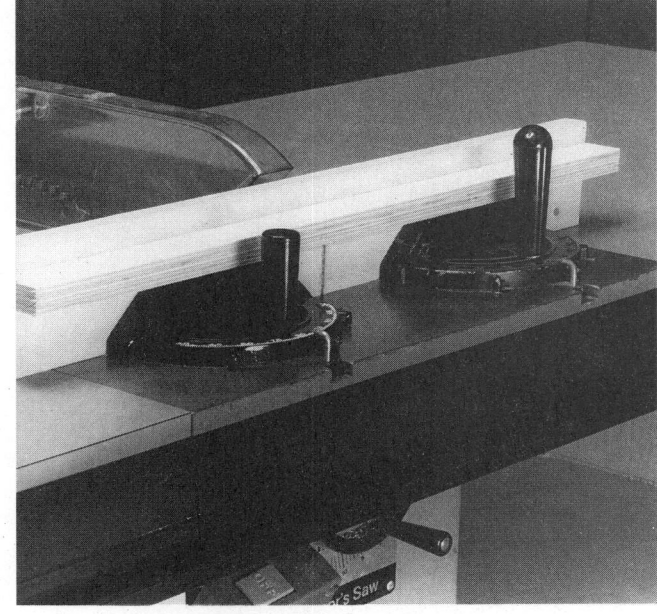

3-3 To provide rigid support directly behind a crosscut, join two miter gauges — one in each slot — with an extension. This setup also works well for miter cuts.

3-4 A sliding table provides additional support *and* eliminates the friction between the work and the saw table. This greatly reduces the tendency of long boards to twist or pivot as you crosscut. You can choose between several commercial sliding tables, or make the one shown. See the "Sliding Table" on page 94.

CUT-OFF BAR

One reason the factory-supplied miter gauge is an inadequate table saw accessory is that it attempts to do too much. Because it's designed to make both crosscuts and miters at a wide range of angles, it trades accuracy for versatility. The cut-off bar makes the opposite trade. It's designed to do just one thing — make 90-degree crosscuts — and it does this precisely.

The long face of the bar is braced to remain absolutely rigid. The bar assembly straddles the saw blade to support the work directly behind the cut. It's mounted to two guide bars — one for each miter gauge slot — for additional stability.

When making this jig, cut the face from solid hardwood and the brace from cabinet-grade plywood. Glue — but *don't* screw — the face to the brace. Let the glue cure completely, then joint the face perfectly straight, flat, and perpendicular to the *bottom* edge. (If you don't have a jointer that's wide enough, have it done at a commercial cabinet shop.) Assemble the mounts and guard box with glue and screws, then fasten these assemblies to the bar assembly with screws only. *Don't* glue them — you may want to remove and replace the bar when it's chewed up.

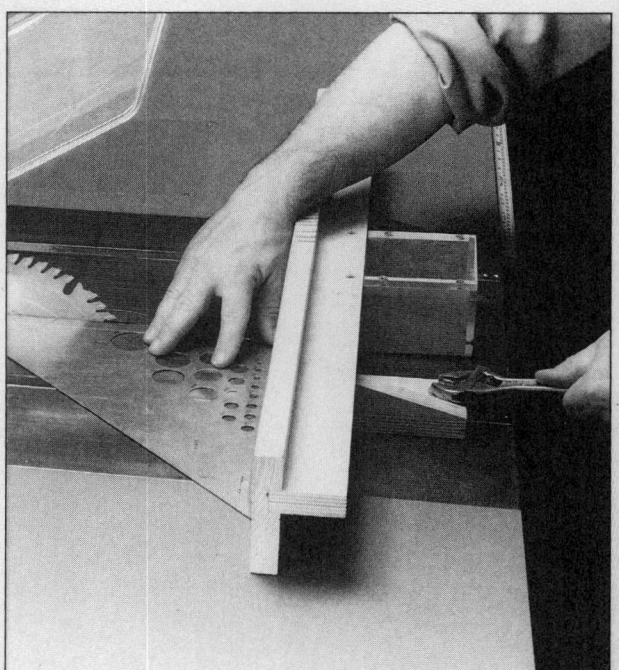

1 **Drill oversize holes in the** mounts for the guide bar mounting bolts. Attach the bars by finger-tightening the bolts. Place the jig on the table saw with the guide bars in the miter gauge slots. Because the bolt holes are oversize, the face will shift back and forth a few degrees. Square it to the blade, then tighten the bolts completely.

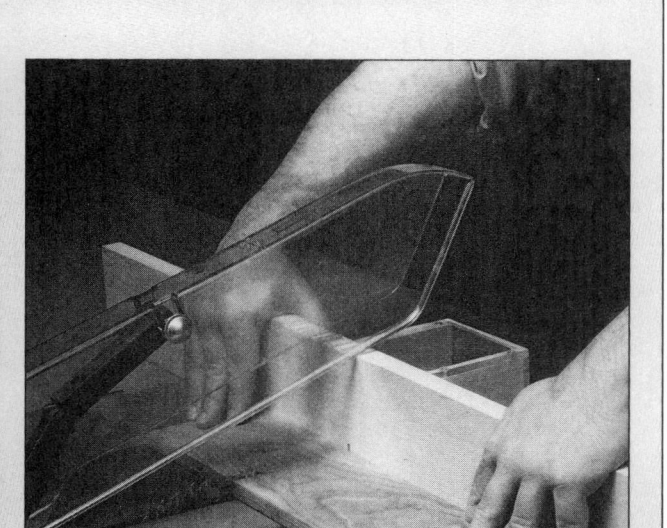

2 **To use the cut-off bar, place** the board you want to cut against the face and align the cut mark with the blade. Turn on the saw and push the bar forward. **Warning:** Do not hold the bar so your hand will pass directly over the saw blade. The sawtooth cuts on the top edge of the face are a tactile reminder of where *not* to place your hands.

(continued) ▷

CUT-OFF BAR — CONTINUED

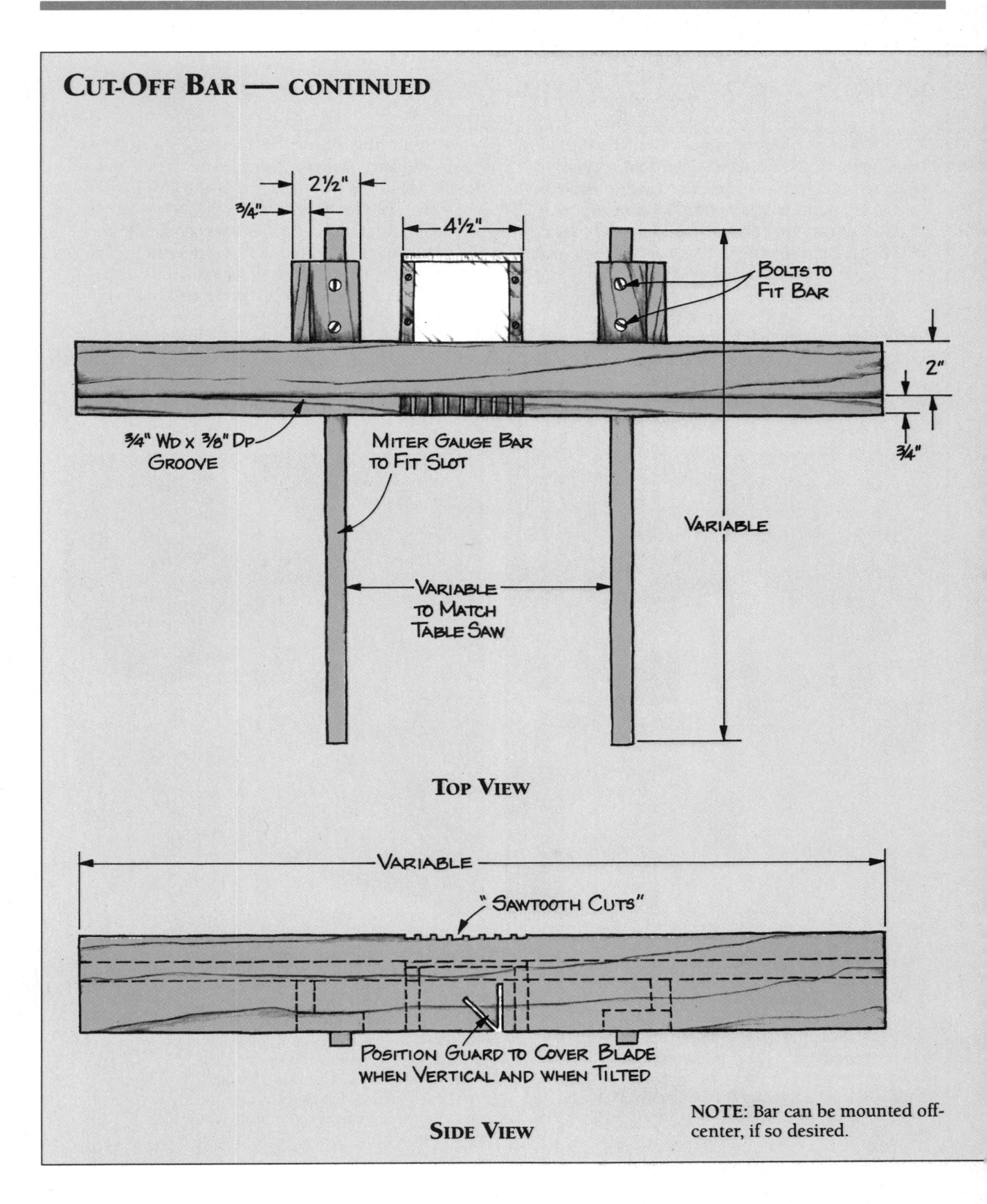

2½"

¾"

4½"

BOLTS TO
FIT BAR

2"

¾"

¾" WD x ⅜" DP
GROOVE

MITER GAUGE BAR
TO FIT SLOT

VARIABLE

VARIABLE
TO MATCH
TABLE SAW

TOP VIEW

VARIABLE

"SAWTOOTH CUTS"

POSITION GUARD TO COVER BLADE
WHEN VERTICAL AND WHEN TILTED

SIDE VIEW

NOTE: Bar can be mounted off-center, if so desired.

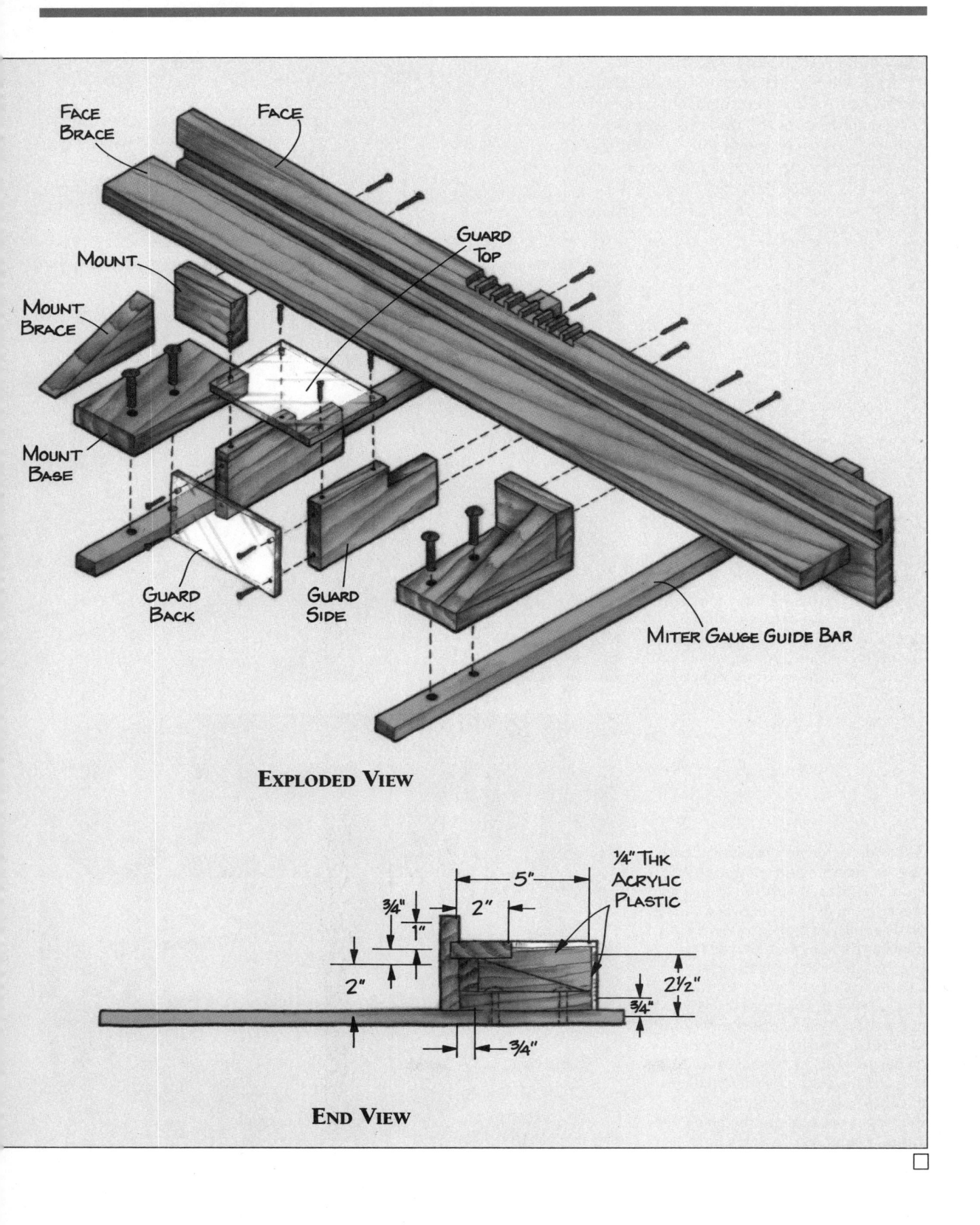

FACE
BRACE

FACE

GUARD
TOP

MOUNT

MOUNT
BRACE

MOUNT
BASE

GUARD
BACK

GUARD
SIDE

MITER GAUGE GUIDE BAR

EXPLODED VIEW

5"

2"

¼" THK
ACRYLIC
PLASTIC

¾"

1"

2"

2½"

¾"

¾"

END VIEW

In addition to making accurate crosscuts, wood-workers often need to make *duplicate* crosscuts. The easiest way to do this is to attach a *stop* to the miter gauge extension or the rip fence. (*SEE FIGURES 3-5 AND 3-6.*) Unfortunately, most table saw manufacturers don't provide even an inadequate stop — you must purchase or make your own, as shown in "Miter Gauge Extension and Stop" on the facing page.

> ## A SAFETY REMINDER
> Never use the rip fence as a stop for crosscutting. The cut-off pieces will be pinched between the blade and the fence, and the saw will fling them back at you.

3-5 To make duplicate crosscuts, clamp a stop to the miter gauge extension. The distance between the blade and the inside *edge* of the stop (closest to the blade) must match the length of the cuts you want to make. To use the stop, butt the end of the stock against it and make the cut. Repeat as many times as needed.

3-6 You can also make duplicate cuts by clamping the stop to the rip fence. Adjust the position of the rip fence so the distance between the blade and the inside *face* of the stop matches the length of the cuts you need to make. Place the stock against the miter gauge extension, butt the end against the stop, and make the cut. Repeat as many times as needed. **Warning:** The stop must be positioned several inches in front of the blade so the work is well clear of the stop as you finish the cut. If the stop is too close to the blade, the cut-off pieces may kick back.

MITER GAUGE EXTENSION AND STOP

This miter gauge extension offers several advantages over a simple board, one of them being the separate mount. The mount remains permanently attached to the miter gauge and replaces the usual bolt holes in the miter gauge with slots. This makes it easier to mount and dismount extensions and other jigs.

Note: A few manufacturers cut slots in their miter gauges rather than drilling bolt holes. If you own one of these, you can dispense with the mount.

Shown are two designs for extensions. The slotted extension can be easily positioned to the right, to the left, or in between, depending on where you need the support. The solid extension straddles the blade whether the miter gauge is in the right or the left slot. This supports the work behind the cut.

The stop will clamp to either extension. You can also attach it to the "Cut-Off Bar" on page 43, the *Long Fence Extension* on page 52, or the "Sliding Table" on page 94.

1 **To attach an extension to** the miter gauge, first screw or bolt the mount to the face. Loosen the wing nuts on an extension and slide the bolts into the slots. If you're using the slotted extension, position it right or left as needed. Then tighten the wing nuts. **Note:** Depending on how your miter gauge is made, you may need extra-long carriage bolts and *spacers.* Make these spacers from short lengths of hardwood dowel.

2 **To attach the stop to an** extension, loosen the wing nut. Slide the clamp over the top of the extension face and tighten the nut. **Note:** The beveled edges of the stop block help to prevent sawdust from becoming trapped between the stop and the work, preserving the accuracy of the cuts.

(continued) ▷

MITER GAUGE EXTENSION AND STOP — CONTINUED

When making the extensions, cut the faces from solid hardwood, and the braces and mount from plywood. Drill or rout the holes and slots required. Glue — but *don't* screw — the faces to the braces. Let the glue cure, then joint the faces straight and flat. (Once again — if you don't have a jointer, have the faces jointed at a commercial cabinet shop.) Cut the shape of the mount on a band saw or with a saber saw.

When making the stop, cut all the parts from solid hardwood. Bevel both edges of the stop block. To make the half-round groove in the clamp, attach the part to a scrap of hardwood. Drill a hole

through *both* pieces of wood, positioning the bit so half the hole is in the clamp and the other half is in the scrap.

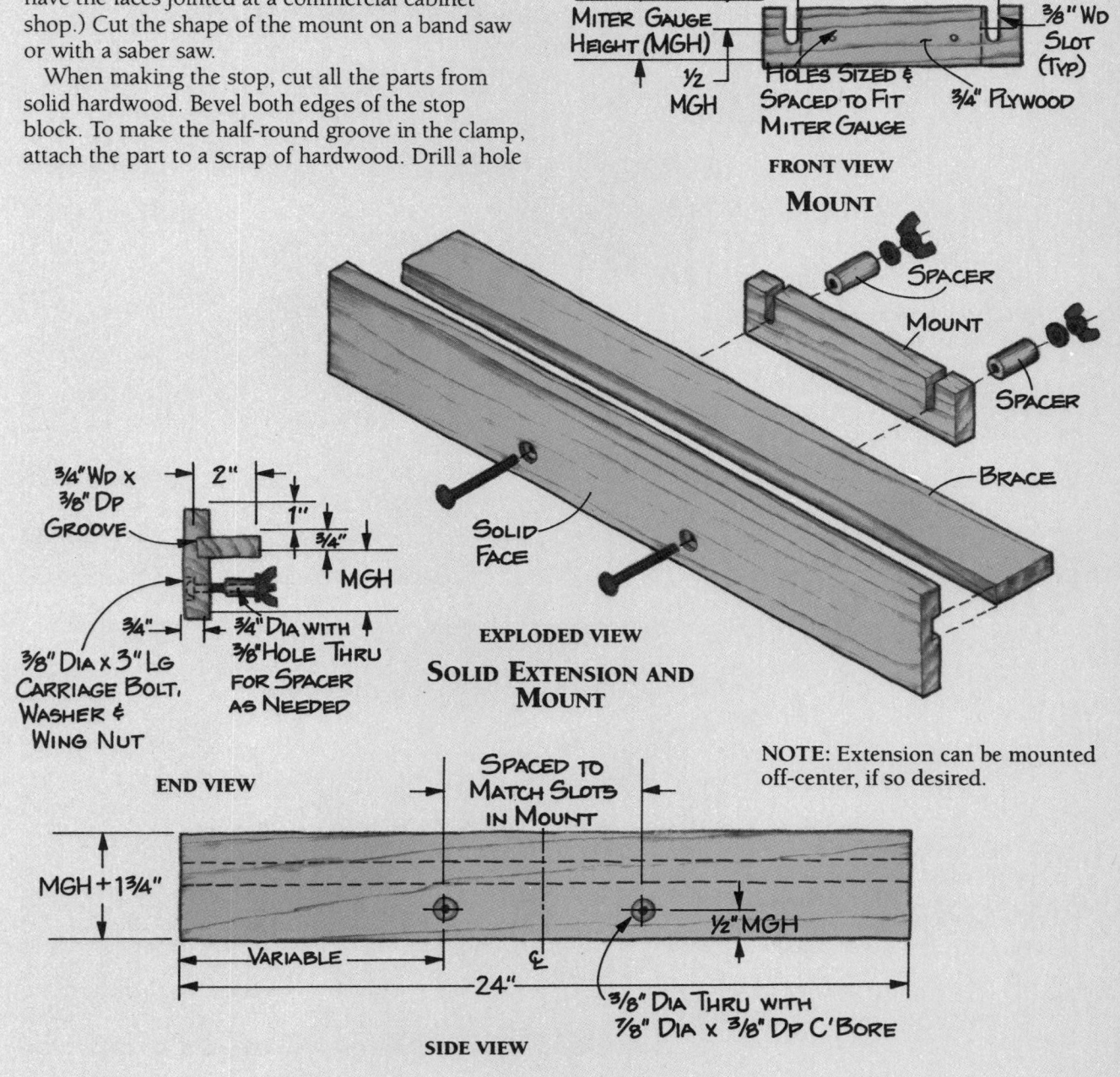

FRONT VIEW

MOUNT

END VIEW

EXPLODED VIEW

SOLID EXTENSION AND MOUNT

NOTE: Extension can be mounted off-center, if so desired.

SIDE VIEW

NOTE: MGH = MITER GAUGE HEIGHT

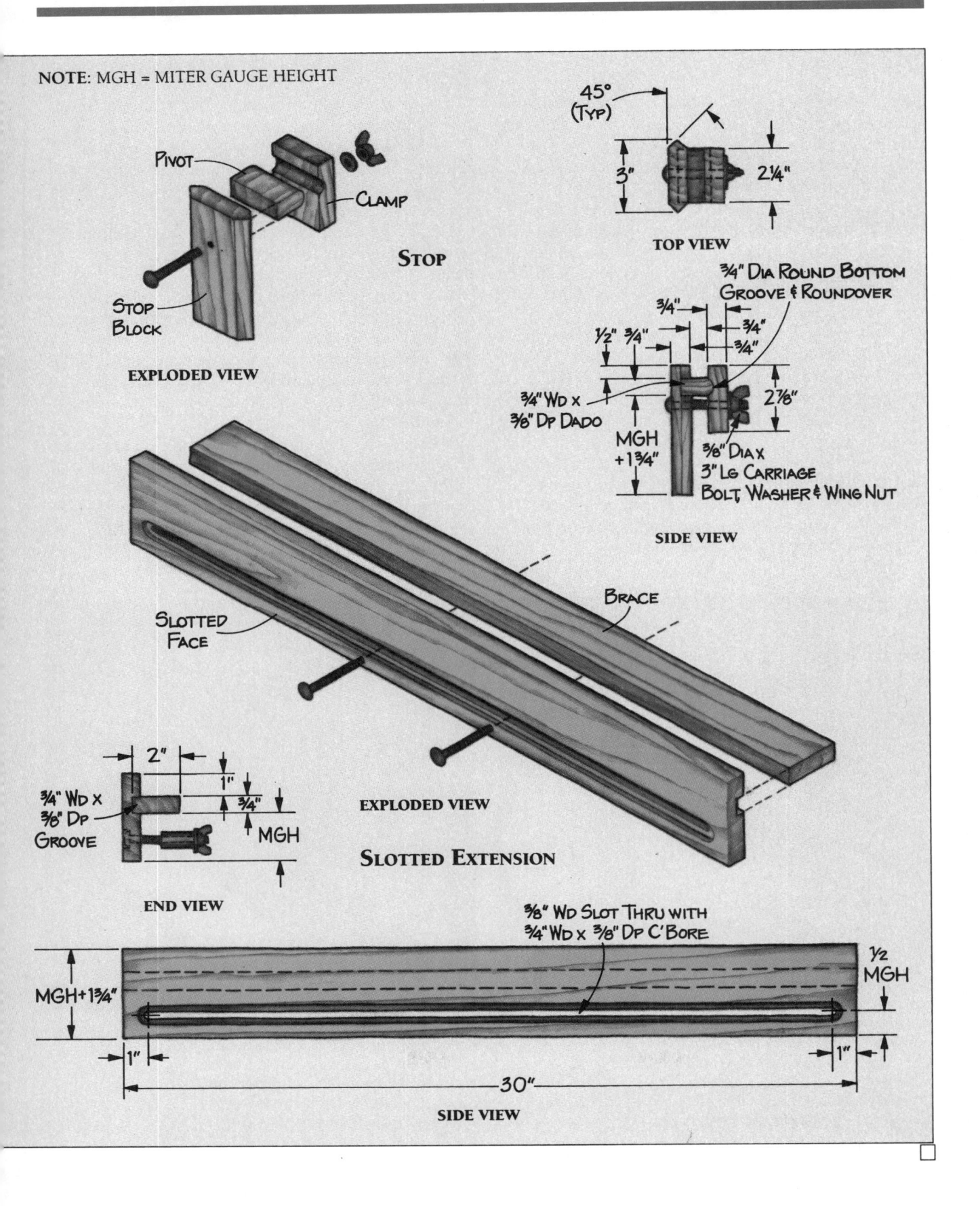

45° (TYP)

3"

2¼"

TOP VIEW

PIVOT

CLAMP

STOP

STOP BLOCK

EXPLODED VIEW

¾" DIA ROUND BOTTOM GROOVE & ROUNDOVER

¾"

½" ¾"

¾"

¾"

2⅞"

¾" WD X ⅜" DP DADO

MGH +1¾"

⅜" DIA X 3" LG CARRIAGE BOLT, WASHER & WING NUT

SIDE VIEW

SLOTTED FACE

BRACE

2"

1"

¾"

¾" WD X ⅜" DP GROOVE

MGH

EXPLODED VIEW

SLOTTED EXTENSION

END VIEW

⅜" WD SLOT THRU WITH ¾" WD X ⅜" DP C'BORE

½ MGH

MGH+1¾"

1"

1"

30"

SIDE VIEW

RIP CUTS

Unlike miter gauges, most factory-supplied fences are adequate guides for rip cuts. They may not remain as parallel to the blade as you could wish for, but you can compensate by quickly checking for parallelism as you position the fence.

Only when ripping unusually long, tall, or narrow stock do you need jigs that provide additional support and control. A *Long Fence Extension* — similar to a miter gauge extension — helps guide long boards or sheets of plywood in a straight line and supports them as they pass over the back edge of the saw. (*SEE FIGURE 3-7.*) When ripping the edge of a wide board, the stock may be too tall (as it sits on the worktable) for the rip fence to hold it in position. A *Tall Fence Extension* prevents the work from tilting or falling over. (*SEE FIGURE 3-8.*) To rip narrow stock, you must hold the stock on the table as it passes between the blade and the rip fence. A *Fence Straddler* rides along the rip fence, holding the stock down and pushing it along. (*SEE FIGURE 3-9.*) These are all simple jigs to build. See "Long and Tall Fence Extensions" on page 52, and the "Fence Straddler" on page 55.

If you rip a bevel or a chamfer, make sure the blade tilts *away from the fence*. (*SEE FIGURE 3-10.*) This gives you more room to safely maneuver the board and reduces the risk of kickback. On most machines, you will have to move the rip fence to the left of the blade (as you face the infeed side of the saw).

There are several other important considerations when ripping a board, no matter what its size or shape or the angle of the blade:

■ The board must have at least one straight edge — a *guiding edge* to rest against the rip fence. To make a guiding edge, joint the board before you rip it.

■ The board must be reasonably straight and flat. A warped or twisted board can bind the blade, ruining the cut. If the board is distorted, joint one face and plane the other before cutting it.

■ Oftentimes, boards warp or twist as you cut them. This is caused by *reaction wood* — internal stresses in the tree. To compensate for reaction wood, many craftsmen rip the stock slightly wider than needed, joint a guiding edge, then rip to the final width.

3-7 A Long Fence Extension extends the length of the fence, and provides a longer guiding surface. If you wish, you can attach a ledge to the rear of the jig that will serve as a table extension. Both the extended fence and the extended table are helpful when ripping extremely long boards or large sheets of plywood.

3-8 Occasionally, woodworkers need to rip the edge of a wide board. If the board is too wide, the rip fence won't be tall enough to properly support it. A *Tall Fence Extension* keeps the board from falling over as you cut it.

TRY THIS TRICK

If you must rip a straight edge in a bowed, rough-cut, or otherwise crooked board, fasten a straight board to it with finishing nails. Don't drive the nails home; you'll want to pull them out later. Rip the edge of the crooked board, keeping the edge of the straight one against the fence. When you've finished, separate the boards.

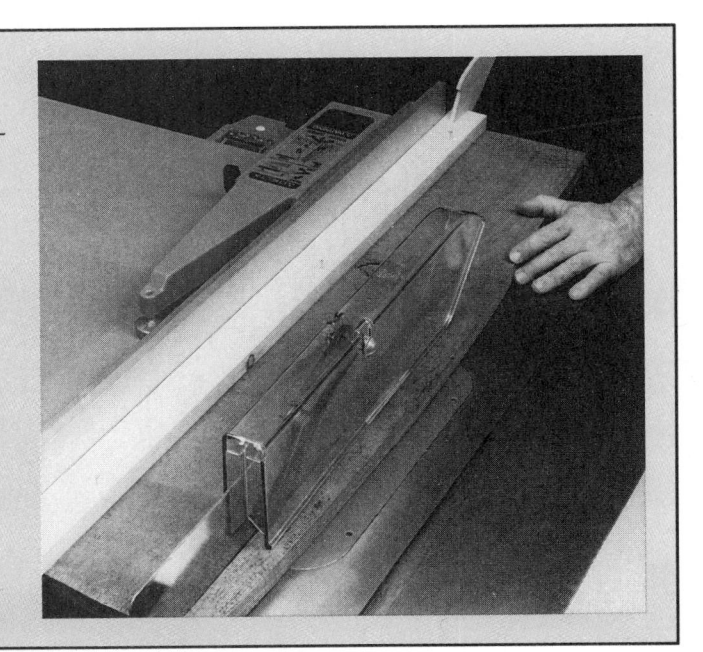

3-9 Making a narrow rip cut presents two dangers. First, the stock can be lifted off the table saw as it passes by the rear of the blade. Second, it can be pinched between the blade and the fence and flung like a spear. To protect yourself, use a *Fence Straddler* to both hold the stock on the table and feed it past the blade.

3-10 When ripping an angle other than 0 degrees — cutting a bevel or a chamfer — be sure the blade tilts *away* from the rip fence. If the blade tilts toward the fence, there is a greater chance that the blade will pinch the board and fling it backward. Furthermore, you may not have the space needed to feed the board safely. And on narrow cuts, there is the added danger that the blade may bite into the fence.

LONG AND TALL FENCE EXTENSIONS

The *Long Fence Extension* lengthens the face of the rip fence *horizontally;* the *Tall Fence Extension* extends it *vertically.* Both jigs attach directly to the face of the rip fence.

They are also built in a similar manner. Cut all the parts from cabinet-grade plywood, taking care to make the faces and braces straight and flat. Rout the joinery, drill the mounting holes, then assemble the parts with glue and screws. Countersink and counterbore the screws so the heads are well below the surface of the wood. If you wish, cover the heads with wooden plugs and sand them flush.

1 **To mount either fence** extension, attach it to the rip fence with carriage bolts and wing nuts. Check that the faces remain perpendicular to the saw table. When mounting the long fence extension, you must also check that the ledge is flush with the table surface.

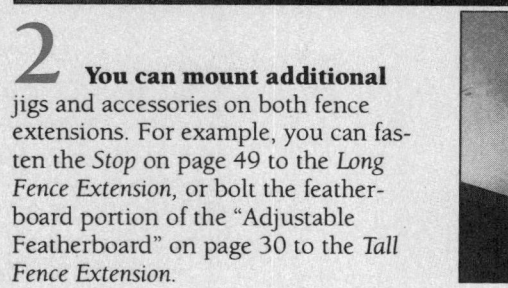

2 **You can mount additional** jigs and accessories on both fence extensions. For example, you can fasten the *Stop* on page 49 to the *Long Fence Extension,* or bolt the featherboard portion of the "Adjustable Featherboard" on page 30 to the *Tall Fence Extension.*

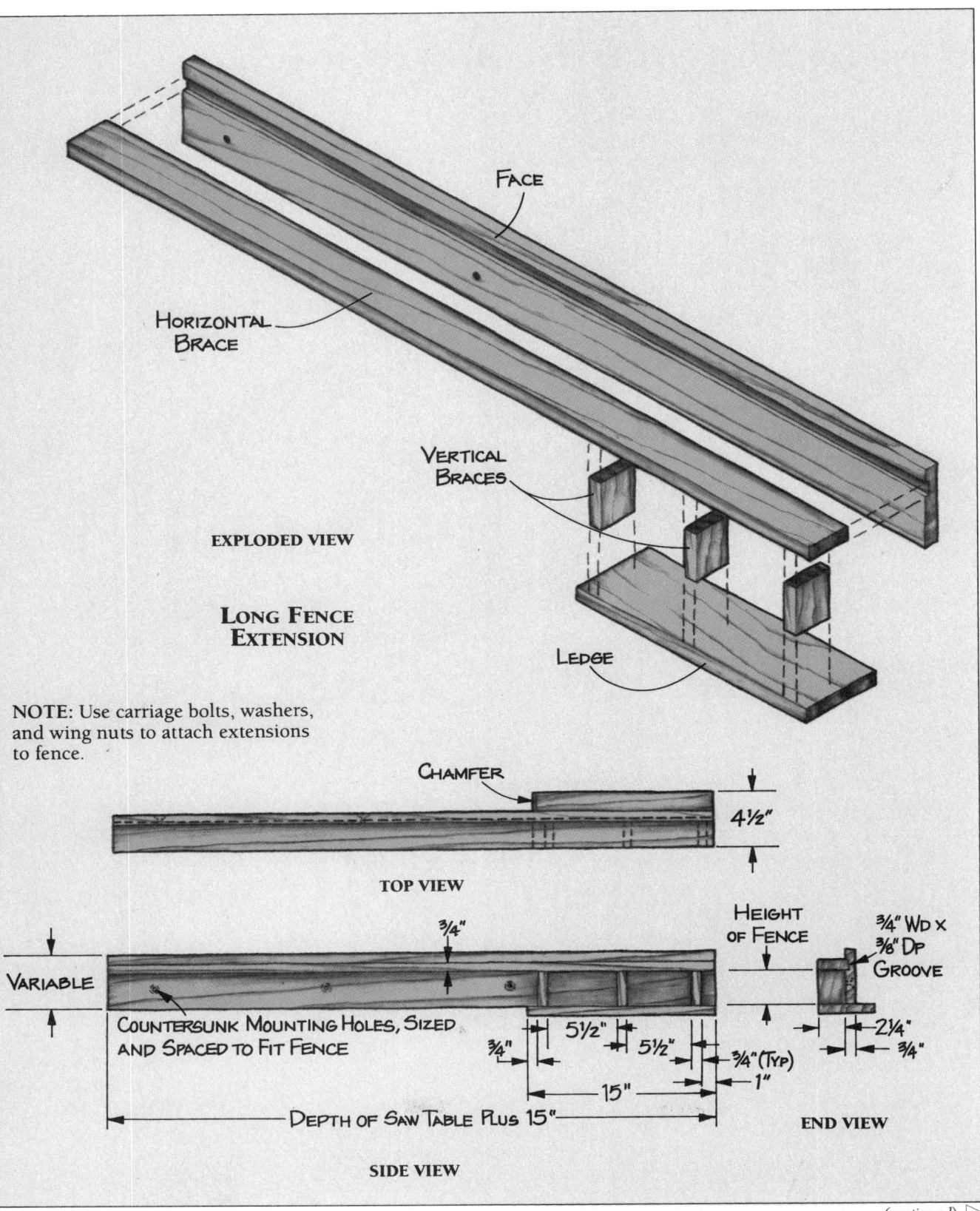

FACE

HORIZONTAL BRACE

VERTICAL BRACES

EXPLODED VIEW

LONG FENCE EXTENSION

LEDGE

NOTE: Use carriage bolts, washers, and wing nuts to attach extensions to fence.

CHAMFER

4½"

TOP VIEW

¾"

VARIABLE

HEIGHT OF FENCE

¾" WD X ⅜" DP GROOVE

COUNTERSUNK MOUNTING HOLES, SIZED AND SPACED TO FIT FENCE

5½"

5½"

¾"

¾"(TYP)

1"

15"

2¼"

¾"

DEPTH OF SAW TABLE PLUS 15"

END VIEW

SIDE VIEW

(continued) ▷

Long and Tall Fence Extensions — continued

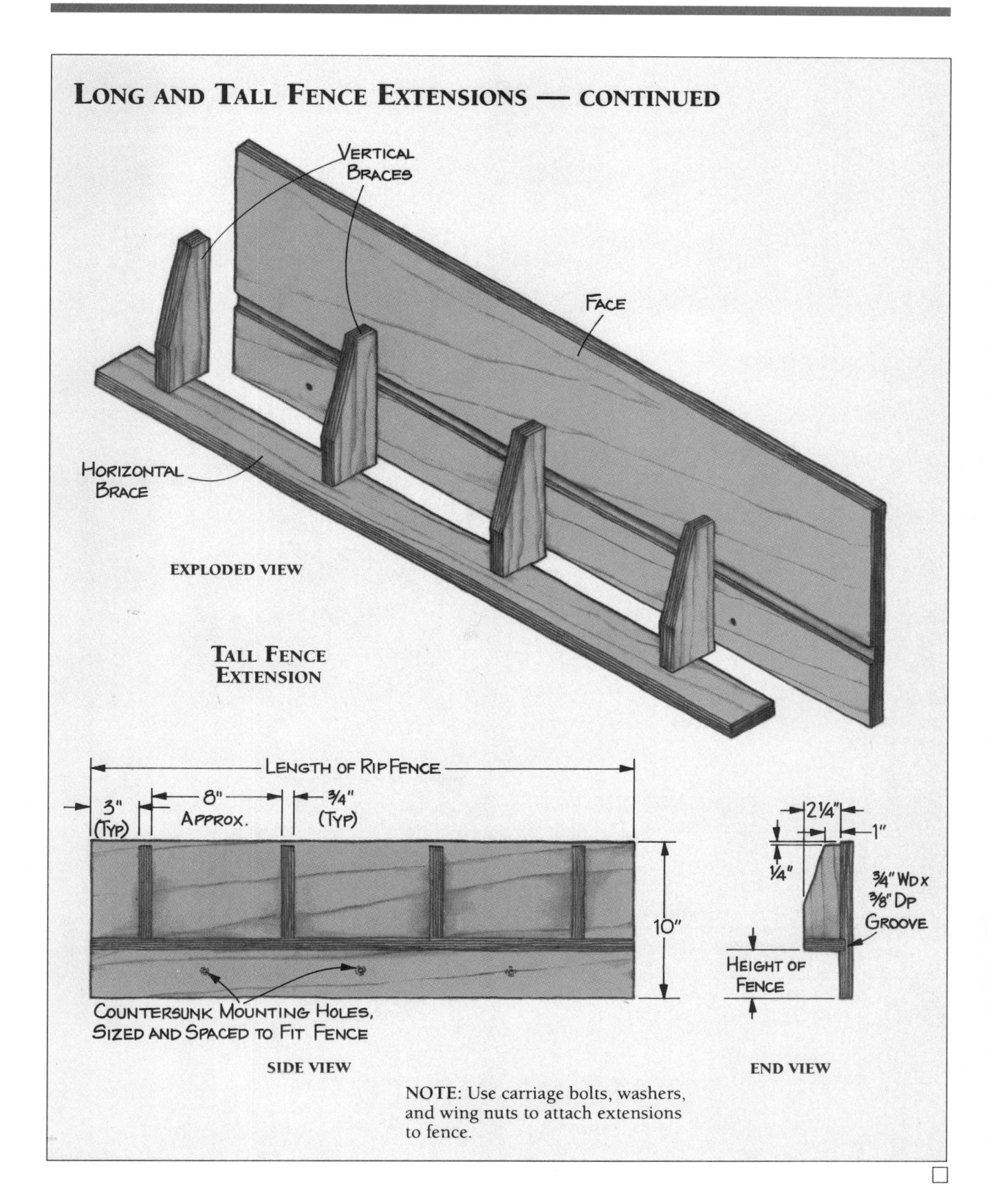

Vertical Braces

Face

Horizontal Brace

EXPLODED VIEW

TALL FENCE EXTENSION

LENGTH OF RIP FENCE

3" (TYP)

8" APPROX.

¾" (TYP)

10"

COUNTERSUNK MOUNTING HOLES, SIZED AND SPACED TO FIT FENCE

SIDE VIEW

2¼"

1"

¼"

¾" WD x ⅜" DP GROOVE

HEIGHT OF FENCE

END VIEW

NOTE: Use carriage bolts, washers, and wing nuts to attach extensions to fence.

FENCE STRADDLER

The fence straddler rides along the top of a rip fence, straddling both the right and left faces. The sides are notched so you can use them to hold the stock down on the table *and* feed it past the blade. **Note:** This jig cannot be used with fences that have only one working face.

The straddler must be made to fit your fence with very little slop. The sides must be precisely ¾ inch taller than the rip fence, and the spacer exactly as wide. Glue the parts together and reinforce them with finishing nails.

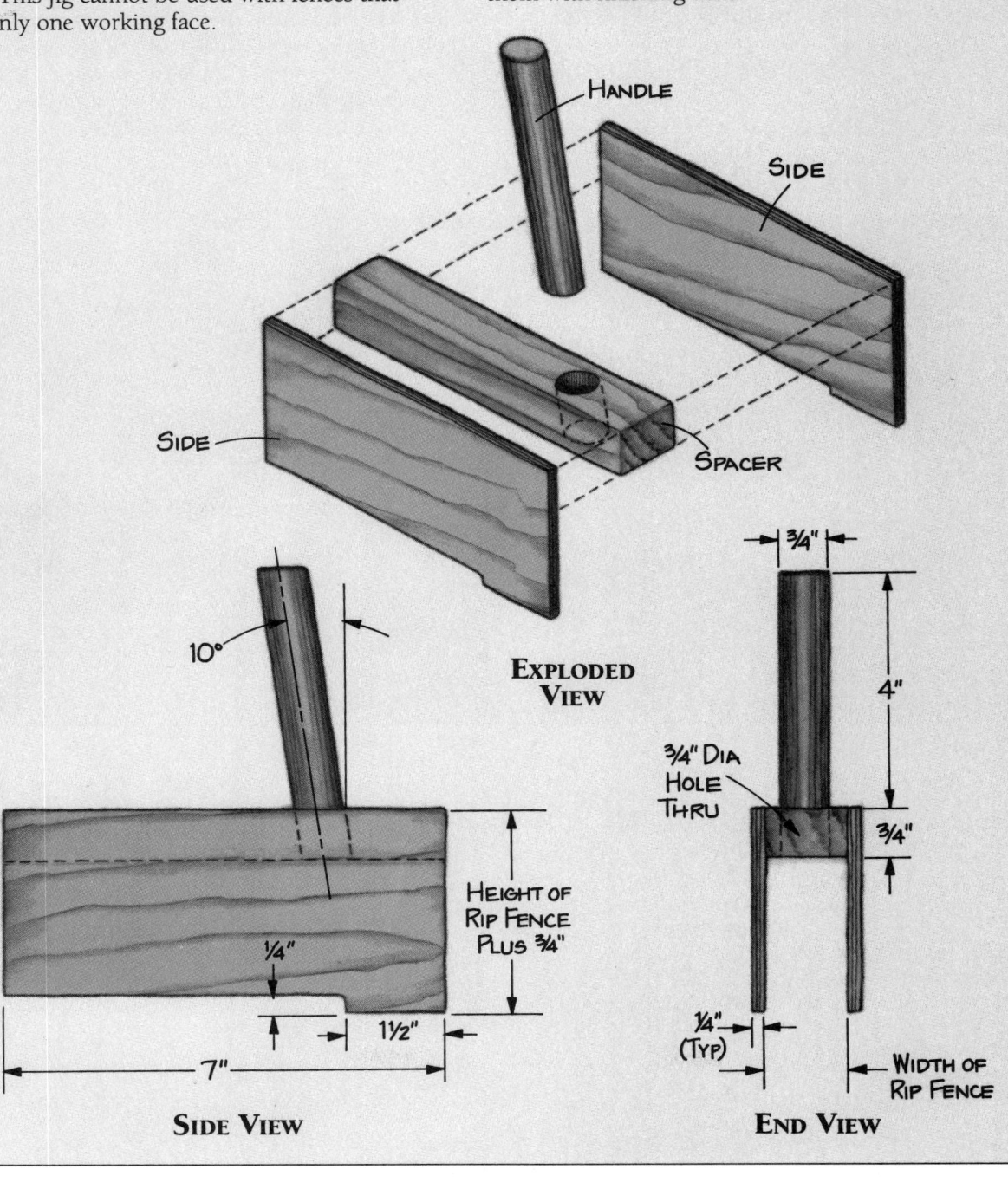

HANDLE

SIDE

SIDE

SPACER

EXPLODED VIEW

10°

HEIGHT OF RIP FENCE PLUS ¾"

¼"

1½"

7"

SIDE VIEW

¾"

4"

¾"

¾" DIA HOLE THRU

¼" (TYP)

WIDTH OF RIP FENCE

END VIEW

CUTTING PLYWOOD AND OTHER COMPOSITES

Technically, you cannot classify cuts made in plywood or particleboard as either crosscutting or ripping. There is no grain direction, so the traditional definitions of these terms do not apply. Nevertheless, craftsmen talk about ripping sheet materials, since they usually use the rip fence to guide the work.

But there the similarity ends. Ripping a solid board and ripping plywood or particleboard are two very different operations and require special techniques.

The most noticeable difference is the sheer bulk of the stock. There isn't a general duty table saw made that will adequately support a 4- by 8-foot sheet of plywood. Craftsmen who constantly must work with sheet materials often convert their table saws into panel saws by surrounding them with enlarged infeed and outfeed tables. Also, since the outer veneers of most grades of plywood are very thin, standard saw blades tend to lift or chip them. Therefore, you must take special precautions to get a good cut.

1 **The most important rule to** remember when cutting plywood and other composites is *don't be a hero*. Get help when handling large sheets. One person should stand on the infeed side of the table, the other on the outfeed side, and both must be clear of the danger zone. You must each understand what is expected of you during the operation, and what you will do if something goes wrong. It's also helpful to agree on some simple hand signals because spoken instructions are difficult to understand over the screaming of a table saw.

2 **Make sure that at least one** of you can easily turn off the saw if needed. A drop switch that hangs from the ceiling or a foot switch that rests on the floor can be a big help. But if you don't have either one, make sure the power cord and the plug are within easy reach. Remember, the switch on the table saw is likely to be obstructed during most of the operation.

3 **Often the easiest and most** accurate way to cut sheet materials is to slice them into easily manageable sizes with a circular saw, then cut them to their final dimensions on the table saw. To support the entire sheet as you cut it up, lay a sheet of fiberboard or builder's board on the floor of your shop and lay the plywood or particleboard on top of that. Lay out the cuts, making the parts slightly bigger than you need. Also be sure that each part has at least one straight "factory" edge. Adjust the depth of cut on the circular saw so it will cut through the top sheet but *not* all the way through the fiberboard, and cut up the sheet.

4 **Trim the smaller sheets to** their final size on the table saw. Use a factory edge as the guiding edge for the first cut, then use either the factory edges or the edges that have been sawed with a table saw to guide subsequent cuts. **Note:** You may want to make your first table saw cut slightly wide, turn the stock, and cut off the factory edge. Although these edges make good guides, they may not be suitable as a final edge. They tend to get beat up during storage and transport.

(continued) ▷

CUTTING PLYWOOD AND OTHER COMPOSITES — CONTINUED

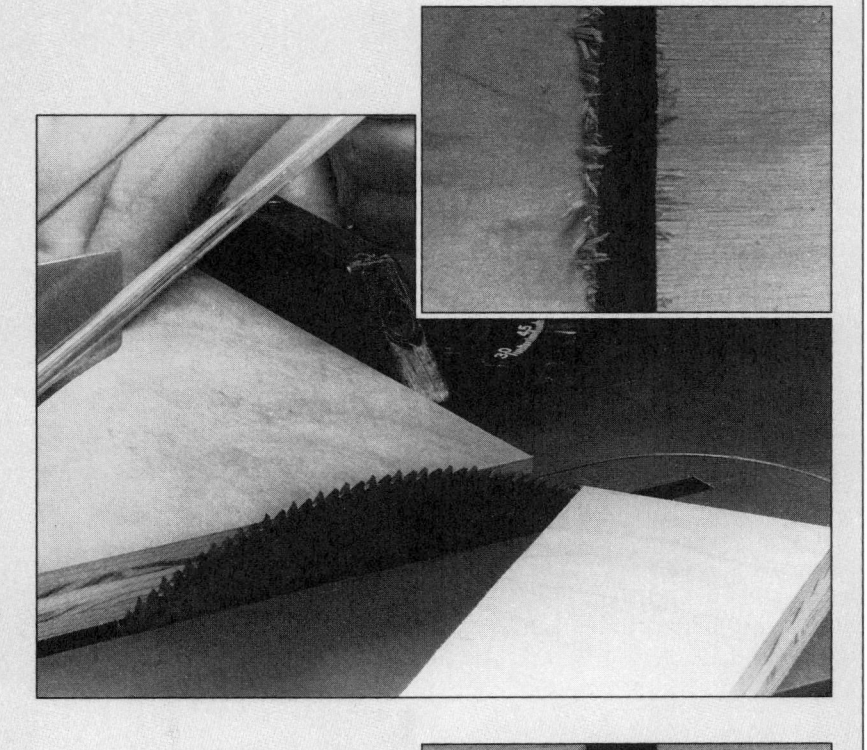

5 **When trimming the stock to** its final dimensions, you must take precautions to ensure the *quality* of the cuts. As the saw blade exits the plywood, the teeth lift the outer layers of veneer, tearing or chipping it. One of the ways to prevent this is to use a plywood blade. As mentioned on page 11, plywood blades have many more teeth than regular saw blades. Each tooth takes a smaller bite, which reduces the amount of tear-out. As shown in the inset, the plywood on the right was cut with a plywood blade, and it is not as badly chipped as the one on the left, which was cut with a regular combination blade.

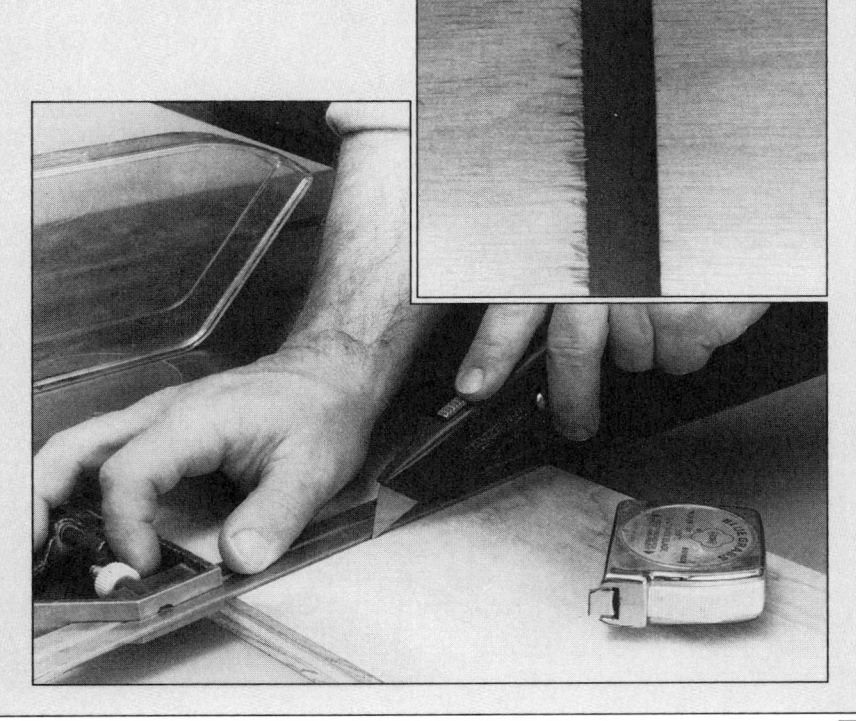

6 **There are several other** things you can do to reduce chipping. Use a zero-clearance table insert to support the stock as it's cut. Back up the plywood with scraps, or put masking tape over the area that will be cut. Perhaps the most effective technique is to score the cut with a marking knife or utility knife *before* you saw it. This cuts the fibers before they can be lifted. In the inset, the plywood on the right was scored before it was cut, while that on the left was not.

MITER CUTS

When you make a miter cut on a table saw, you run into the same problem associated with crosscuts — the factory-supplied miter gauge is an inadequate accessory for guiding most boards. To properly sup- port the work, you must fit the gauge with an exten- sion or replace it with a sliding table. (The "Sliding Table" on page 94 includes an attachment for miter cuts.)

You also run up against a new problem. The miter gauge and blade tilt scale on most table saws — even the best ones — are notoriously inaccurate. And you can't use a drafting triangle to set every angle that you might want to cut. You must use the scales to *estimate* the degree setting, then thoroughly test the setup. Use the testing technique outlined in "Making a Cut" on page 21, or make a test frame. (*SEE FIGURES 3-11 THROUGH 3-13.*)

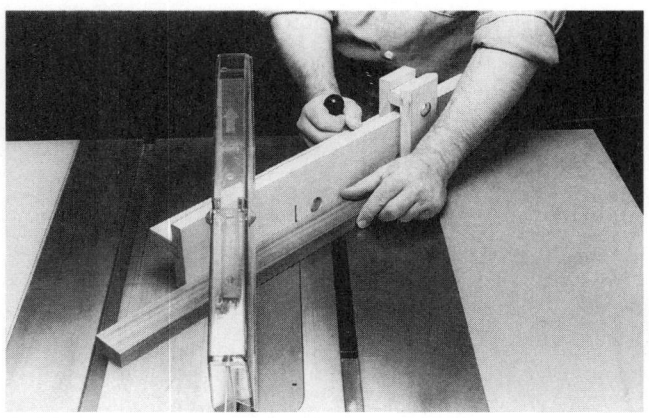

3-11 As you set up to make a miter cut, you must decide which way to angle the miter gauge. There really is no right or wrong way, although most craftsmen prefer turn- ing the face of the gauge *away* from the blade — this helps to keep their hands out of danger.

3-13 Most often, woodworkers use miter cuts to make a frame or join two or more boards at an angle that will divide evenly into 360 degrees. For example, 22½-degree miter cuts will produce an octagonal (eight-sided) frame, 30-degree cuts, a hexagonal (six-sided) frame, and 45-degree cuts, a rectangular (four- sided) frame. Check the setup for these sorts of cuts by making a test frame. Cut all the parts to exactly the same length and fit them together. If any of the frame joints gap on the *inside, increase* the miter gauge angle. If they gap on the *outside, reduce* the angle. Unless the gaps are extremely large, do not adjust the angle by more than ½ degree between each test.

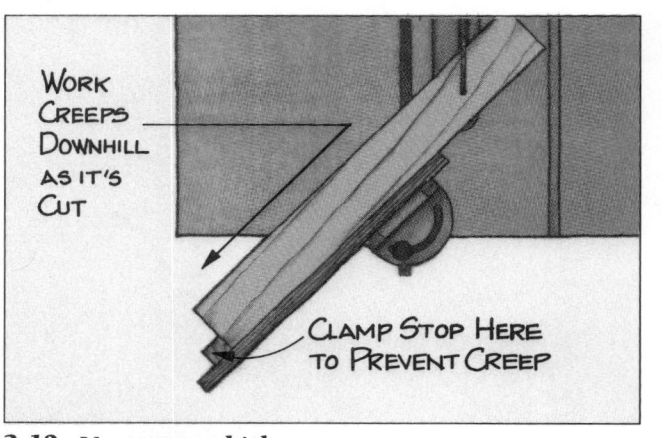

WORK CREEPS DOWNHILL AS IT'S CUT

CLAMP STOP HERE TO PREVENT CREEP

3-12 No matter which way you angle the miter gauge, the stock tends to creep "downhill" as you cut it. To prevent this, you must hold the work firmly against the miter gauge face or extension. You can also clamp the work to the miter gauge, glue a piece of abrasive emery cloth to the face, or butt the downhill end of the board against a stop.

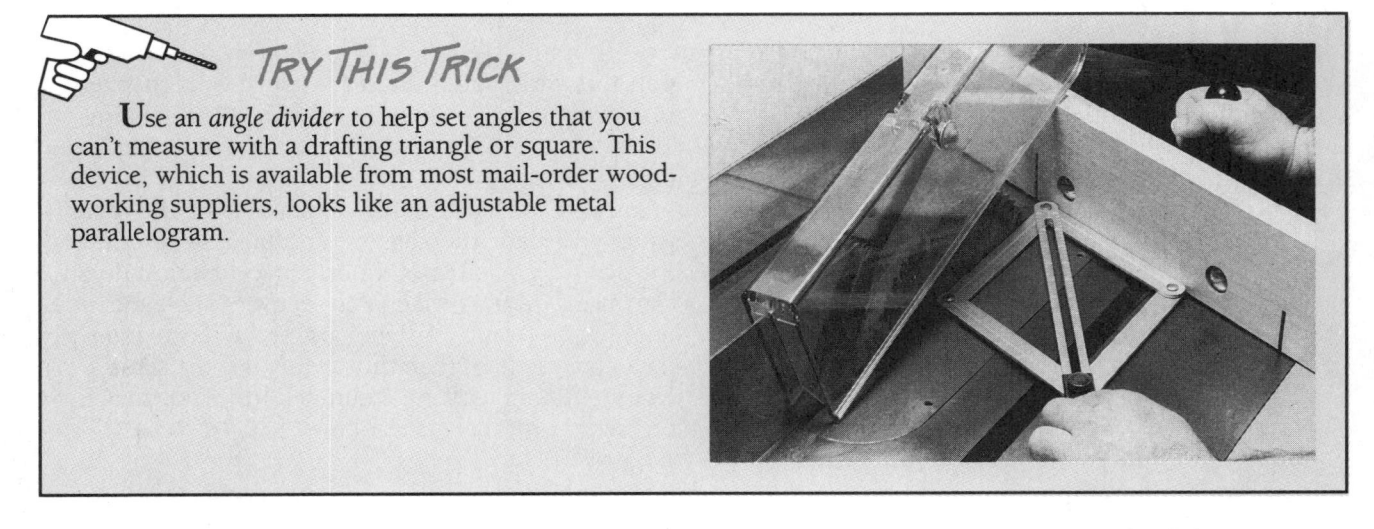

Once the miter gauge angle is properly set, make the miter cuts. If the mitered boards are to be joined by miter joints (like the members of a frame), you must make mirror-image miters — often called "left" and "right" miters. (A single miter joint is comprised of one left and one right miter.) To do this, flip each board end-for-end, *keeping the same edge against the gauge* as you cut the ends. (*SEE FIGURE 3-14.*) Only in rare instances — when you can't flip the board —

should you have to readjust the angle of the miter gauge to cut left and right miters.

You can also cut a miter by tilting the saw blade rather than angling the miter gauge. The procedure is similar, but there is an important difference when cutting left and right miters. As you flip the board end for end, *the same face must rest against the table.* (*SEE FIGURE 3-15.*) **Note:** You *can* switch faces if you first change the miter gauge to the other slot.

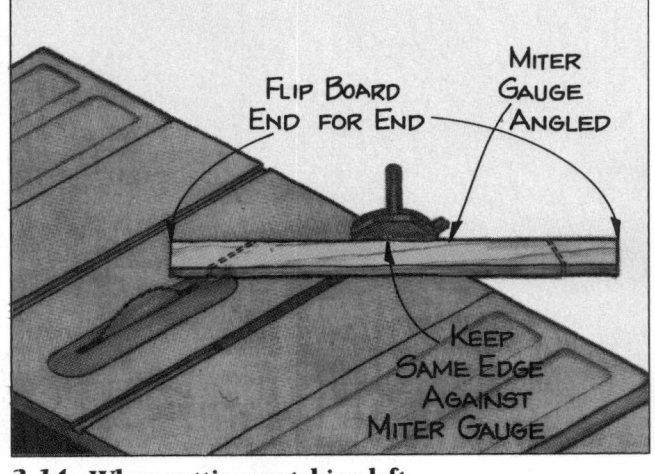

3-14 When cutting matching left and right miters, you must flip each board between cuts. How you make this flip depends on whether you've angled the miter gauge or tilted the blade. If the miter gauge is angled, flip the board end for end, keeping the *same edge* against the *miter gauge* when cutting both miters. To prevent mistakes, mark this edge plainly.

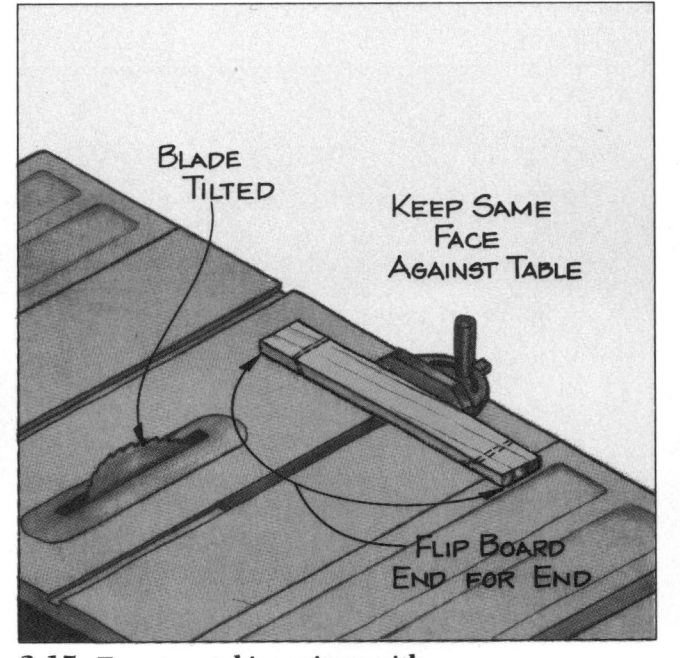

3-15 To cut matching miters with the blade tilted, flip the board end for end, keeping the *same face* against the *table.* Mark the face that looks up.

Finally, you can cut a miter with *both* the blade tilted and the miter gauge angled. This is called a *compound miter*. (SEE FIGURE 3-16.) When joined by compound miters, the boards "slope" rather than resting flat on an edge or a face. This slope and the number of sides of the frame determine the blade tilt and the miter gauge angle. Refer to "Compound Miter Settings" on page 62 to find the settings needed for rectangular, hexagonal, and octagonal frames of various slopes.

To test a compound-miter setup, cut enough identical pieces to make a small frame. Tape the pieces together and inspect the joints. (SEE FIGURE 3-17.) To make matching left and right compound miters, flip each board face for face so a *different edge* rests against the miter gauge and a *different face* rests against the table when cutting each end. (SEE FIGURE 3-18.)

3-16 To make a *compound miter,* angle the miter gauge *and* tilt the blade. Compound miters are used to join boards whose faces slope, such as crown moldings or the members of shadowbox picture frames.

3-17 To test a compound miter setup, cut enough pieces, all the same length, to make a small frame. Tape the parts together, then inspect the joints and measure the slope. If the joints gap on the *inside, decrease the blade tilt.* If they gap on the *outside, increase the blade tilt.* If the slope is *greater* than expected (as measured from horizontal), *decrease the miter gauge angle.* If it's *less* than expected, *increase the angle.* Don't change any one setting more than 1/2 degree between tests.

3-18 To make matching left and right compound miters, flip the board face for face *and* move the miter gauge from one slot to the other. A *different edge* should rest against the miter gauge and a *different face* should rest against the table when cutting each end of the board.

COMPOUND MITER SETTINGS

To find the proper miter gauge and blade tilt settings for a compound miter cut, first decide whether the frame you want to make will have four, six, or eight sides, and what the slope of the sides will be. **Note:** The *slope* is measured from horizontal; its reciprocal is sometimes called the *work angle.* Find the proper arc for the number of sides, and follow that arc to find the desired slope. From there, follow a horizontal line to find the blade tilt, and follow a vertical line to find the miter gauge angle. For example, if you want to build a four-sided frame with a slope of 65 degrees, you must set the miter gauge to approximately 71 degrees and the blade tilt to approximately 41 degrees.

You can also use simple formulas to find the settings precisely, provided you understand a little trigonometry (or know how to beat on a scientific calculator and produce an intelligible result):

For a four-sided frame:
　　Blade tilt angle = *sin* (slope) x 45°
　　Miter gauge angle = 90 - [*cos* (slope) x 45°]

For a six-sided frame:
　　Blade tilt angle = *sin* (slope) x 30°
　　Miter gauge angle = 90 - [*cos* (slope) x 30°]

For an eight-sided frame:
　　Blade tilt angle = *sin* (slope) x 22½°
　　Miter gauge angle = 90 - [*cos* (slope) x 22½°]

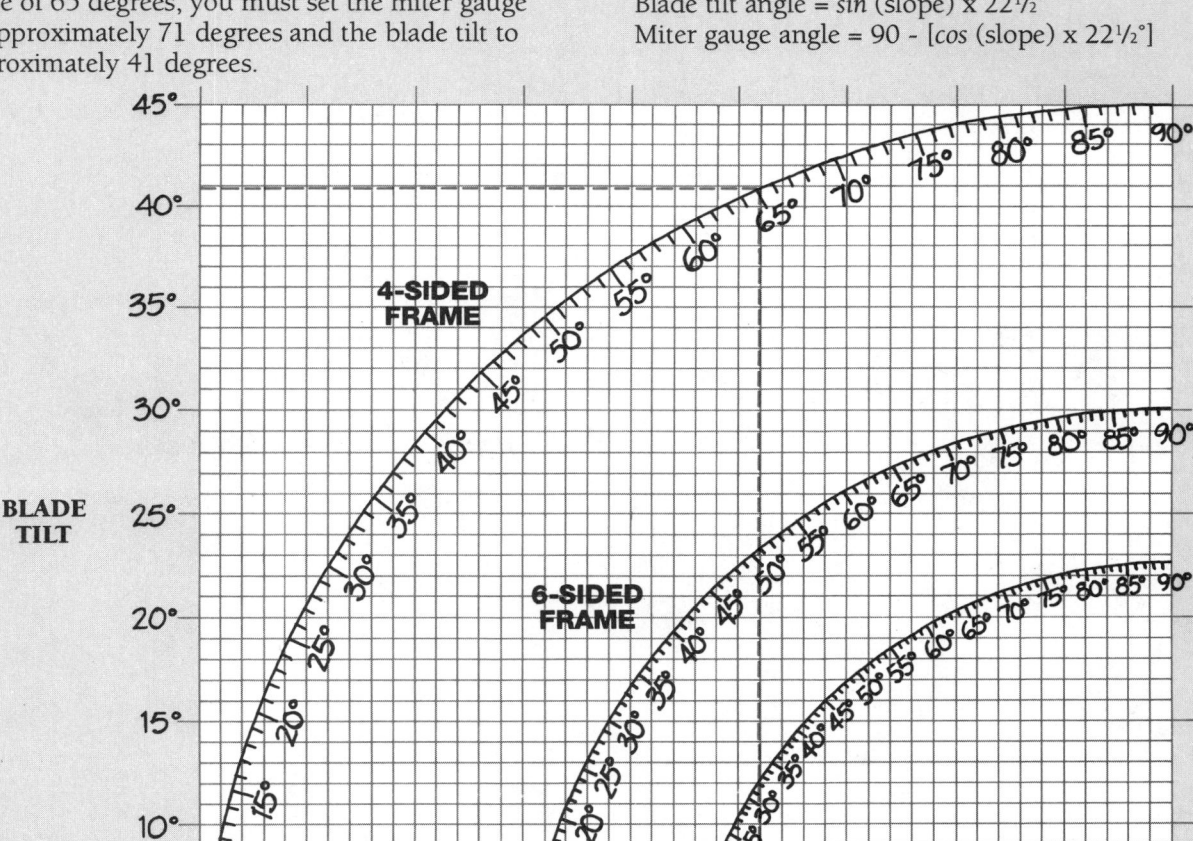

4

DADOING AND MOLDING

Although the table saw was invented to cut large boards into smaller ones, that's not all it will do. With the proper accessories, you can use it to cut a variety of woodworking joints and decorative shapes.

A *dado cutter* mounts on the saw arbor like a blade, but makes a much broader cut. An ordinary saw blade cuts a narrow kerf — 1/8 inch wide or less — to reduce waste and the effort required to saw through the stock. But a dado cutter isn't meant to saw completely through a board. It cuts a wide kerf with a flat bottom and square shoulders. Depending on how you arrange these kerfs in the wood, you can create dadoes, grooves, rabbets, and a number of other joints.

A molding head or *molder* also mounts on the saw arbor and makes broad cuts. But unlike the dado cutter, the kerf left by a molder is rarely square. There are a variety of knives that fit in the molding head, and each cuts a different shape. With a good selection of molding knives, you can make decorative cuts or complex joints.

SETTING UP FOR DADOING AND MOLDING

Although the results are different, the table saw setups for dadoing and molding are very similar. Unplug the saw, remove the saw blade, and replace it with a dado cutter or a molder. Both of these accessories are mounted just like a saw blade, although some molders may require a bushing and/or a spacer to position them properly on the arbor. And because both tools cut a much wider swath than an ordinary saw blade, you must replace the table insert with a special dadoing or molding insert. (SEE FIGURES 4-1 AND 4-2.) You can also make your own inserts, following the procedures for making a *Zero-Clearance Table Insert* described in *Figures 2-24* and *2-25* on page 32. (SEE FIGURE 4-3.)

For many dadoing and molding operations, you must also attach a wooden face to the fence. This face must have a semicircular cutout that's the same radius as the dado cutter or molder. (SEE FIGURES 4-4 AND 4-5.) The cutout face serves two purposes. It protects the metal rip fence during those operations in which you must position the fence very close to the cutters or knives. And when you don't want to cut the full width of the accessory, it covers the unused portion.

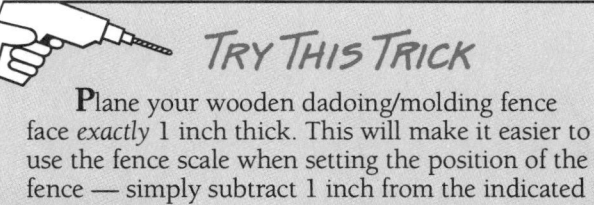

TRY THIS TRICK

Plane your wooden dadoing/molding fence face *exactly* 1 inch thick. This will make it easier to use the fence scale when setting the position of the fence — simply subtract 1 inch from the indicated measurement.

Your final step is to detach the splitter-mounted saw guard from the table saw and attach a featherboard to the table or the wooden face. (SEE FIGURE 4-6.) Because you don't use a dado cutter or a molder to cut all the way through a board, the splitter will get in the way. Unfortunately, without the splitter and its anti-kickback pawls (fingers), there is nothing to stop kickback.

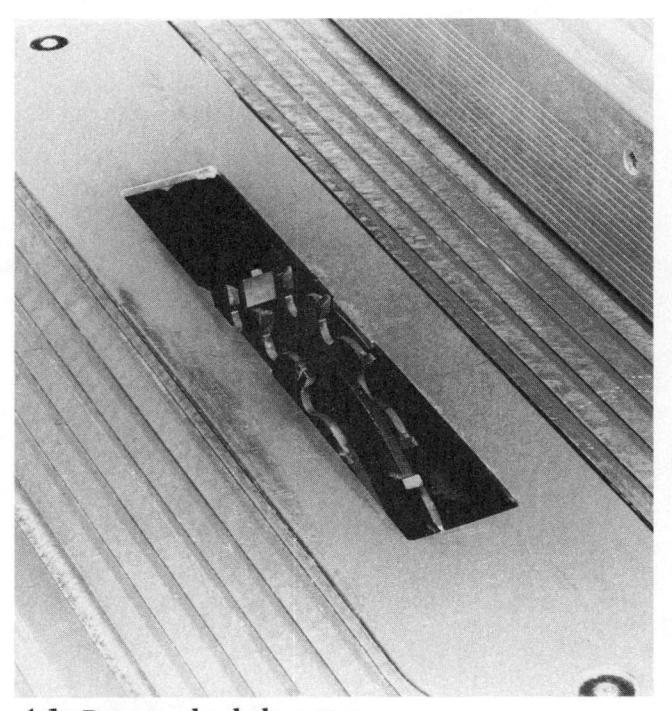

4-1 Because the dado cutter makes a wider kerf than the saw blade, you must replace the normal table insert with one that has a wider opening. This insert is necessary even if you use a wobble dado with a single 1/8-inch-wide blade.

4-2 You must also use a different insert with a molder for the same reason. Although they look very similar, dadoing inserts and molding inserts are not the same. Because molders make a wider cut and don't project as far above the table as dado cutters, molding insert openings are typically wider and shorter than those on dado inserts.

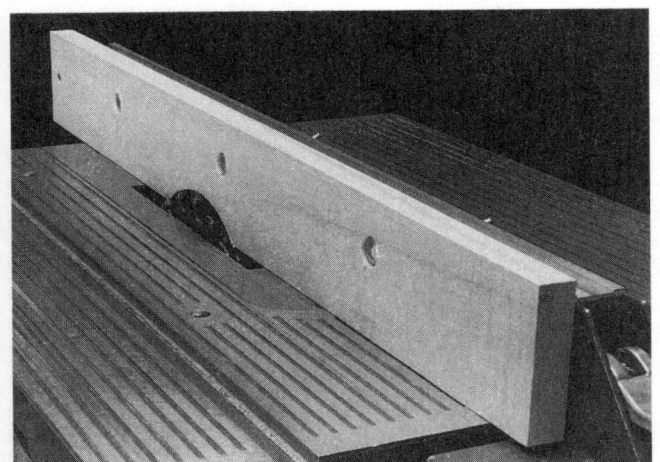

4-3 If there are no available inserts for the dado cutter or molder you wish to use, you can easily make your own by following the procedure for making *Zero-Clearance Table Inserts*. For some operations, you may *prefer* to make your own. A zero-clearance dadoing or molding insert provides better support for small or narrow stock, and greatly reduces chipping and tearing.

4-4 Many dadoing and molding operations require a wooden fence face with a semicircular cutout. To make this cutout, lower the dado cutter or molder below the surface of the table. Attach the wooden face to the fence, and position the fence so the face partially covers the accessory. Turn on the saw and slowly raise the accessory, cutting the wooden face. Be careful not to cut the metal fence.

4-5 If you don't wish to cut the full width of the accessory, cover the *unused* portion with the cutout in the wooden face. Here, a craftsman cuts just two beads with three-bead molding knives. The cutout covers one of the beads. *Never leave the unused portion of the dado cutter or molder uncovered* — your hand might slip into the exposed cutter or knives.

4-6 Attach a featherboard to the fence or table when dadoing and molding. A featherboard does two things — it helps prevent kickback and holds the wood against the fence or table. This, in turn, makes the operation safer and more accurate.

Furthermore, because the dado cutter and the molder remove more stock than a saw blade, kickback is more likely. To guard against this, use a featherboard.

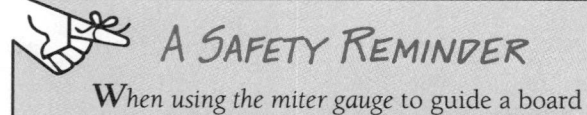

A SAFETY REMINDER

When using the miter gauge to guide a board across the dado cutter or molder, you cannot use a featherboard to prevent kickback. To be safe, you must be doubly careful. Keep the on/off switch within easy reach, stand clear of the danger zone, and feed the wood very slowly and steadily. You may want to make a deep cut in several passes, raising the accessory slightly with each pass.

USING A DADO CUTTER

DADOES, GROOVES, AND RABBETS

You can create many different joints with a dado cutter, but there are really only two types of dado cuts — an L-shaped cut or *rabbet* in an edge or end of a board, and a U-shaped cut in the face. This U-shaped cut is called a *dado* if it runs across the grain, and a *groove* if it runs with the grain. (SEE FIGURE 4-7.)

The two common types of dado cutters, as mentioned in "Table Saw Accessories" in chapter 1, are a *wobble dado* and a *stacked dado*. A wobble dado con-

sists of a single blade mounted between two tapered or wedge-shaped washers. The washers cause the blade to move back and forth as it cuts, making a wide kerf. By turning the washers, you can control this side-to-side motion. A stacked dado is made up of two types of blades, *trimmers* and *chippers*. The trimmers are normally 1/8 inch wide, while chippers come in several different widths — 1/16, 1/8, and 1/4 inch. Stack these blades on the arbor with the trimmers on the outside and the chippers in between.

As you set up the dado cutter, you must adjust the *width* and the *depth* of the cut. Adjusting the width depends partly on the type of cutter, and partly on the type of cut. If you're making a dado or a groove (a U-shaped cut) with a wobble dado, turn the tapered washers that hold the blade to the proper setting. (SEE FIGURE 4-8.) If you're using a stacked dado, select the chippers needed to build a stack of the required width. (SEE FIGURE 4-9.) To make a rabbet (an L-shaped cut) with either tool, set the dado cutter to make a kerf slightly wider than needed. Position the fence so the wooden face covers part of the cutter, reducing the cut to the width required. (SEE FIGURE 4-10.)

To adjust the depth of cut, simply raise or lower the dado cutter. To set the height accurately, you can use a *height gauge*. (SEE FIGURE 4-11.) Set the gauge to the desired measurement, then use it to set the cutter height. You can purchase any of several commercial gauges, or you can easily make your own "Height Gauge" following the plans on page 69.

4-7 A dado cutter makes U-shaped and L-shaped cuts of varying widths and depths. A U-shaped cut is called a *dado* if it runs across the grain and a *groove* if it runs with the grain. An L-shaped cut is called a *rabbet,* no matter how it's oriented to the wood grain. You can create many different woodworking joints, both simple and complex, by making one or more cuts in the adjoining surfaces of two boards.

4-8 To adjust the width of cut
of a wobble dado, simply turn the
tapered washers to the proper setting. You can adjust a wobble dado
to cut any width between the minimum and maximum allowed, but
you may have to make several test
cuts to check your setting — the
scales on the washers are not always
accurate. If you make a lot of cuts at
the same setting, check the width
from time to time. Wobble dadoes
tend to slip during constant use.

4-9 To adjust the width of cut
on a stacked dado, simply select the
trimmers (1) and *chippers* (2) needed
to make a stack of the desired width.
Unfortunately, because the width of
these blades is fixed, the width of cut
can only be adjusted to the nearest
1/16 inch. You can compensate for this
somewhat by placing metal *shims* (3)
of varying thicknesses between the
blades.

4-10 Use the fence to adjust the
width of cut when making a rabbet.
Set the dado cutter to make a kerf
slightly wider than needed, then
position the fence so the wooden
face partially covers the cutter.
Measure from the face to a tooth that
angles *away* from the fence.

4-11 To use a height gauge to set
the depth of cut, first set the gauge,
raising or lowering the "shoulder"
to the required distance above the
table. Lower the dado cutter below
the shoulder and place the gauge
with the shoulder over the cutter.
Slowly raise the cutter, spinning it by
hand until the teeth just brush the
shoulder. If the gauge "walks" —
that is, the teeth catch it and push it
sideways — then you've raised the
cutter too far.

When making a dado or a groove, you must also adjust the position of the cut on the face of the board. If you use the fence to guide the board, position the fence the proper distance from the cutter. If you use the miter gauge to guide the board, you have several choices:

■ Line up the layout marks on the board with the cutter.

■ Fasten a stop to the miter gauge extension the proper distance from the cutter.

■ Position the fence the proper distance from the cutter and use it as a stop. (*SEE FIGURE 4-12.*)

Note: The "Height Gauge" on page 69 can also be used to gauge the distance between the fence and a cutter or blade.

When cutting a rabbet or a dado *across the grain* of a board, take precautions to prevent splintering. This is especially important when cutting across the veneer grain of plywood. There are several techniques you can use, as shown in "Cutting Plywood and Other Composites" on page 56. Of these, the simplest and most effective is to lay out the dado cuts with an awl or marking knife, scoring the shoulders of each cut before you make it.

If you regularly make dado cuts in plywood, you may want to purchase a *laminate dado cutter.* A laminate cutter is to a regular cutter what a plywood blade is to a combination blade. The trimmer blades in a laminate cutter have a great many more teeth than usual — often 40 or more — ground at a slightly steeper bevel. As a result, each tooth takes a smaller bite and lifts less grain. This reduces the tendency for the cutter to tear out or chip the surface of the stock, and you get a cleaner, smoother cut.

FOR BEST RESULTS

After you've made the necessary adjustments, *always* make a test cut in a scrap before cutting good stock. Measure the position of the cut on the board with a ruler or tape measure, and gauge the width and depth of the cut with a calipers or depth gauge.

4-12 Although you cannot safely use the fence as a stop when cross-cutting, you can when dadoing. Because you don't cut all the way through the board, there is no cut-off piece to be pinched between the blade and the fence.

HEIGHT GAUGE

This simple gauge has a wide base to stand on its own, leaving both hands free to make adjustments. The large shoulder makes it easy to position the gauge over the blade or cutter. And you can adjust the width of the base to gauge the distance between the fence and the cutter.

To make the gauge, cut the parts to the sizes and shapes needed. Drill the bases for bolts and dowels, and rout a groove in the slide. Glue the dowels to the short base, and fasten the plastic shoulder to the slide with screws. Cut slots in the tall base, sawing from the ends into the holes. Also, glue a scale to the tall base so the measurements run from the bottom edge up.

Fasten the shoulder/slide assembly to the tall base with carriage bolts and screws. Insert the dowels through the holes in the tall base. To clamp the tall base to the dowels, drive screws through the slots from the top edge.

1 **To use the gauge, adjust the** height of the shoulder according to the scale. Loosen the screws that clamp the tall base to the dowels and slide it closer to or further away from the short base. Measure the distance between the bases at *both* ends to make sure they're parallel, then tighten the screws.

2 **To position the rip fence,** place the gauge between the cutter and the fence, with the face of the tall base against the cutter. Move the fence sideways until it touches the short base. To set the depth of cut, raise the cutter until it brushes the shoulder. **Warning:** Make sure you've removed the gauge before turning on the saw!

(continued) ▷

HEIGHT GAUGE — CONTINUED

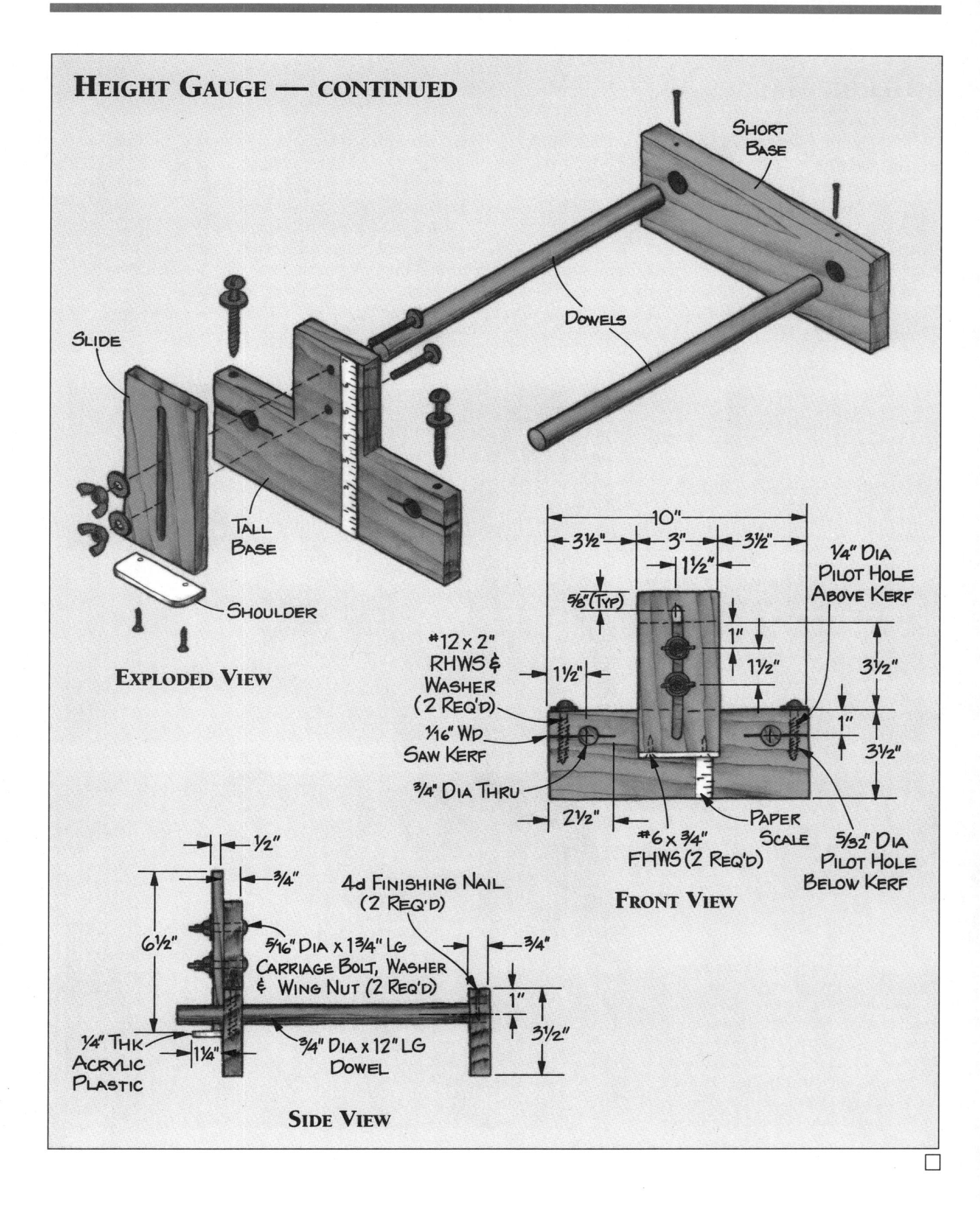

SHORT BASE

DOWELS

SLIDE

TALL BASE

SHOULDER

EXPLODED VIEW

10"

3½"   3"   3½"

1½"

5⁄8" (TYP)

¼" DIA PILOT HOLE ABOVE KERF

#12 x 2" RHWS & WASHER (2 REQ'D)

1"

1½"

1½"

3½"

1"

3½"

1⁄16" WD SAW KERF

¾" DIA THRU

2½"

#6 x ¾" FHWS (2 REQ'D)

PAPER SCALE

5⁄32" DIA PILOT HOLE BELOW KERF

FRONT VIEW

½"

¾"

4d FINISHING NAIL (2 REQ'D)

¾"

6½"

5⁄16" DIA x 1¾" LG CARRIAGE BOLT, WASHER & WING NUT (2 REQ'D)

1"

3½"

¼" THK ACRYLIC PLASTIC

1¼"

¾" DIA x 12" LG DOWEL

SIDE VIEW

SPECIAL DADO TECHNIQUES

In addition to cutting basic dadoes, grooves, and rabbets, there are many other useful dado techniques. Here are three of the most often used:

Making wide cuts — To cut a joint that's wider than the dado cutter itself, make two or more passes over the tool. This seems simple enough if you only have to make one joint — make the first pass, move the rip fence or reposition the board on the miter gauge, and make another. But oftentimes, you must make several precise copies of the joint. To do this, use spacers to help position the board for the cuts. Remove the spacers one at a time as you make each pass. (*SEE FIGURE 4-13.*)

Making blind cuts — Sometimes you must halt a dado cut before it exits the end or edge of a board. This is called a *blind* cut. If the cut is halted at both ends and has no entrance or exit, it's *double blind*. To make a blind rabbet, dado, or groove, use a stop to halt the board when the cutter is the proper distance from the end or edge. (*SEE FIGURES 4-14 THROUGH 4-16.*) To make a double-blind cut, use two stops — one to begin the cut and the other to end it. (*SEE FIGURE 4-17.*)

4-13 To make a dado cut that's wider than the dado cutter itself, clamp one or more spacers to the rip fence. The combined thickness of the spacers (ST) should be equal to the width of the dado cut you want to make (DW) minus the width of the cutter (CW): the formula would be DW - CW = ST. For example, if you want to cut a 2-inch-wide groove using a $\frac{3}{4}$-inch-wide cutter, the combined width of the spacers should be $1\frac{1}{4}$ inches: $2 - \frac{3}{4} = 1\frac{1}{4}$. Cut the groove in several passes, removing one spacer with each pass. **Note:** If you use the miter gauge instead of the rip fence to guide the stock, place the spacers between the stop and the workpiece. The formula for figuring the thickness of the spacers remains the same.

4-14 Before you can make a blind dado cut, you must first know where the dado cutter *starts* to cut as the wood passes across the table saw. To find out, first adjust the cutter to the desired height and position the rip fence. Affix a piece of tape to the fence beside the cutter. Select a scrap with at least one square corner and place it on the *infeed* side of the table with the square corner against the fence and facing the cutter. Slide the scrap toward the dado accessory as you spin the cutter by hand. When the teeth brush the scrap, mark the position of the corner on the tape. **Note:** You can use this same technique to find where the dado cutter *stops* cutting by placing the scrap on the *outfeed* side of the table.

4-15 Clamp a stop to the *outfeed* end of the rip fence to halt the cut. To calculate where to position the stop (SP), subtract the desired distance between the blind end of the cut and the end of the board (BD) from the length of the board (BL): the formula would be BL - BD = SP. The result is the distance between the edge of the stop and the "start mark" you made on the rip fence. For example, if you want to halt a groove $3/4$ inch before the end of a 12-inch-long board, place the stop $11\frac{1}{4}$ inches from the start mark on the outfeed side: $12 - 3/4 = 11\frac{1}{4}$.

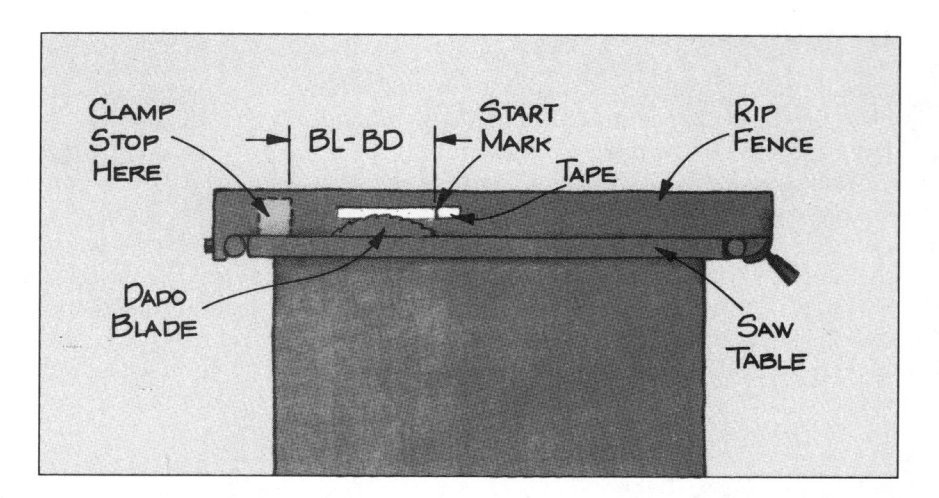

4-16 Lay out the cut on a *visible* surface of the board so you can monitor the progress of the cut. Place the board on the table, against the rip fence. Turn on the saw and feed the board across the cutter until it contacts the stop. When the cut halts, the layout mark that indicates the blind end of the cut should be even with the start mark on the rip fence. Turn off the saw, remove the board, and, if necessary, square the blind end of the cut with a chisel.

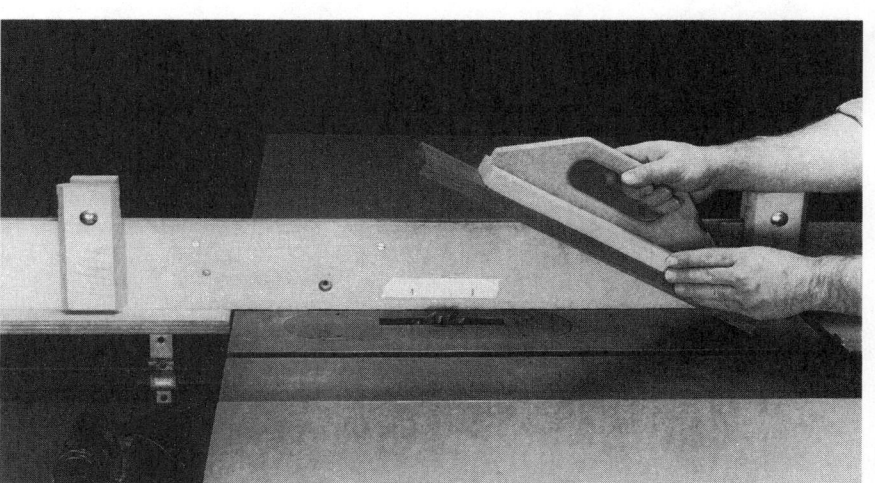

4-17 To make a double-blind cut, you must make *both* a start mark and a stop mark on the rip fence, and attach stops to both the infeed and outfeed ends. The procedure for positioning the infeed stop is exactly the same as for the outfeed stop, except that you measure from the stop mark instead of the start mark. For example, if you want to make a blind groove in an 18-inch-long board, starting 2 inches from one end and stopping 1 inch from the other, place the *outfeed* stop 17 inches from the *start* mark $(18 - 1 = 17)$, and the *infeed* stop 16 inches from the *stop* mark $(18 - 2 = 16)$. To begin the cut, hold the board at an angle above the cutter with the infeed end resting on the table and against the infeed stop. Turn on the saw, then slowly and carefully lower the board onto the cutter, keeping one edge firmly against the rip fence. When the board is flat on the table, feed it forward until it contacts the outfeed stop. **Note:** To help perform the operation safely, affix a push block to the workpiece with double-faced carpet tape.

Making vertical cuts — When cutting tenons or slots in the end of a board, it's often necessary to hold the board vertically. To do this, you must use a *tenoning jig*. *(See Figure 4-18.)* There are several commercial jigs that you may purchase, or you can make your own. The tenoning attachment to the "Sliding Table" on page 94 is a tenoning jig, and will work with a dado cutter or a molder, as well as with an ordinary saw blade.

4-18 To make a dado cut in the end of a board, hold it vertically in a tenoning jig. There are several commercial jigs that you can purchase, but you might choose to make your own — see the "Sliding Table" on page 94.

Using a Molder

A molder is used very much like a dado cutter, with one important difference. While there are only two basic dado cuts, there are dozens of possible molding cuts — as many different cuts as there are molding knives. The shape of each molding cut is determined by the shape of the knives used to make it. Furthermore, you can create hundreds of additional shapes by passing a board over the molder two or more times, using different knives for each pass.

Although there are many different molding knives, they can all be grouped into three categories (*See* *Figure 4-19.*):

■ *Single-purpose knives* cut just one shape, such as a cove, a bead, or an ogee.

■ *Multi-purpose knives* cut two or more shapes. Usually, one side of the knife is ground to cut one shape, and the other side is ground to cut another. This saves the setup time required to change knives.

■ *Coping knives* cut interlocking joints. They come in matched sets. One part of the set cuts one half of the joint, while the other part of the set cuts the other half.

Some knives in each category are shown in "Common Molding Knives" on page 76.

4-19 The ogee knife (left) is a *single-purpose knife*; it only cuts the ogee shape. The ogee-and-bead knife (middle) is a *multi-purpose knife* that will cut two different shapes, depending on how you set up for the molding cut. The tongue-and-groove *coping knives* (right) are precisely matched — one knife cuts a groove and the other cuts a tongue to fit it.

Molding knives normally come in sets of three; each knife in a set is ground identically to the others. (Coping knives come in six-knife sets containing two matching sets of three.) To mount the knives in the molding head, slip them into the slots. Make sure that the *flat* surfaces all face in the direction of rotation.

(*SEE FIGURE 4-20.*) Tighten the screws that hold the knives in the head, *then* check each screw again.

Set the position of the rip fence and the depth of cut as you would for a dado cutter, and cut test pieces to check your setup. If you plan to cut two or more shapes in the same workpiece — for example, if you

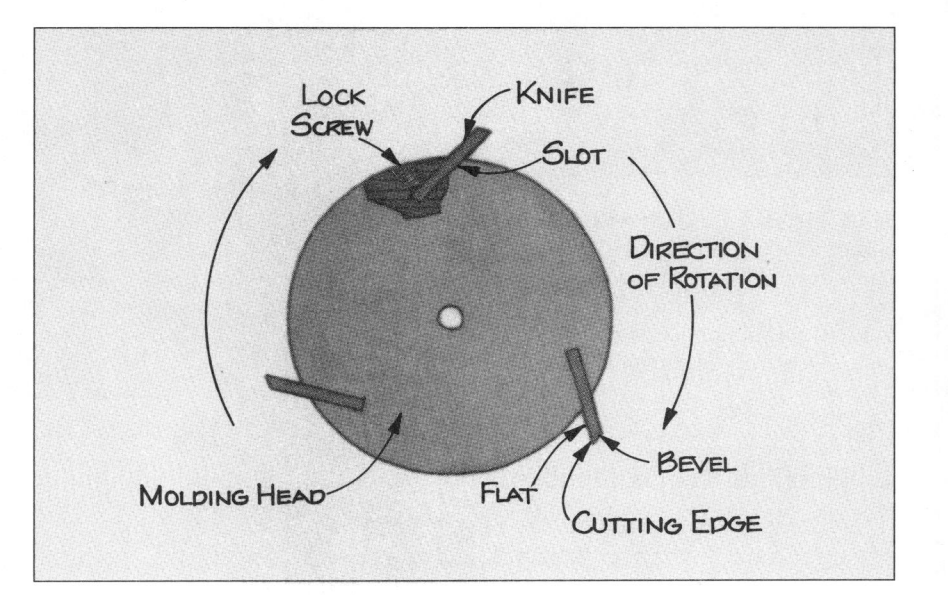

4-20 Mount the knives in the molding head slots and tighten the lock screws. When the knives are mounted, their cutting edges should all face the same way. The flat surfaces must face in the direction of rotation, and the beveled surfaces must face in the opposite direction.

4-21 To cut a molded shape in the edge or end of a board, position the rip fence next to or partially covering the knives. Place the face of the board on the saw table and the edge or end of the board against the fence. Slowly feed the stock over the cutter. Here, a molder forms part of a corner bead in the bottom edge of a table apron. **Note:** When molding the end of a board, use the rip fence to guide the workpiece and the miter gauge to feed it.

4-22 You can also mold an edge with the face of the board against the rip fence and the edge on the saw table. Here, the same apron board has been turned up on its edge to cut the second part of the corner bead. **Note:** If the board is very much wider than the rip fence is tall, use a tall fence extension to help support it.

want to cut an ogee and a cove in the same board to form a crown molding — cut several test pieces *after* you fine-tune the first setup. Use these pieces to test successive setups.

Feed the wood slowly over the cutter — more slowly than you would when making a saw cut or a dado cut. If you feed the wood too fast, the shaped surface will show ridges or *mill marks*. By using a slower feed, you allow the molder to make more cuts per inch so the molded shape appears perfectly smooth. However, be careful not to feed the wood *too* slowly, especially when molding hardwoods. If the molder dwells too long in any one spot, it will heat up and burn the wood.

The advantage of a molder over other shaping tools (such as a router or a shaper) is that it will cut all three surfaces — the *face* of a board as well as the ends and edges. Shapers only cut ends and edges, and the decorative face cuts you can make with a router are limited. To mold the ends or edges, position the rip fence next to or partially covering the molder. (*SEE FIGURES 4-21 THROUGH 4-23.*) To cut the face, move the fence away from the molder or use the miter gauge to guide the work. (*SEE FIGURE 4-24.*)

A SAFETY REMINDER

Do *not* attempt to mold narrow stock or any workpiece that's too small to safely control on the table saw. Instead, mold a larger board and cut the smaller piece from it. *Or* temporarily attach the small piece to a large scrap, mold it, and remove it from the scrap.

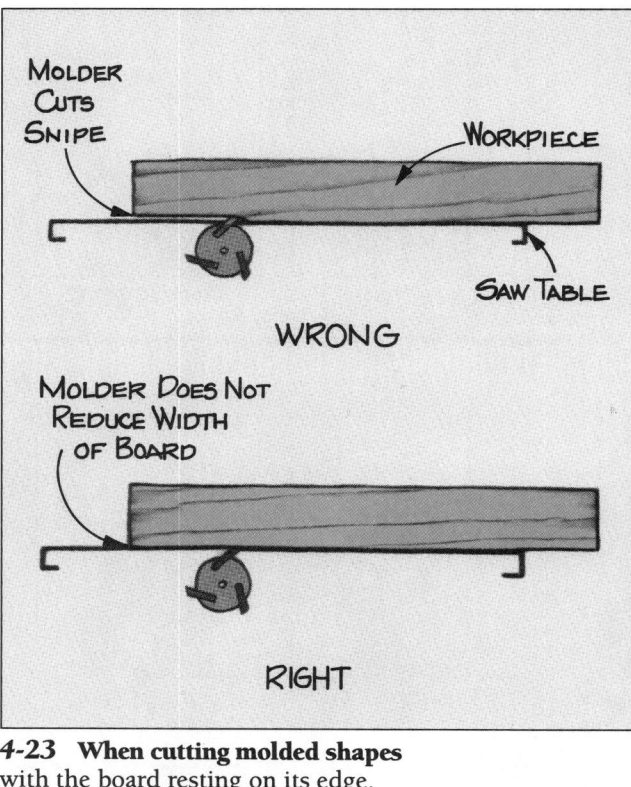

4-23 When cutting molded shapes with the board resting on its edge, *you must not reduce the width of the board.* If you don't cut the entire edge, this won't be a problem. But if you do, carefully set the depth of cut so the molder does not plane the board. If the molder removes too much wood, the board will rock forward toward the end of the cut, making the molded edge crooked. This is especially important when cutting coped edge joints, such as glue joints, rule joints, and tongue-and-groove joints.

4-24 When molding the face of a board, use a miter gauge to guide the board if cutting across the grain, and a rip fence if cutting with the grain. Here, a molder cuts three beads down the center of a table apron, using the same knives that made the corner bead shown in *Figures 4-21 and 4-22.*

Common Molding Knives

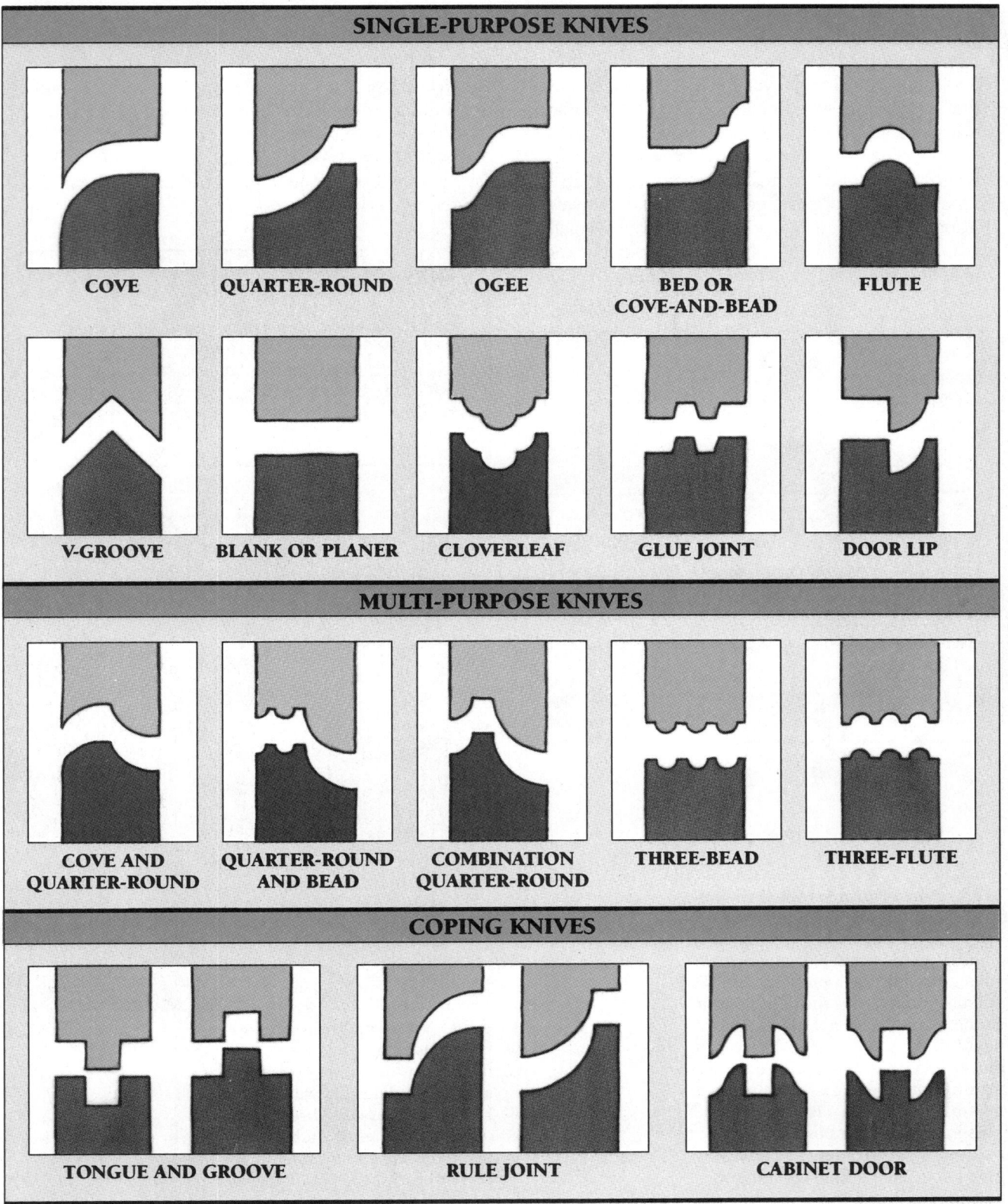

SINGLE-PURPOSE KNIVES

COVE   QUARTER-ROUND   OGEE   BED OR COVE-AND-BEAD   FLUTE

V-GROOVE   BLANK OR PLANER   CLOVERLEAF   GLUE JOINT   DOOR LIP

MULTI-PURPOSE KNIVES

COVE AND QUARTER-ROUND   QUARTER-ROUND AND BEAD   COMBINATION QUARTER-ROUND   THREE-BEAD   THREE-FLUTE

COPING KNIVES

TONGUE AND GROOVE   RULE JOINT   CABINET DOOR

5

SPECIAL TABLE SAW TECHNIQUES

The uses of a table saw go well beyond cutting, dadoing, and molding. Like most simple tools, it's remarkably versatile.

For instance, there are jigs and accessories that allow you to cut decorative panels, to taper table legs and other wooden parts, and to duplicate straight-sided, non-rectangular shapes such as triangles, trapezoids, and pentagons quickly and exactly. By cutting a series of evenly spaced saw kerfs partway through a board, you can bend that board around a corner — or in a complete circle! Pass a board across the saw at an angle and you can create wide coves and other contours.

And these are just a few examples. Although the table saw was originally designed for sizing wood, you can push it to do so much more.

MAKING RAISED PANELS

When using the table saw for specialty work, such as raising panels, it's important to remember that pushing a table saw to perform tasks that it wasn't originally designed to do can create a problem. If you *overextend* the table saw — push it beyond its safe limits — you can easily lose control of the workpiece. This, in turn, makes the operation dangerous, inaccurate, or both. When trying new techniques, you must maintain safety, accuracy, and control.

Often, the easiest way to do this is to build a simple, sturdy jig to hold or guide the workpiece. A well-made jig is a tool in its own right, with its own capabilities and limits. Some of the special table saw operations that follow would be impossible without the jigs shown; all of these jobs are made safer and more accurate by the jigs.

A raised panel is a board whose edges and ends have been beveled or tapered so the stock is thicker in the center than it is at the perimeter. This panel is usually mounted in a frame that allows it to expand and contract without stressing or distorting the project. You can raise a panel on a table saw by beveling the ends and edges.

Before you can do so, you must decide what angle to cut the bevels. Most raised panels are designed to fit into grooves in their frames. If you make the bevel too steep, it will act as a wedge in the groove — when the panel expands, the bevel will split the sides of the groove. If you make the bevel too shallow, the panel will be loose in the groove. The bevel must be angled to just touch the groove's side when the edge of the panel rests in the groove's bottom. (*SEE FIGURES 5-1 AND 5-2.*) When you've determined the proper bevel, tilt the saw blade to that angle.

Next, decide whether the raised panel will have a step between the field (raised area) and the bevels, and how large that step will be. Most craftsmen

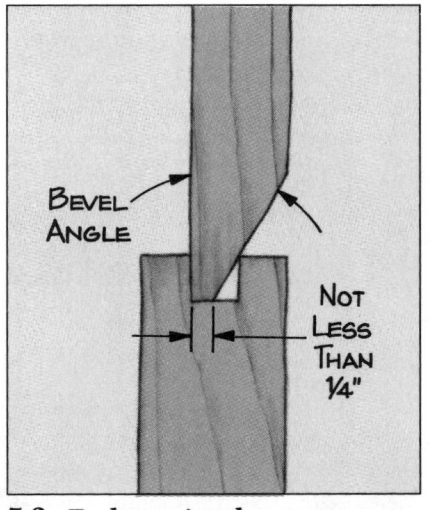

5-2 To determine the proper bevel angle of a raised panel, draw a full-size cross-section of the panel construction, showing both the groove and the panel on edge. Decide how thick the panel should be at the perimeter. (Most craftsmen prefer not to cut it thinner than 1/4 inch; if the beveled area becomes too thin, the panel will be weak.) Measure that thickness along the bottom of the groove from the left corner and make a mark. From this mark, draw a line that just touches the top right corner of the groove. With a protractor, measure the angle between the side of the groove and the last line you drew — that's the bevel angle you want to cut. Tilt the saw blade to that angle.

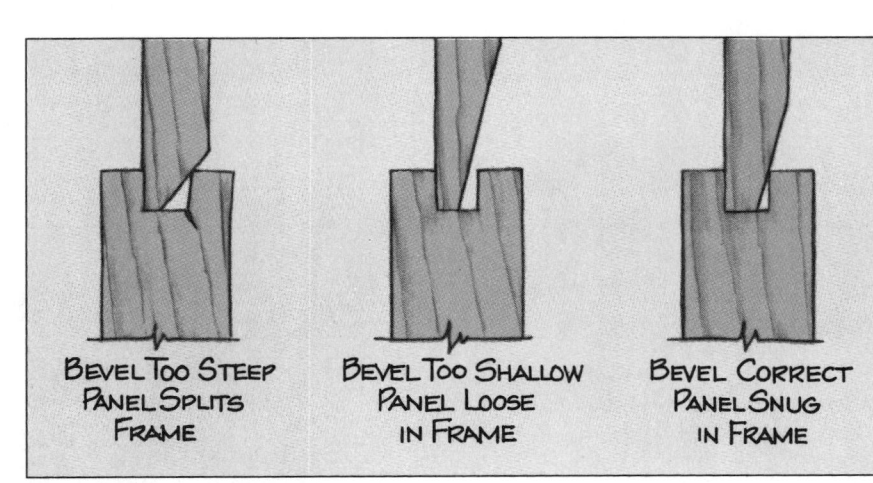

5-1 When making a raised panel, the bevel angle is critical. If it's too steep, as shown on the *left,* the panel could split the frame that it's mounted in. If it's too shallow, as shown in the *middle,* the panel will be too loose — it will rattle every time the frame is moved. The bevel should be angled so it barely touches the groove's side when the edge of the panel rests in the groove's bottom, as shown on the *right.*

prefer to make a $\frac{1}{16}$- to $\frac{1}{8}$-inch-deep step — about the same width as the sawteeth. (SEE FIGURE 5-3.) This helps delineate the field from the bevels, and makes the visual effect of the raised panel more dramatic.

If you decide to make a step on the panel, place the rip fence so just the outside corners of the teeth break through the wood as you cut. Make several test cuts to get the fence positioned just right, then saw the bevels in the ends and edges of the panel. (SEE FIGURE 5-4.)

Because the saw blade was tilted when you cut the bevels, the step won't be square to the field. Depending on the grind of the sawteeth, it may not even be flat. You can easily correct this by filing, scraping, or sanding the step to the proper angle. (SEE FIGURE 5-5.)

5-4 Before you cut, attach a *Tall* *Fence Extension* (see page 86) to the rip fence — this will help support the panels as they rest on their ends and edges. Bevel-cut the ends of the panel first, then the edges. If there's any tear-out while you're cutting across the wood grain, it will be removed when you cut parallel to the grain. **Note:** On most table saws, the blade tilts to the right. For safety, the fence must be placed to the left of the blade (away from the tilt) when raising panels.

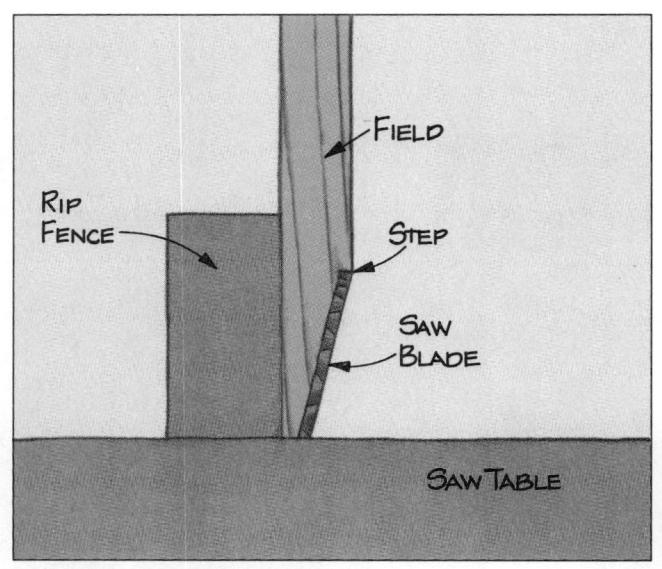

5-3 Raised panels often have a step between the field and the bevels — this emphasizes the design. If you decide to make a step, you must carefully position the rip fence so just the *outside* corners of the sawteeth break through the surface of the wood as you cut. The tops of the teeth will create the step. To make the step shallower, move the rip fence away from the blade — the teeth will protrude farther from the side of the panel. To make it deeper, move the fence closer. If you move the fence too close, however, the teeth won't cut completely through the wood. Using this technique, you can only make the step as deep as the sawteeth are wide.

5-5 After it's cut, the step will not be square to the field. Some craftsmen prefer to correct this by trimming it with a second series of saw cuts. However, the step is so small that all it really needs is a little special attention with a file, scraper, or sandpaper. If you use sandpaper to correct the angle of the step, wrap the paper around a hard, square block to make the step as flat as possible.

MAKING TAPER CUTS

To taper a board, you must reduce its width gradually from one end of the board to the other. That requires holding the board with its *length* at a slight angle to the blade as you *rip* it. The "Tapering Jig" on page 82 can be a big help.

To set up for a taper cut, you must know the *slope* of the taper. You should also know whether you will cut a single taper (on a single side or two *adjacent* sides) or a double taper (with tapers on two or more *opposing* sides).

The slope is determined by the length and width of the taper (sometimes called the *rise* and *run*). To find the rise of a taper, measure from the starting point to the end. To determine the run of a single taper, calculate the amount by which the width of the board is reduced. For a double taper, divide that amount by 2. (*See Figure 5-6.*)

To set the tapering jig to the proper angle, draw a right triangle on a large sheet of paper. The *base* on the triangle must be the same length as the *rise*, and the side of the triangle must be equal to the *run*. Place the jig over the triangle, then adjust it so one arm is parallel to the base and the other is parallel to the hypotenuse. (*See Figure 5-7.*)

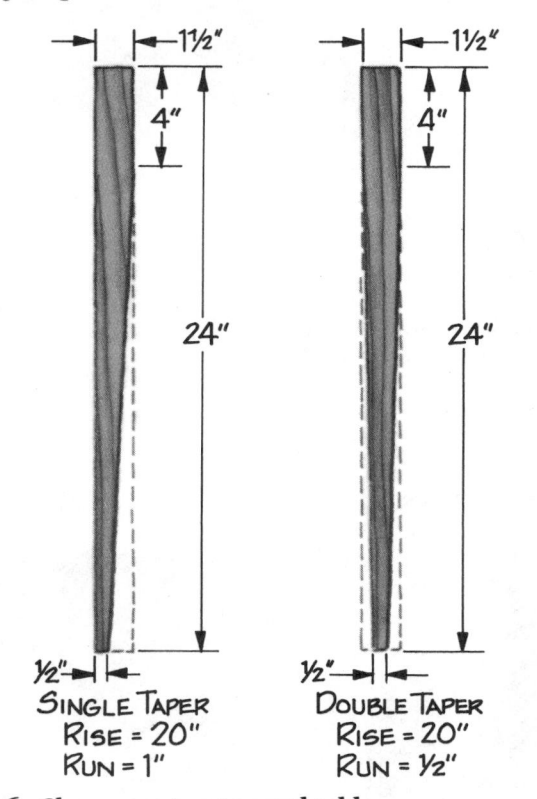

5-6 Shown are two tapered table legs, each 24 inches long. The one on the left has a single taper; the one on the right, a double taper. The taper on both legs is the same length and narrows to the same width. The rise is equal — on both legs, the taper begins 4 inches from the top and continues to the bottom, making the rise 20 inches (24 - 4 = 20). The run is *not* equal. Although both legs are 1½ inches wide at the top and then narrow to ½ inch at the bottom, the single-taper run is 1 inch (1½ - ½ = 1), and the double-taper run is ½ inch ([1½ - ½] / 2 = ½).

5-7 On a sheet of wrapping paper, draw a large right triangle with the same slope as the taper. Use this as a gauge to set the tapering jig to the proper angle — align one arm with the base of the triangle and the other with the hypotenuse.

Note: If the slope of a taper is given in degrees, you don't have to calculate the rise. Simply draw the triangle so the angle between the base and the hypotenuse matches that given for the slope.

Lay out the taper on a test piece. Place the jig on the table saw with the guiding arm against the fence. Position the fence so the taper will begin at the proper point and make a test cut in a scrap. *(SEE*

FIGURES 5-8 AND 5-9.) If test results are acceptable, cut the good stock.

To cut a double taper, make the first pass as if you were making a single taper. Then flip the board so the cut edge faces the jig. Place a wedge-shaped shim between the workpiece and the jig to hold the stock at the proper angle, and make the second pass. *(SEE FIGURES 5-10 AND 5-11.)*

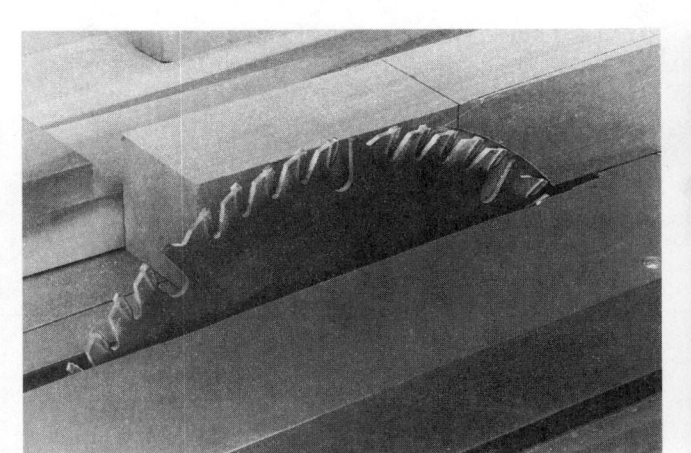

5-8 Using scrap stock, cut several test pieces to exactly the same dimensions as the workpieces you will taper. Carefully lay out the tapers on each of these pieces. Place the jig on the table saw with the guiding arm against the fence, and place a test piece against the ledge on the other arm of the jig. Position the fence so the *inside* edges of the sawteeth (those closest to the fence) brush the layout line that marks the start of the taper.

5-9 Turn on the saw and slowly push the jig forward, feeding the stock into the blade. As you do so, monitor the cut to make sure the blade follows the layout line. If it does, the setup is correct. If not, readjust the angle of the jig or the position of the rip fence.

5-10 To cut a double taper, you must make two passes, using a wedge-shaped shim to position the stock on the *second* pass. The dimensions and slope of this shim are the same as the right triangle you drew to set the angle of the jig. Lay out the shim on scrap stock, place the scrap in the tapering jig, and cut the shim. Saw to the *inside* of the layout line (the side nearest the jig). **Note:** The scraps from the first pass of a double taper may look to be the same size as the shim, but they will be too narrow because of the saw kerf.

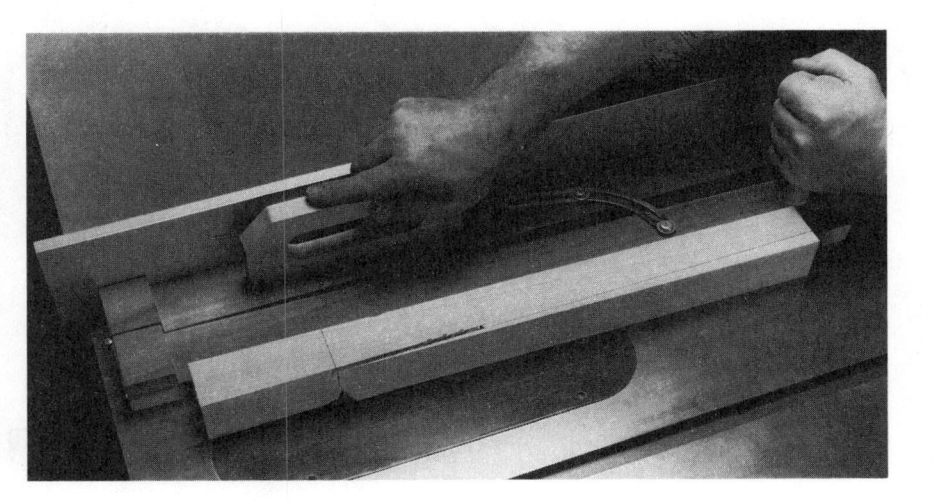

5-11 Make the first pass of the double taper as if you were cutting a single taper. Turn the board so the cut side faces the jig and place the shim between the workpiece and the jig. The wide end of the shim must be flush with the narrow end of the stock. This will hold the workpiece at the same angle to the blade as it was for the first pass. Make the second pass, holding both the workpiece and the shim against the ledge on the jig. **Note:** If the ledge isn't as wide as the shim, there is a danger the workpiece will slip as you cut it. To prevent this, adhere the shim to the workpiece with double-faced carpet tape.

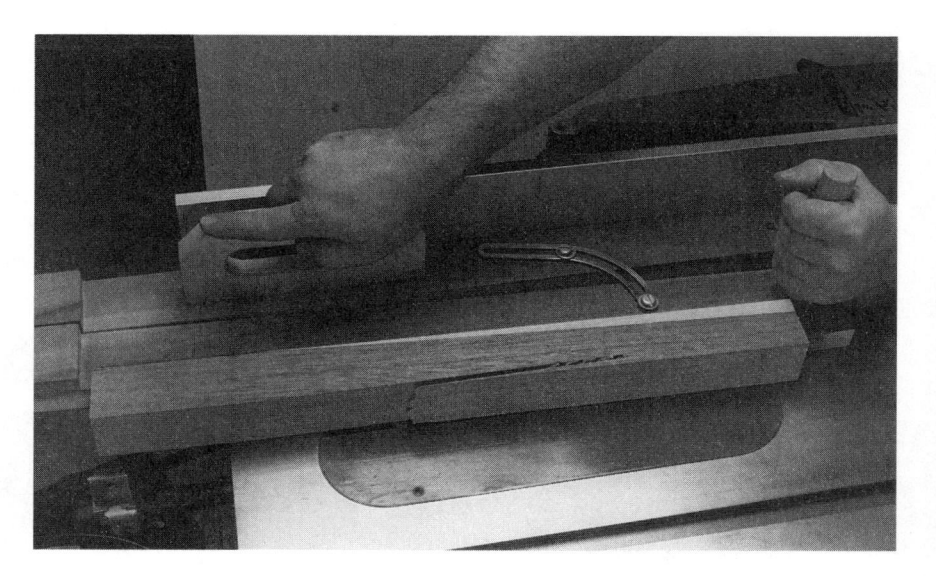

TAPERING JIG

A tapering jig consists of two long arms, hinged together at one end. A ledge is glued to one arm near the end opposite the hinge. A metal brace lets you adjust and lock the angle between the two arms. The arm without the ledge guides the jig along the rip fence, while the other holds the stock at an angle to the saw blade.

To make the jig, cut the parts to size and drill a hole for the handle in the holding arm. Glue the ledge to the holding arm and the grip to the guiding arm. When the glue is dry, install the hinge that holds the two arms together.

Purchase a *curved* box lid support and remove the metal mounts from the brace. Using a panhead screw, fasten the *fixed* end of the brace (the end with the hole) to the holding arm, a few inches from the

HINGE
BLOCKS

HANDLE

LEDGE

GRIP

HOLDING
ARM

GUIDING
ARM

EXPLODED VIEW

PATTERN SAWING

Many woodworking projects require that you make duplicate copies of certain parts. This is easy enough to do when the parts are rectangular — simply rip the stock to the same width, then cut the parts to the same length. But what if the parts are cut to a triangle, pentagon, or some other odd shape? As long as all the sides of that shape are straight, you can reproduce precise copies by *pattern sawing*.

To saw a pattern, first cut a single part to the shape you want. This will serve as the *template* for duplicate parts. Then cut rectangular *blanks* for the duplicates, making each blank slightly larger than needed.

Adjust the height of the saw blade to cut through the thickness of a blank. Mount a *Tall Fence Extension* (see page 86) to the rip fence and attach a *pattern*

sawing guide to the extension. (Refer to "Pattern Sawing Guide" on page 86 for plans and instructions.) Align the outside edge of the guide (farthest from the rip fence) with the outside edges of the saw-teeth, then adjust the height of the guide so the bottom surface is 1/4 to 1/2 inch above the saw blade. *(SEE FIGURE 5-12.)* The distance between the guide and the saw table should be slightly more than the thickness of one blank.

Fasten the template to a blank with nails, screws, or double-faced carpet tape. Holding the edges of the template against the guiding edge of the jig, saw each side. *(SEE FIGURE 5-13.)* Repeat for each blank until you've made all the parts needed.

ledge. Tighten the screw until it's snug, but not so tight that the brace can't pivot. Insert another screw through the slot in the brace and drive it into the guiding arm. You may have to experiment with the placement of this second screw. Find the location that allows you to open the arms as wide as pos-

sible, but keeps the end of the brace from straying over the outside edge of the guiding arm when you close the jig.

To lock the arms in place, open or close them to the desired angle. Then tighten *both* of the panhead screws.

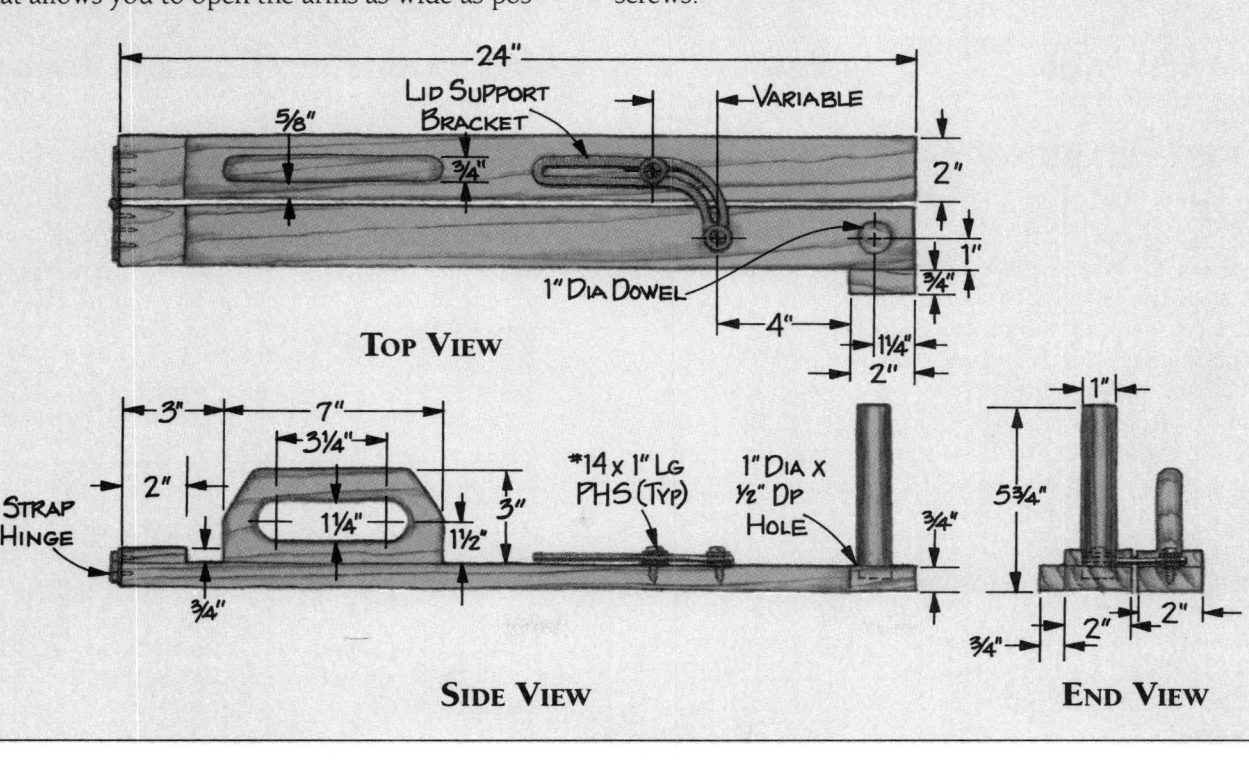

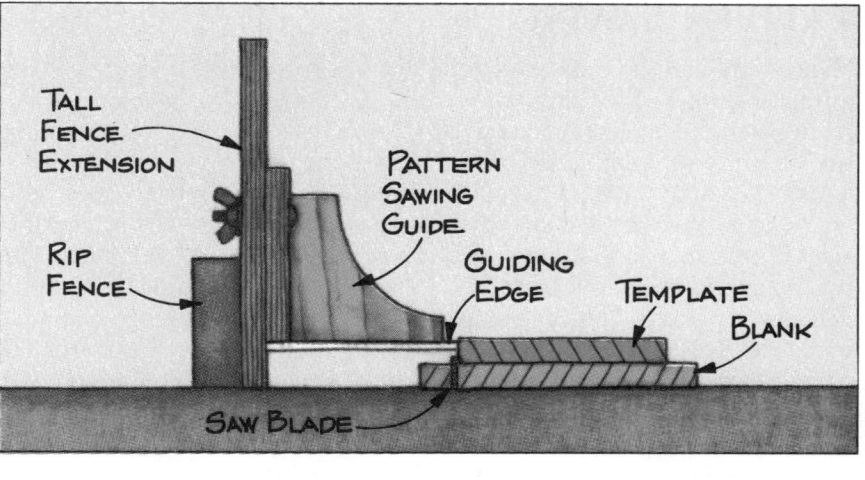

5-12 Position the pattern sawing guide so the outside edge is parallel to the saw blade plate and flush with the outside edges of the sawteeth. The guiding edge of the jig must be high enough above the saw so that it will contact the edge of the template, but *not* the blank.

5-13 Attach the template to a blank and rest it in front of the saw blade (on the infeed side). Butt one of the template edges against the guiding edge of the jig. Turn on the saw and push the template forward, cutting one edge of the blank. Turn the template and cut another edge. Repeat for each edge.

KERF BENDING

You can bend a board of any thickness if you first cut several kerfs in one side — preferably a side you won't see on the assembled project. These kerfs must not sever the board, but should leave about $1/16$ to $1/8$ inch of stock at the bottom of each cut.

The radius of the curve you want to bend determines the spacing of the kerfs — the tighter the radius, the closer the kerfs. *(SEE FIGURE 5-14.)* To get a smooth, even bend, the kerfs must be evenly spaced. Gauge the spacing of each kerf by driving a small nail into the face of the miter gauge extension and using it as a stop. *(SEE FIGURE 5-15.)*

Note: The depth of the cut and the thickness of the stock at the bottom of the kerf will depend on the species of wood — some must be cut thinner than others to bend easily. Experiment with scraps until you can make a smooth, even bend without cracks or splinters.

Cut the kerfs only in the area where you want to bend the wood. After kerfing, carefully bend the wood to the radius needed. To prevent it from straightening out again, brace it or fasten it to the project. *(SEE FIGURE 5-16.)*

TRY THIS TRICK

If the wood is hard to bend or breaks when you bend it, wrap the kerfed portion of the board in a towel. Soak the towel with boiling water and let it sit for 10 to 15 minutes. Unwrap the towel and bend the wood *immediately*, before it has a chance to cool or dry.

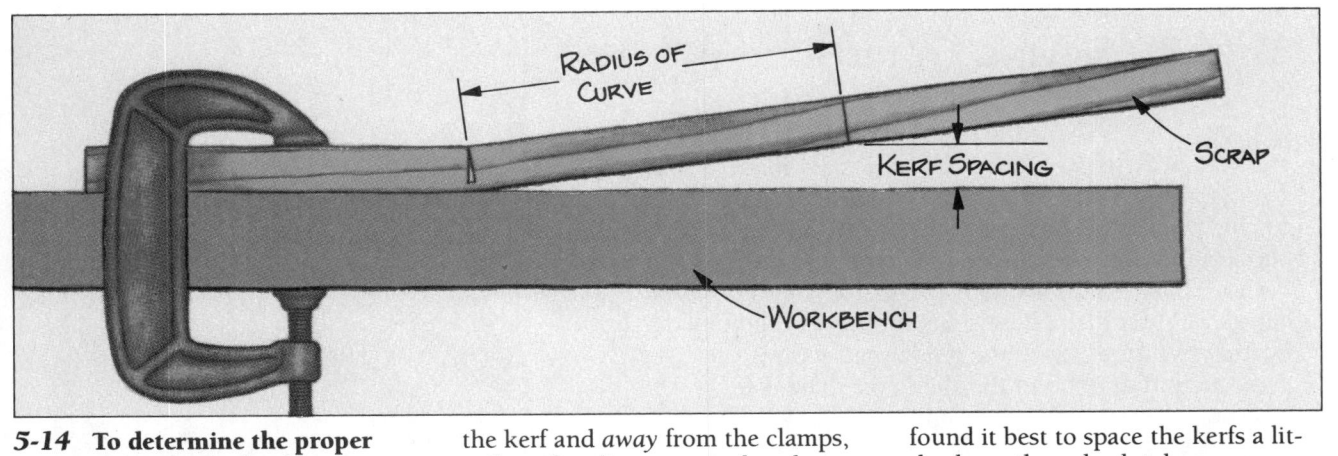

RADIUS OF CURVE

KERF SPACING

SCRAP

WORKBENCH

5-14 To determine the proper spacing between the kerfs, cut a single kerf in a long scrap board of the same thickness and species as the wood you want to bend. Fasten the board to a workbench, placing the clamps to one side of the kerf. Measure along the board out from the kerf and *away* from the clamps, and mark a distance equal to the *radius* of the bend you want to make. Lift the free end of the board until the kerf closes. Measure the distance from the board to the workbench at the radius mark — this will give you the spacing. **Note:** In practice, I've found it best to space the kerfs a little closer than absolutely necessary, so the kerfs don't quite close when you bend the wood. Also, I never space the kerfs any *farther* apart than 1". If they're too far apart, the bend won't look smooth.

5-15 Fasten an extension to the miter gauge, positioning it to pass over the blade when you cut. Cut a single kerf in the workpiece and through the extension. Drive a small brad into the extension to the right or left of this cut. The distance between the brad and the cut must be equal to the spacing between the remaining kerfs you want to cut. Place the workpiece against the extension with the first kerf over the brad. Cut a second kerf, move the board so the second kerf is over the brad, and repeat. Continue until you've made all the kerfs needed.

5-16 When you bend the wood, you must fasten it to something to hold the curve. If you can't fasten the board to the project itself, fasten a brace to the board.

PATTERN SAWING GUIDE

This jig is an L-shaped bracket with several braces
to stiffen it. The mount and the braces are made
from hardwood, but the guide is made from clear
acrylic plastic. This lets you see the saw blade and
monitor the saw cuts as you make them.

Cut the parts to size and rout the slots in the
mount. Fasten the braces to the mount with glue
and screws, then attach the guide with screws.
Drill mounting holes in the *Tall Fence Extension*
and bolt the jig to the extension.

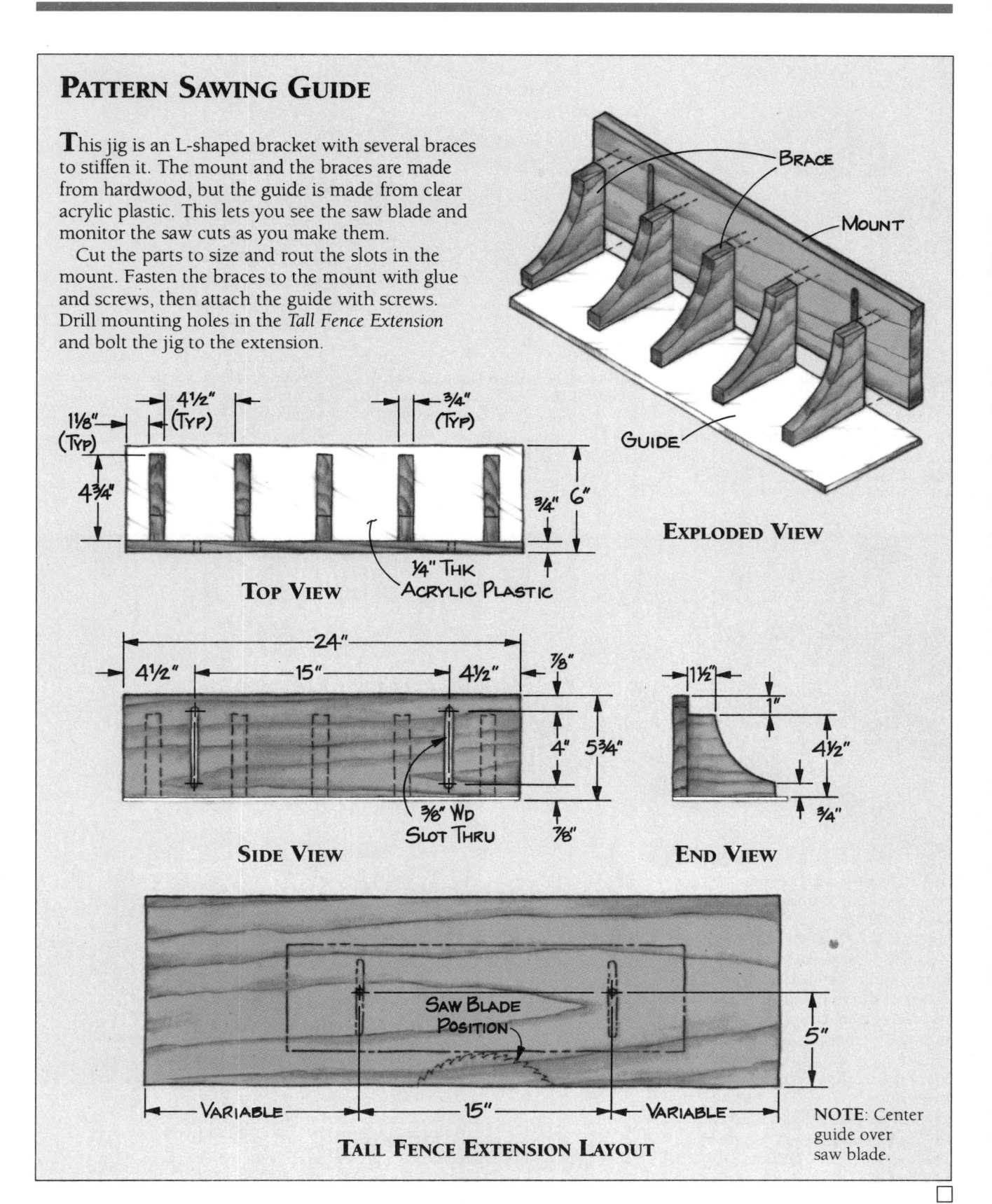

BRACE

MOUNT

GUIDE

EXPLODED VIEW

1⅛"
(TYP)

4½"
(TYP)

¾"
(TYP)

4¾"

¾"   6"

¼" THK
ACRYLIC PLASTIC

TOP VIEW

24"

4½"   15"   4½"   ⅞"

4"   5¾"

⅜" WD
SLOT THRU

⅞"

SIDE VIEW

1½"

1"

4½"

¾"

END VIEW

SAW BLADE
POSITION

5"

VARIABLE   15"   VARIABLE

TALL FENCE EXTENSION LAYOUT

NOTE: Center
guide over
saw blade.

CUTTING COVES

To cut a cove in the face or edge of a board, pass it over the saw blade *at an angle*. The depth of the cove is determined by the height of the blade above the table, and the width of the cove by the angle of the board to the saw. Determine this angle with a *Parallel Rule*. (*SEE FIGURE 5-17.*) See "Coving Jigs" on page 88 for instructions on how to make a parallel rule.

Clamp a straightedge to the saw table or position a *Coving Fence* at the proper angle and distance from the blade. (*SEE FIGURES 5-18 AND 5-19.*) "Coving Jigs" on page 88 also includes plans for making a coving fence. Lower the blade until it barely projects above the table. Cut the cove in several passes, raising the blade slightly with each pass until the cove is the desired depth and width. (*SEE FIGURE 5-20.*)

A SAFETY REMINDER

Place the fence or straightedge on the *infeed* side of the blade. The rotation of the blade will help hold the stock against the guide as you cut.

5-17 **To find a *coving angle* —** the angle at which the board should cross the blade to cut a particular cove — first raise or lower the saw blade to the desired depth of cut. Adjust a *Parallel Rule* (see page 88) to the width of the cove you want to cut and place it on the saw table so the rules straddle the blade, front and back. Turn the rules at various angles to the blade while slowly spinning the blade by hand. Find the position where the teeth of the saw blade brush *both* rules. Holding the parallel rule in that position, draw *two* pencil lines across the saw table that trace the *inside* edge of each rule. The angle between the blade plate and either one of these lines is the coving angle. **Note:** If an ordinary pencil won't leave a visible mark on your saw table, use a grease pencil.

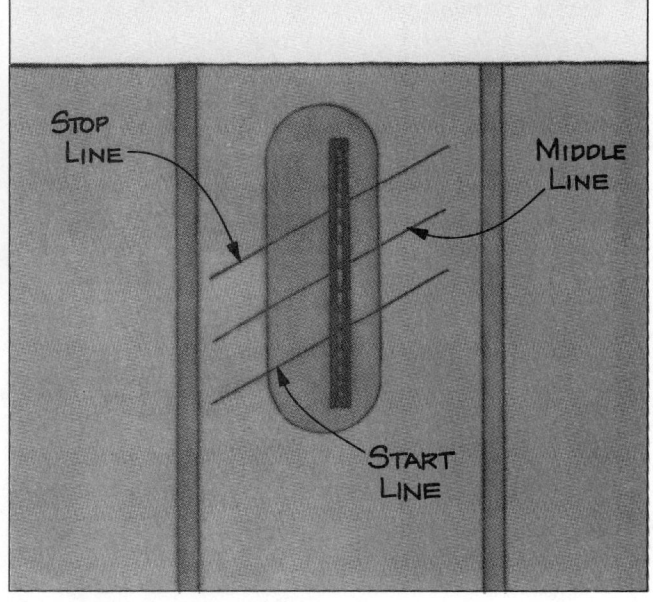

5-18 **Measure the distance** between the two lines, then draw a *third* line halfway between and parallel to them. This marks the precise middle of the cove cut. Use all three marks as references to determine both the angle and the position of the coving fence on the saw table. For example, if you want to cut a cove down the middle of a 5-inch-wide board, the fence must be parallel to and 2½ inches away from the middle reference line.

5-19 Fasten the coving fence to
the rip fence and adjust the angle
parallel to the three reference lines.
Then move the rip fence sideways
until it's the proper distance away
from the lines. If you need to position the coving fence over the saw
blade, lower the blade beneath the
surface of the table. When the fence
is properly positioned, turn on the
saw and raise the blade. This will cut
a kerf in the coving fence. **Note:** If
you don't want to make a coving
fence, you can also use a long,
straight board instead. Clamp the
board to the table saw in the proper
position.

COVING JIGS

There are two tools you need to cut a cove on a
table saw — a *parallel rule* to measure the coving
angle and a *coving fence* to guide the board across
the blade at the proper angle.

The parallel rule consists of four pieces of wood
— two rules and two stretchers. Cut the parts from
straight, clear hardwood. Join them at the ends
with screws, making a parallelogram. Tighten the
screws until they're snug, but not so tight that the

parts won't pivot easily. **Note:** For the parallel rule
to work accurately, all the screw holes must be
centered between the edge of the rules and
stretchers, and they should be precisely the same
distance from the ends of the boards.

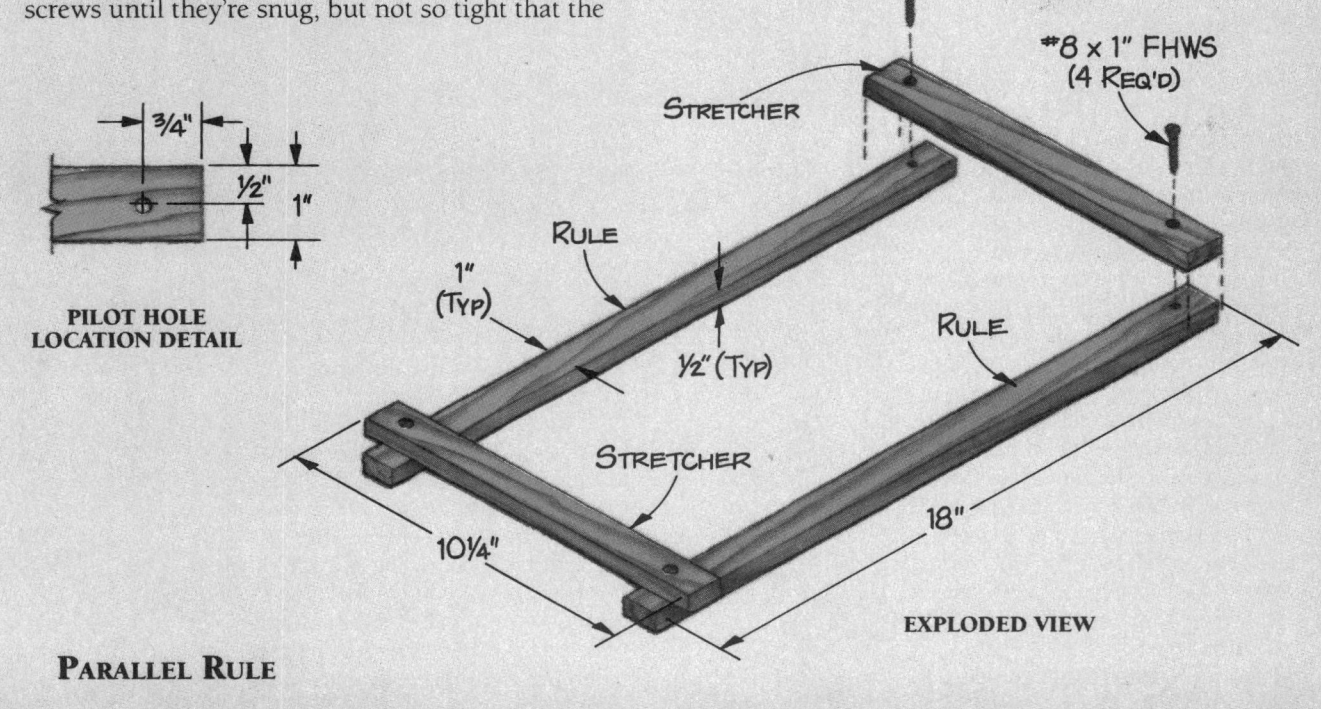

PILOT HOLE
LOCATION DETAIL

PARALLEL RULE

5-20 Adjust the saw blade so it projects no more than ¹/₁₆ inch above the saw table. Turn on the saw and place the workpiece against the fence. Slowly feed the workpiece from the infeed side of the saw and *against* the direction of rotation. After completing the first pass, raise the saw blade another ¹/₁₆ inch and make a second pass. Repeat until you have cut the cove to the desired depth and width. On the last pass, feed the wood very slowly — this will make the surface of the cove as smooth as possible and reduce the amount of sanding needed.

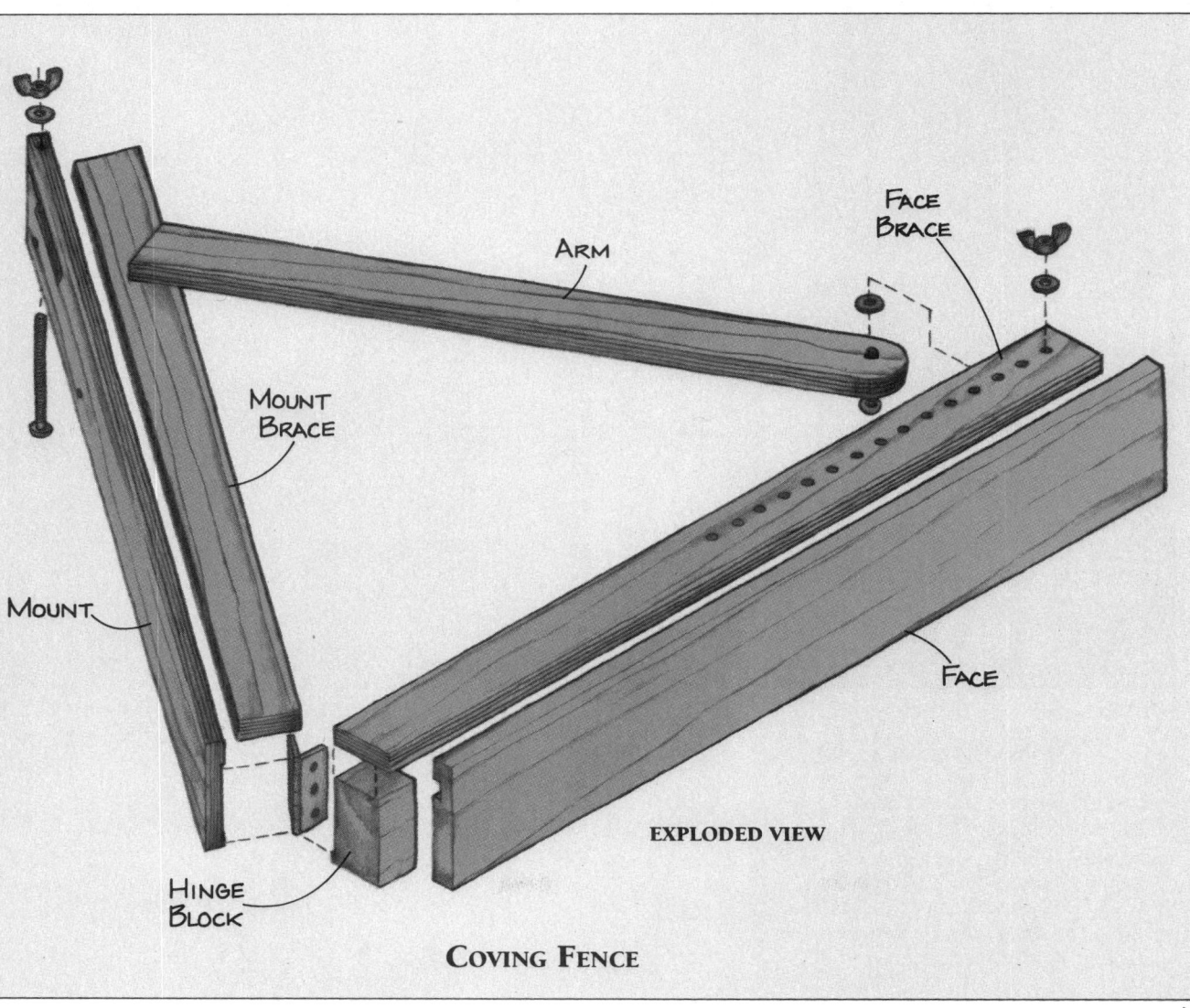

ARM

FACE
BRACE

MOUNT
BRACE

MOUNT

FACE

EXPLODED VIEW

HINGE
BLOCK

COVING FENCE

(continued) ▷

COVING JIGS — CONTINUED

A coving fence can be a single long, straight board clamped to the saw table. However, a single board can be difficult to position accurately. And depending on how your table saw is constructed, the board may also be difficult to clamp securely. To avoid these problems, make a coving fence that mounts to the rip fence. The fence shown consists of two long assemblies, hinged at one end. The mount assembly remains stationary, while the face assembly swings out from it and can be locked at any angle.

Cut the face from hardwood and the remaining parts from plywood. Rout the grooves for the braces and drill the holes required. Cut a recess and a slot in the mount to hold the arm.

Glue the mount and the mount brace together to make the mount assembly, then glue the face, face brace, and hinge block together to make the face assembly. Hinge the two assemblies together and attach the arm to the face brace with a carriage bolt, washers, and wing nut.

1 **To use the coving fence, bolt** the mount to the rip fence. Insert the free end of the arm in the mount recess, adjust the face to the desired angle, and clamp the arm in the mount using the carriage bolt. If necessary, you can also adjust the position of the pivoting end of the arm by fastening it to another hole in the face brace.

2 **When you are not using the** coving fence, remove the mount from the rip fence and the arm from the mount recess. Fold together the face assembly, mount assembly, and arm as shown.

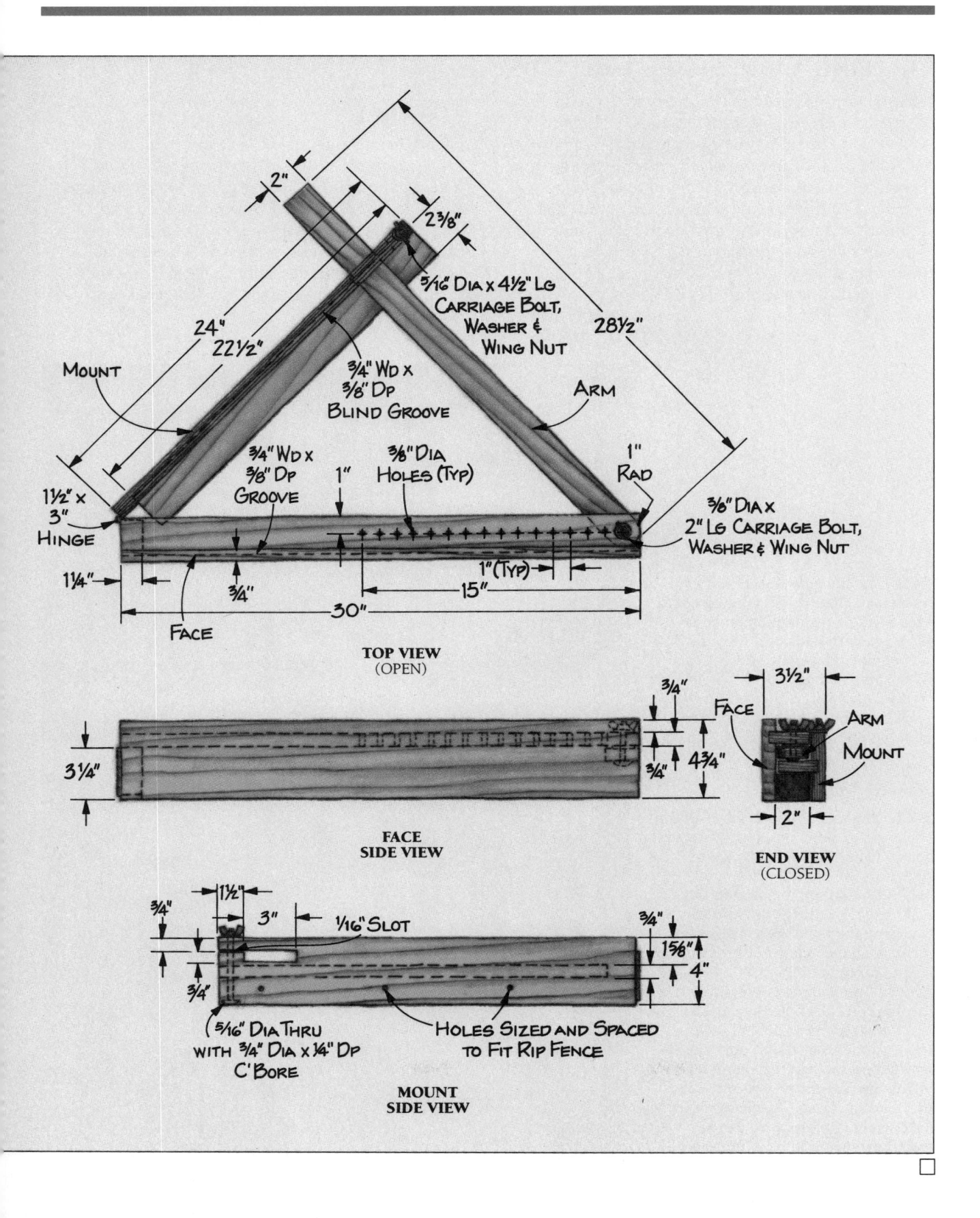

2"

2⅜"

⁵⁄₁₆" Dia x 4½" Lg
Carriage Bolt,
Washer &
Wing Nut

24"
22½"

28½"

Mount

¾" Wd x
⅜" Dp
Blind Groove

Arm

¾" Wd x
⅜" Dp
Groove

⅜" Dia
Holes (Typ)

1"

1"
Rad

1½" x
3"
Hinge

⅜" Dia x
2" Lg Carriage Bolt,
Washer & Wing Nut

1¼"

¾"

1" (Typ)

15"

30"

Face

TOP VIEW
(OPEN)

3¼"

¾"

Face

¾"

4¾"

3½"

Arm

Mount

2"

**FACE
SIDE VIEW**

END VIEW
(CLOSED)

¾"

1½"

3"

¹⁄₁₆" Slot

¾"

1⅝"

4"

¾"

⁵⁄₁₆" Dia Thru
with ¾" Dia x ¼" Dp
C'Bore

Holes Sized and Spaced
to Fit Rip Fence

**MOUNT
SIDE VIEW**

CUTTING ODD-SHAPED BOARDS

Occasionally, you need to rip or crosscut a board that doesn't have an edge straight or square enough to hold against the rip fence or miter gauge. Sometimes the board is crooked or warped, other times it's cut or shaped to a particular pattern or contour. The best solution would be to straighten one edge, but there are times when, for one reason or another, you can't.

To safely cut an odd-shaped board, mount it on a "holder" that has at least one good guiding edge. This holder needn't be a complex affair; a scrap of plywood with several straight edges makes an excellent holder.

Nail the workpiece to the plywood or secure it with double-faced carpet tape. Place the holder against the rip fence or the miter gauge, and feed both the holder and the workpiece past the saw blade. (*SEE FIGURE 5-21.*)

You can also use the "Sliding Table" shown on page 94 to hold an odd-shaped workpiece. Secure the workpiece to the jig using the built-in disk-shaped clamps, letting a portion overhang the sliding table's edge. Place the jig in the miter gauge slot and slide both the jig and the workpiece forward, past the saw blade. (*SEE FIGURE 5-22.*)

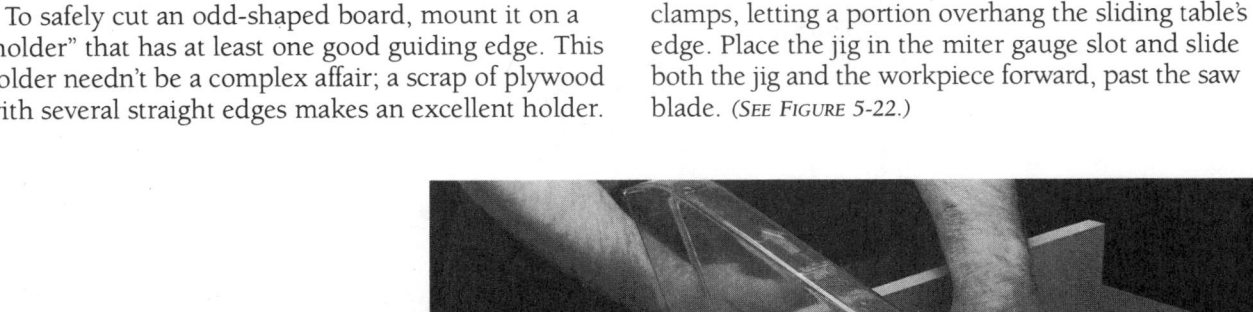

5-21 To cut an odd-shaped workpiece that has no guiding edge, secure it to a rectangular scrap of plywood with nails or double-faced carpet tape. Place one straight edge of the plywood against the rip fence or the miter gauge, then guide the workpiece over the blade, cutting *both* the plywood and the workpiece.

5-22 You can also use the "Sliding Table" jig to cut an unusually-shaped board. (The plans for this jig are shown in the *Projects* section on page 94.) Clamp the board to the sliding table, letting one portion overhang the table's edge. Don't let the disk-shaped clamps tilt or tip when you tighten them. If they do, they will put sideways pressure on the workpiece and it may shift as you cut. To prevent this, place a spacer under the clamp, opposite the workpiece, to keep the clamp level. When the workpiece is secured to the "Sliding Table," fit the jig in the miter gauge slot, turn on the saw, and feed the workpiece past the blade.

PROJECTS

6

SLIDING TABLE

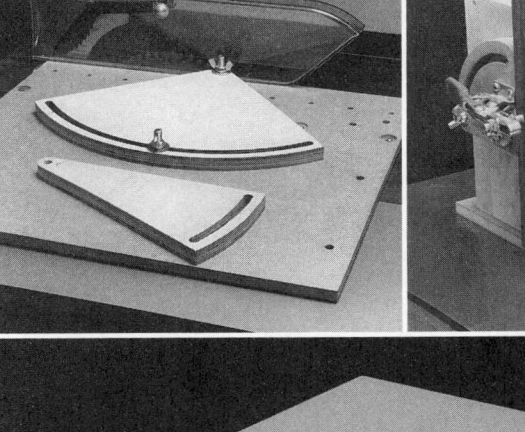

A sliding table is a cut-off accessory. Like a miter gauge, it slides back and forth in a slot in the saw table, guiding the wood as you make crosscuts and miters. But unlike a miter gauge, it supports *two* adjacent sides of a workpiece — a face and an edge — preventing the wood from rubbing directly on the saw table. Furthermore, the supporting surfaces are much larger than those of a miter gauge. Because of these differences, a sliding table is easier to use than a miter gauge, and produces more accurate results.

The sliding table shown is more capable than most. It has several attachments for many different saw operations. Each of these quickly mounts to the table with carriage bolts and wing nuts:

■ The *cut-off fence* holds the wood perfectly square to the blade while you make 90 degree crosscuts. It cannot be adjusted to any other position, but provides excellent support for small and medium-size workpieces at this one much-used angle.

■ Small and large *miter fences* let you make both crosscuts and miters. With the small miter fence, you can make extremely acute miters — as little as 15 degrees right and left. (Ordinary miter gauges can only be angled to 30 degrees.) You can adjust the large fence to make crosscuts, right and left 45-degree miters, or reciprocal

miters (with angles that add up to 90 degrees).

■ A *tenoning attachment* holds a workpiece vertically at various angles while you cut its end. This allows you to make tenons, slot mortises, and spline grooves.

■ *Clamping attachments* will hold odd-shaped and curved workpieces to the sliding table. This lets you crosscut or rip them, even though they may not have a suitable guiding edge.

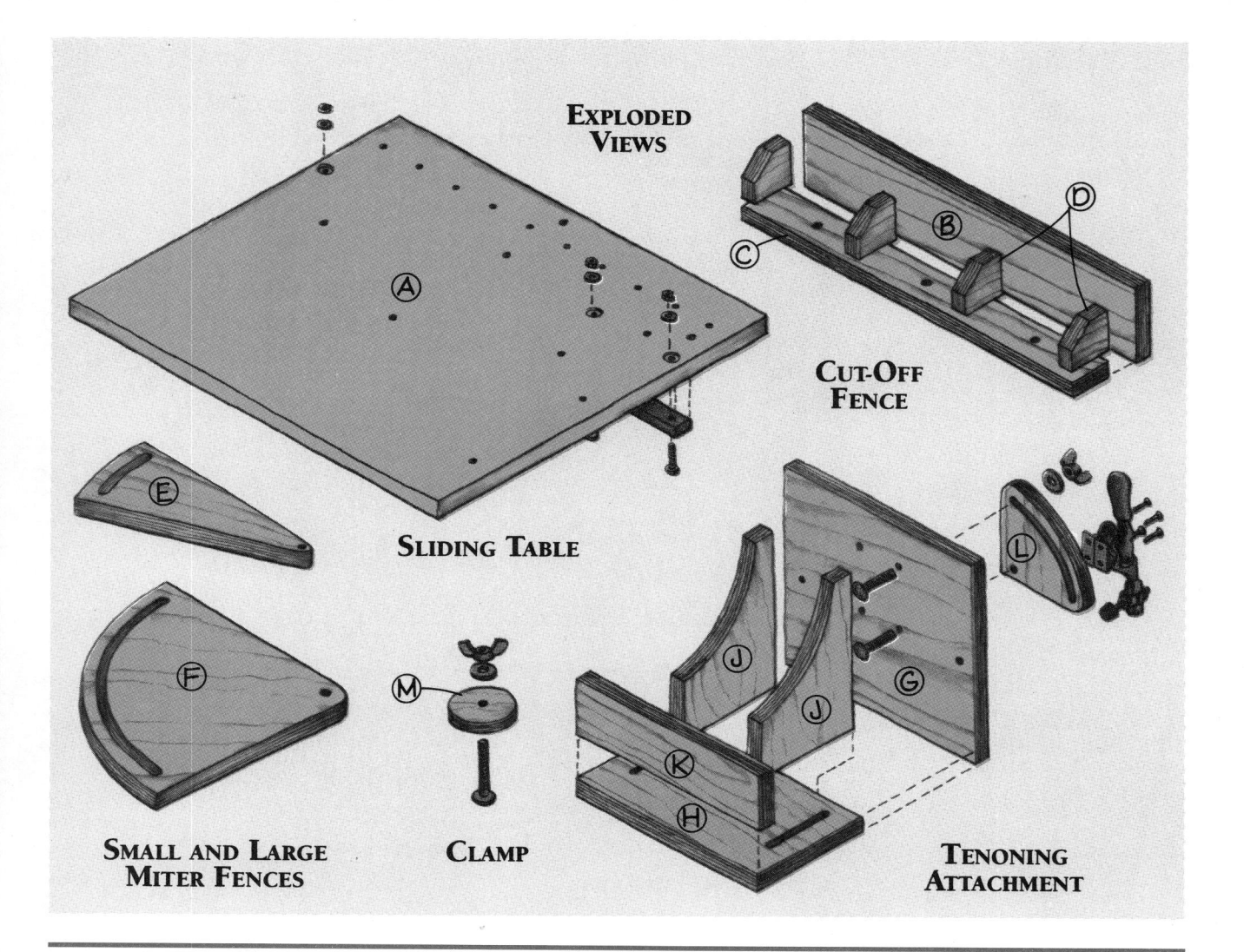

EXPLODED VIEWS

CUT-OFF FENCE

SLIDING TABLE

SMALL AND LARGE MITER FENCES

CLAMP

TENONING ATTACHMENT

MATERIALS LIST (FINISHED DIMENSIONS)

Parts *(Make all parts from cabinet-grade plywood unless otherwise noted.)*

Sliding table

A. Table*   ½" x 18" x 20"

Cut-off fence

B. Face†   ¾" x 3¾" x 18"
C. Base   ¾" x 2" x 18"
D. Braces (4)   ¾" x 2" x 2"

Miter fences

E. Small fence   ¾" x 5" x 10⅜"
F. Large fence   ¾" x 10⅜" x 10⅜"

Tenoning attachment

G. Face   ¾" x 10" x 10"
H. Base   ¾" x 5¾" x 10"
J. Braces (2)   ¾" x 5" x 7¾"
K. Back   ¾" x 2¾" x 10"
L. Quadrant   ¾" x 5" x 5"

Clamping attachment

M. Clamps
    (2–4)   (Variable) dia. x ¾"

*Make this part from medium-density
fiberboard (MDF).*
†*Make this part from solid hardwood.*

Hardware

#8 x 1¼" Flathead wood screws
   (30–36)

⅜" x 2" Carriage bolts, washers,
   and wing nuts (3)

⅜" x 2½" Carriage bolts, washers,
   and wing nuts (2)

5/16" x 3" Carriage bolts, washers,
   and wing nuts (2)

Miter gauge bar and mounting
   hardware

Toggle clamp and mounting screws

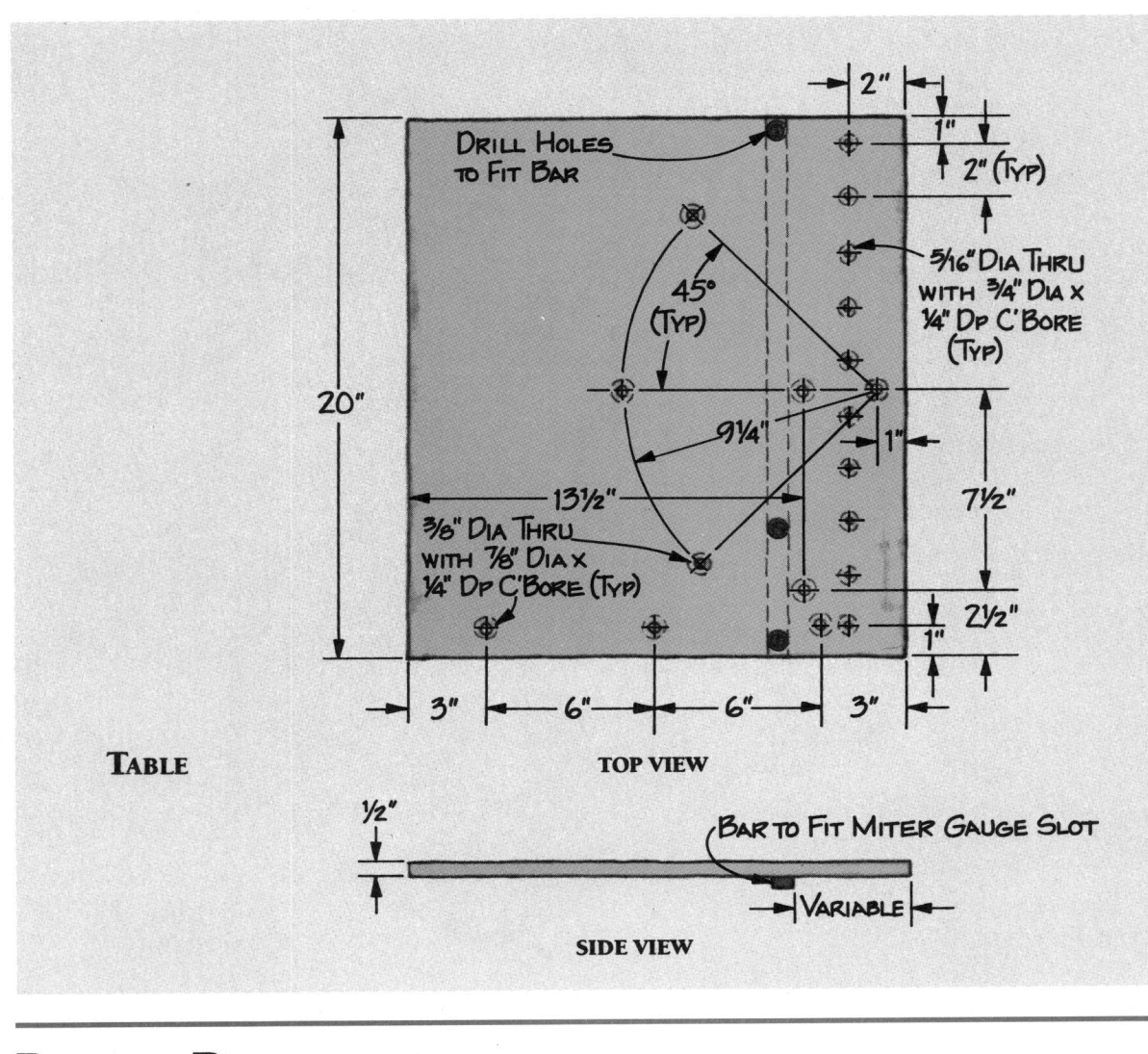

DRILL HOLES TO FIT BAR

45° (TYP)

5/16" DIA THRU WITH 3/4" DIA X 1/4" DP C'BORE (TYP)

20"

9¼"

13½"

⅜" DIA THRU WITH ⅞" DIA X ¼" DP C'BORE (TYP)

2"

1"

2" (TYP)

1"

7½"

2½"

1"

3"   6"   6"   3"

TABLE   **TOP VIEW**

½"

BAR TO FIT MITER GAUGE SLOT

VARIABLE

SIDE VIEW

PLAN OF PROCEDURE

1 Cut the parts to size. To make this project, you need a scrap of clear hardwood (such as maple or oak), a scrap of ½-inch medium-density fiberboard (available on special order at most lumberyards), and one 2- by 4-foot sheet of ¾-inch cabinet-grade plywood. Cut all the parts to the sizes shown in the Materials List *except* the table, miter fences, and quadrant. Make the table 1 inch wider than specified, and cut the miter fences and quadrant slightly wider *and* longer than specified.

Note: I used medium-density fiberboard for the table because it's extremely stable and has little tendency to distort or expand — and because I had a scrap kicking around my shop. If you can't purchase a small piece, you probably don't want to buy a whole

4- by 8-foot sheet to make this one project. Instead, purchase a laminate-covered sink cutout from a cabinet shop. Your sliding table will be slightly heavier, but it will be just as stable.

2 Cut the table to size. The table serves as a base for all of the attachments. It's a simple assembly — just a piece of fiberboard with a miter gauge bar attached to it.

To determine the position of the bar, measure from the table saw blade over to the *left* miter slot (as you face the infeed side of the saw). Add 1 inch to this measurement — this is the distance from the *right* side of the table to the bar.

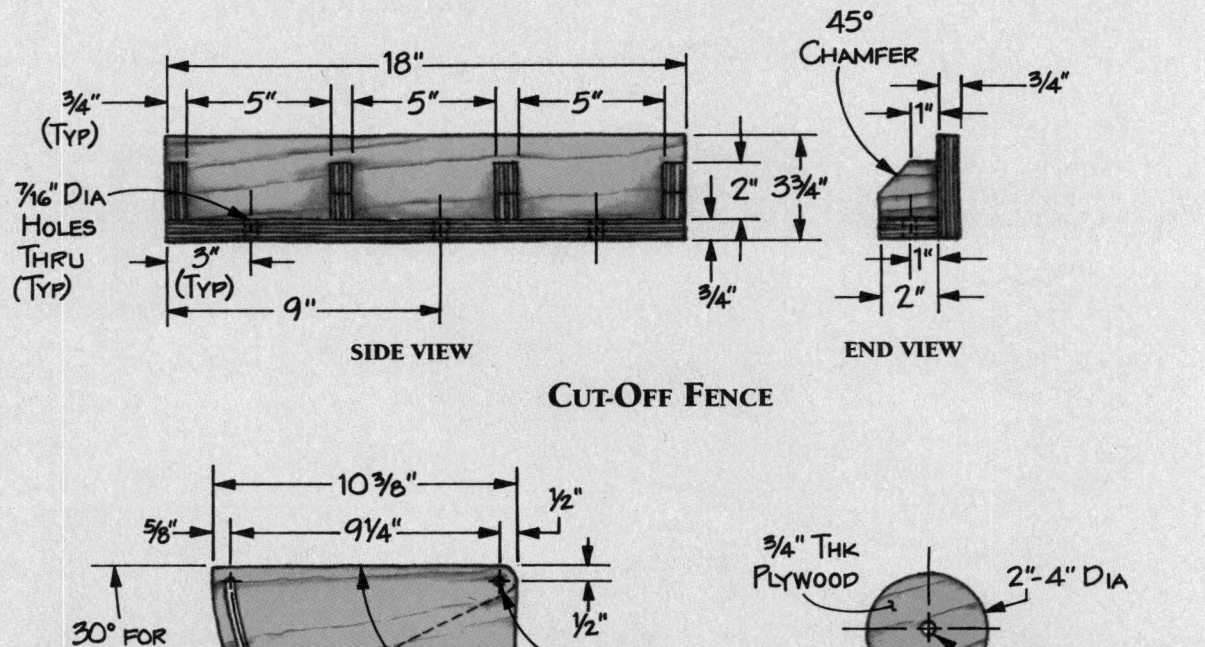

CUT-OFF FENCE

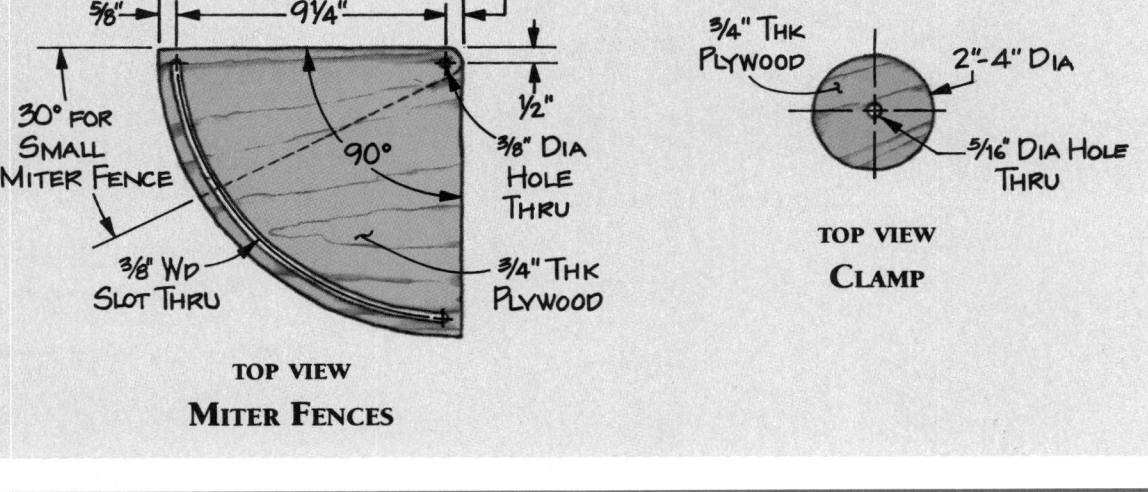

TOP VIEW
MITER FENCES

TOP VIEW
CLAMP

Mark the position of the bar on the table, drill the necessary mounting holes, and bolt the bar to the underside of the table. The positions of the bolt holes are *not* specified in the drawings; they will vary depending on the make of the miter gauge bar.

Place the table on the table saw, slipping the bar into the left miter gauge slot. Turn on the saw and push the table forward, trimming the right side. After it's cut, the table should be 18 inches wide.

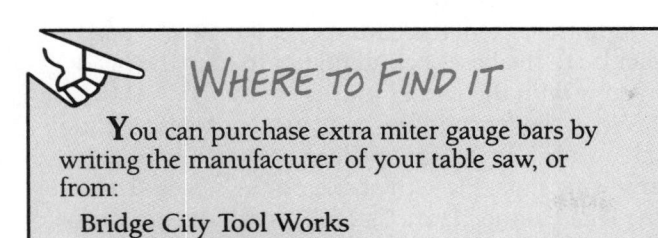

WHERE TO FIND IT

You can purchase extra miter gauge bars by writing the manufacturer of your table saw, or from:

Bridge City Tool Works
1104 N.E. 28th Avenue
Portland, OR 97232

3 Drill the mounting holes in the table.
Remove the bar from the table and carefully lay out the positions of the mounting holes, as shown in the *Table/Top View* drawing. Try to make sure that none of the mounting holes will be covered by the bar when you reinstall it. If this isn't possible, you may have to move the location of the attachment on the table right or left — or move the location of the mounting holes in the attachment.

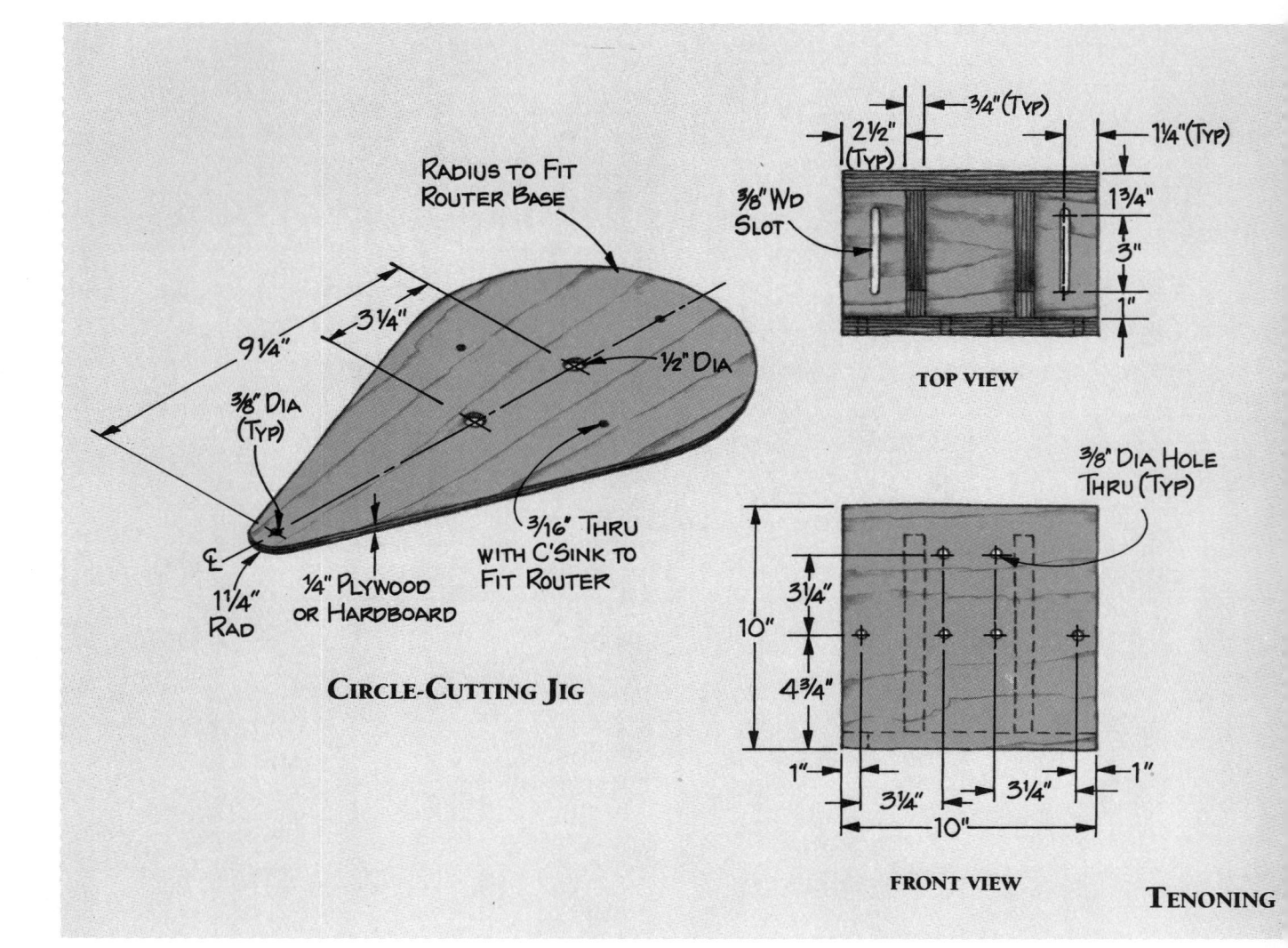

RADIUS TO FIT ROUTER BASE

3/8" WD SLOT

9¼"

3¼"

½" DIA

3/8" DIA (TYP)

¢

1¼" RAD

¼" PLYWOOD OR HARDBOARD

3/16" THRU WITH C'SINK TO FIT ROUTER

CIRCLE-CUTTING JIG

2½" (TYP)

¾" (TYP)

1¼" (TYP)

1¾"

3"

1"

TOP VIEW

3/8" DIA HOLE THRU (TYP)

10"

3¼"

4¾"

1"

3¼"

3¼"

1"

10"

FRONT VIEW

TENONING

Note that each hole is counterbored on the underside. The heads of the carriage bolts that hold the attachments in place are recessed in these counterbores so they won't rub on the saw table. Drill the holes and counterbores on a drill press, then replace the bar.

4 Make the cut-off fence. Lay out the mounting holes on the fence base as shown in the *Cut-Off Fence/ Side View.* Check your layout against the holes in the table to make sure that both sets will line up. When the marks are properly aligned, drill the holes.

Note: The mounting holes in the fence base are slightly oversized. This allows you to adjust the angle of the cut-off fence a few degrees right or left to square it to the blade.

Cut the chamfers in the back top corners of the braces, as shown in the *Cut-Off Fence/End View.* Glue the parts of the fence together, let the glue set, and reinforce the glue joints with flathead wood screws. Countersink the heads of the screws well below the surface of the wood.

Joint the face of the fence perfectly flat and perpendicular to the base. Be careful not to nick the head of a screw with the jointer knives.

When the fence is finished, attach it to the sliding table with 2-inch-long carriage bolts, flat washers, and wing nuts. Place the table on the saw and square the fence to the blade. Carefully mark the position of the fence on the sliding table. This mark will make it easier to realign the fence each time you reattach it to the table.

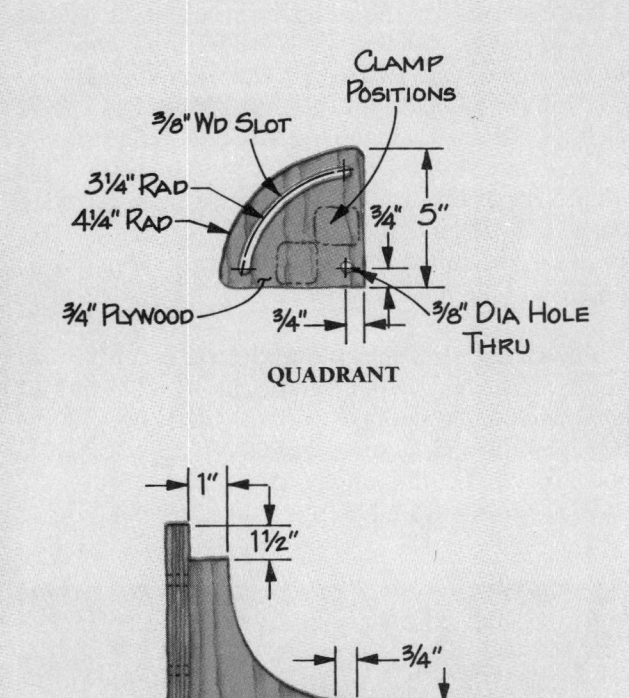

CLAMP POSITIONS

3/8" WD SLOT

3 1/4" RAD

4 1/4" RAD

3/4" 5"

3/4" PLYWOOD   3/4"

3/8" DIA HOLE THRU

QUADRANT

1"

1 1/2"

3/4"

2 3/4"

3/4"   5 3/4"   3/4"

SIDE VIEW

ATTACHMENT

6-1 Rout the curved slots in the miter fences with a router and a *Circle-Cutting Jig.* This simple jig is a piece of 1/4-inch plywood cut to fit the base of your router. Drill two 3/8-inch-diameter pivot holes in the plywood, 9 1/4 inches and 3 1/4 inches from the router bit. Place the miter fence on a routing pad or affix it to your workbench with double-faced carpet tape. Insert a bolt through the far pivot hole in the *Circle-Cutting Jig* and the pivot hole in the miter fence. Swing your router in an arc, rout the slot in several passes, cutting 1/8 inch to 1/4 inch deeper with each pass. (Later, you'll use the near pivot hole in the *Circle-Cutting Jig* to rout the slots in the tenoning attachment quadrant.) Be careful not to cut into your bench as you make the final pass.

5 Make the miter fences. Lay out the large and small miter fences as shown in *Miter Fences/Top View.* Compare the layouts to the appropriate mounting holes in the sliding table to be sure the holes and slots will match up. Cut the shapes of the fences with a band saw or coping saw and sand the sawed edges.

Drill 3/8-inch-diameter pilot holes in both fences. Make a *Circle-Cutting Jig* and attach it to the base of a router. Using the jig to guide the router in an arc, rout the curved slots in the fences. (*SEE FIGURE 6-1.*) Using the 2-inch-long carriage bolts, secure the small and large miter fences to the sliding table one at a time, making sure that they pivot easily. If the mounting bolts rub in the slots, widen the slots slightly with a file.

6 Make the tenoning attachment quadrant.
While you're set up to rout curved slots, make the tenoning quadrant. Lay out the part as shown in the *Tenoning Attachment/Quadrant* drawing. Cut the shape, sand the sawed edges, and drill the pivot hole. Rout the curved slot using the *Circle-Cutting Jig.*

Note: Because the near pivot hole in the *Circle-Cutting Jig* is just 3 1/4 inches away from the router bit, you must use a small router with a base no more than 6 inches in diameter. Large routers will cover the pivot hole. If your router won't work with this jig, cut the curved slot with a scroll saw or coping saw.

7 **Assemble the tenoning attachment.** Lay out the shapes of the tenoning braces as shown in the *Tenoning Attachment/Side View* and cut them with a band saw or coping saw. Sand the sawed edges. Rout the slots in the tenoning base as shown in the *Tenoning Attachment/Top View,* and drill the holes in the tenoning face as shown in the *Tenoning Attachment/ Front View.*

Glue the face, base, back, and braces together. Let the glue set, then reinforce the glue joints with flathead wood screws. Countersink the heads of the screws beneath the wood surface.

Mount the quadrant to the tenoning attachment with 2½-inch-long carriage bolts, making sure the quadrant pivots easily. Note that the quadrant can be attached in two different positions, facing either forward or back. Secure a toggle clamp to the quadrant with screws. This toggle clamp can also be mounted in two different positions, overhanging one face of the quadrant or the other. (*See Figure 6-2.*)

Mount the tenoning attachment to the sliding table with 2-inch-long carriage bolts and check that it slides right and left easily, without binding.

8 **Make the clamps.** Lay out the clamps on the stock. Depending on the woodworking you do, you may need several different sizes — I find that two 2-inch-diameter and two 4-inch-diameter clamps work well for me. Drill the mounting holes and cut the circular shapes with a band saw or coping saw. Sand the sawed edges.

Mount the clamps to the sliding table with 5/16-inch carriage bolts. Unlike the other attachments, the clamps can be shifted to several positions along the right edge of the table. (*See Figure 6-3.*)

9 **Finish the sliding table and attachments.** Remove all the hardware from the sliding table and its attachments. Lightly round-over any hard edges with sandpaper, then apply several coats of tung oil to all wood surfaces. Let the tung oil dry, apply a coat of paste wax, and buff well. Replace the hardware.

6-2 Not only can you mount the quadrant facing forward or back, you can also mount it to the upper or lower portion of the jig. This allows you to cut both long and short boards. **Note:** If you mount it to the lower portion, as shown, make sure the saw blade doesn't nick the clamp.

6-3 The clamps are designed to be mounted in any of the 5/16-inch-diameter holes along the inside edge (closest to the blade) of the sliding table. However, you can also mount them in any of the 3/8-inch-diameter holes. Or you can drill additional holes, as needed.

7

CORNER CUPBOARD

Acorner cupboard presents an appealing alternative to the usually "flat" or rectangular variety. Aesthetically, it softens the corner of a room, giving the eye some relief from all the hard 90-degree angles. Practically, it turns difficult-to-use space into a handy storage area. The front of the cupboard is set at 45 degrees to the walls, making the contents easy to see and to reach.

This particular cupboard can be built almost entirely with a table saw. Much of the simple joinery that holds the parts of the cases and the doors together can be made with either a saw blade or a dado cutter. Many of the decorative cuts — the raised panels in the doors, the rounded edges of the base top, and the cove moldings — are also created with a table saw. Only the door knobs, the mortises in the door stiles, and a few contoured cuts must be made with other tools.

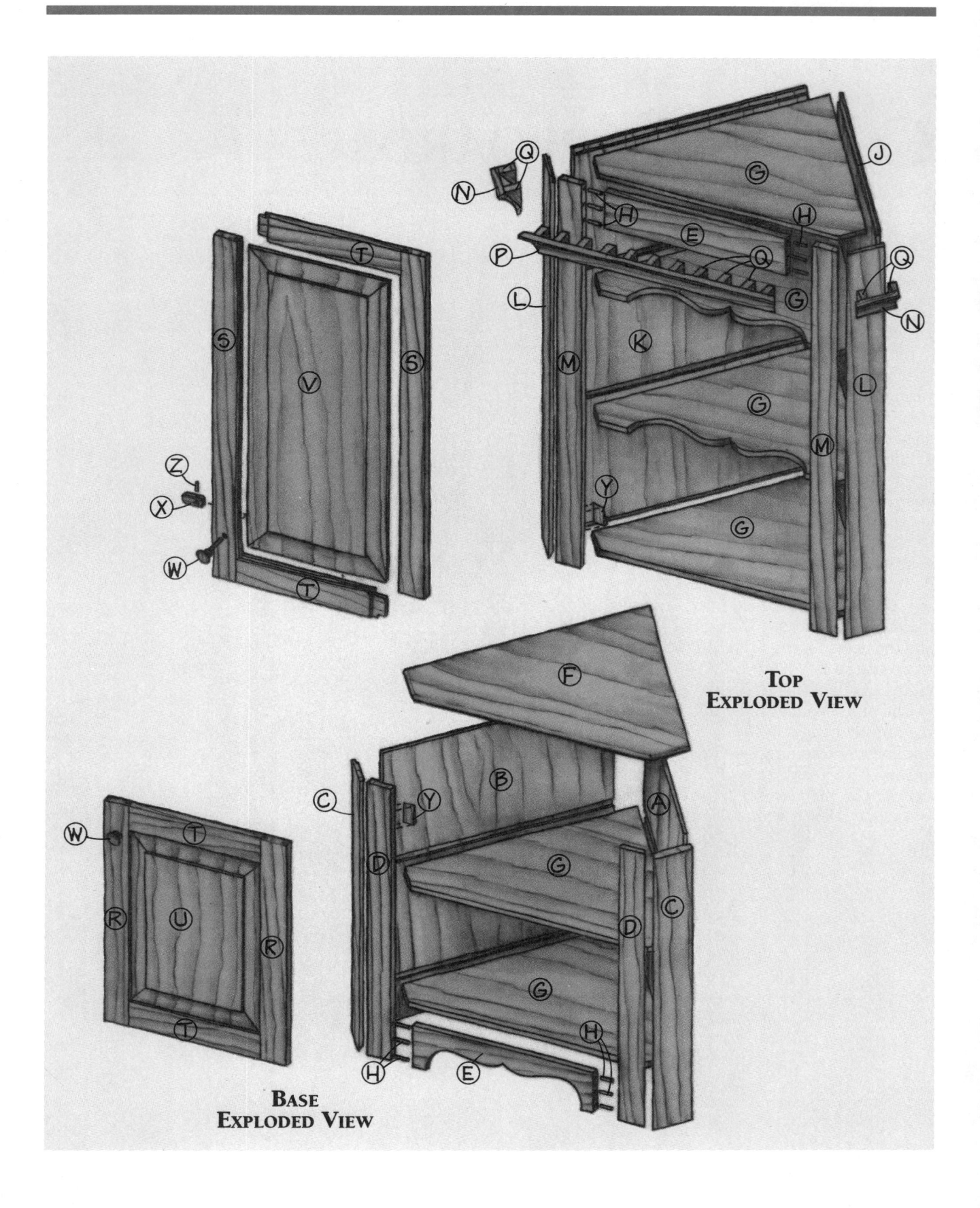

TOP EXPLODED VIEW

BASE EXPLODED VIEW

MATERIALS LIST (FINISHED DIMENSIONS)

Parts

Base

A. Right back* $\frac{1}{2}$" x 23$\frac{5}{8}$" x 31"
B. Left back* $\frac{1}{2}$" x 23$\frac{3}{8}$" x 31"
C. Sides (2) $\frac{3}{4}$" x 4$\frac{1}{4}$" x 31"
D. Front stiles (2) $\frac{3}{4}$" x 3" x 31"
E. Front rail $\frac{3}{4}$" x 5" x 21$\frac{7}{8}$"
F. Top 1" x 20$\frac{15}{16}$" x 35"
G. Shelves (2) $\frac{3}{4}$" x 18$\frac{3}{4}$" x 33$\frac{1}{16}$"
H. Large dowels (6) $\frac{3}{8}$" dia. x 2"

Top

E. Front rail $\frac{3}{4}$" x 5" x 21$\frac{7}{8}$"
G. Shelves (4) $\frac{3}{4}$" x 19" x 33$\frac{1}{16}$"
H. Large dowels (6) $\frac{3}{8}$" dia. x 2"
J. Right back* $\frac{1}{2}$" x 23$\frac{5}{8}$" x 46"
K. Left back* $\frac{1}{2}$" x 23$\frac{3}{8}$" x 46"
L. Sides (2) $\frac{3}{4}$" x 4$\frac{1}{4}$" x 46"
M. Front stiles (2) $\frac{3}{4}$" x 3" x 46"

N. Side cove moldings (2) $\frac{3}{4}$" x 4$\frac{1}{4}$" x 5$\frac{3}{4}$"
P. Front cove molding $\frac{3}{4}$" x 4$\frac{1}{4}$" x 30$\frac{1}{4}$"
Q. Glue blocks (15) $\frac{3}{4}$" x 2$\frac{3}{16}$" x 2$\frac{3}{16}$"

Doors

R. Base stiles (2) $\frac{3}{4}$" x 3" x 25$\frac{15}{16}$"
S. Top stiles (2) $\frac{3}{4}$" x 3" x 40$\frac{15}{16}$"
T. Rails (4) $\frac{3}{4}$" x 3" x 18$\frac{9}{16}$"
U. Base panel $\frac{1}{2}$" x 16$\frac{7}{16}$" x 20$\frac{9}{16}$"
V. Top panel $\frac{1}{2}$" x 16$\frac{7}{16}$" x 35$\frac{9}{16}$"
W. Knobs (2) 2" dia. x 2$\frac{3}{4}$"
X. Latches (2) $\frac{3}{4}$" x 1$\frac{1}{4}$" x 3"
Y. Wedges (2) $\frac{1}{4}$" x 1$\frac{1}{2}$" x 2$\frac{1}{2}$"
Z. Small dowels (2) $\frac{1}{4}$" dia. x 1$\frac{1}{4}$"

Make these parts from plywood.

Hardware

1$\frac{1}{2}$" x 3" Hinges and mounting screws (4)
4d Finishing nails ($\frac{1}{4}$ lb.)
1" Wire brads (1 box)
Tabletop clips (10)
#8 x $\frac{3}{4}$" Flathead wood screws (10)

PLAN OF PROCEDURE

1 Select the stock and cut the parts to size.
To make this project, you need one 4- by 8-foot sheet of $\frac{1}{2}$-inch cabinet-grade plywood, approximately 50 board feet of 4/4 (four-quarters) stock, 6 board feet of 5/4 (five-quarters) stock, and a few scraps of 8/4 (eight-quarters) stock. You can make the cupboard from almost any wood, but the solid stock and the veneer on the plywood should either match or complement one another. The cupboard shown is made from white pine and spruce-veneer plywood.

Plane the 5/4 lumber to 1 inch thick and glue up the stock needed to make the base top. Plane all the 4/4 lumber to $\frac{3}{4}$ inch thick. Glue up stock to make a 2-foot-wide, 10-foot-long board to make the shelves, and set this aside. With the exception of the shelves and moldings, cut all the $\frac{3}{4}$-inch-thick parts to size. As you do so, bevel the adjoining edges of all the sides and the front stiles at 22$\frac{1}{2}$ degrees. Cut a piece 4$\frac{1}{4}$ inches wide and 48 inches long to make the moldings, but don't cut them to length.

Set aside some $\frac{3}{4}$-inch-thick stock to use as test pieces, then plane the remaining stock to $\frac{1}{2}$ inch thick. Glue up the stock needed to make the door panels, and cut them to size.

From the 8/4 scraps, cut turning blocks to make the door knobs. **Note:** If you don't want to turn your own knobs, you can use commercial wooden knobs.

2 Cut the joinery in the backs and sides.
Because the construction of the base and top cases are similar, it's much easier to build both of them at the same time. Lay out the rabbets and dadoes on the backs and sides as shown in the *Joinery Layout*. Score the layout lines with an awl or marking knife; this will help prevent torn grain and veneer. Using a dado cutter or a router, make these joints:

■ $\frac{3}{4}$-inch-wide, $\frac{1}{4}$-inch-deep rabbets in the top and bottom edges of both the right and left top backs
■ $\frac{3}{4}$-inch-wide, $\frac{1}{4}$-inch-deep dadoes in the backs
■ $\frac{3}{4}$-inch-wide, $\frac{1}{4}$-inch-deep dadoes in the sides
■ $\frac{1}{2}$-inch-wide, $\frac{1}{4}$-inch-deep rabbets in the back edges of the right backs
■ $\frac{1}{2}$-inch-wide, $\frac{1}{4}$-inch-deep rabbets in the back edges of the sides
■ $\frac{1}{4}$-inch-wide, $\frac{1}{4}$-inch-deep dadoes in the base backs and base front stiles

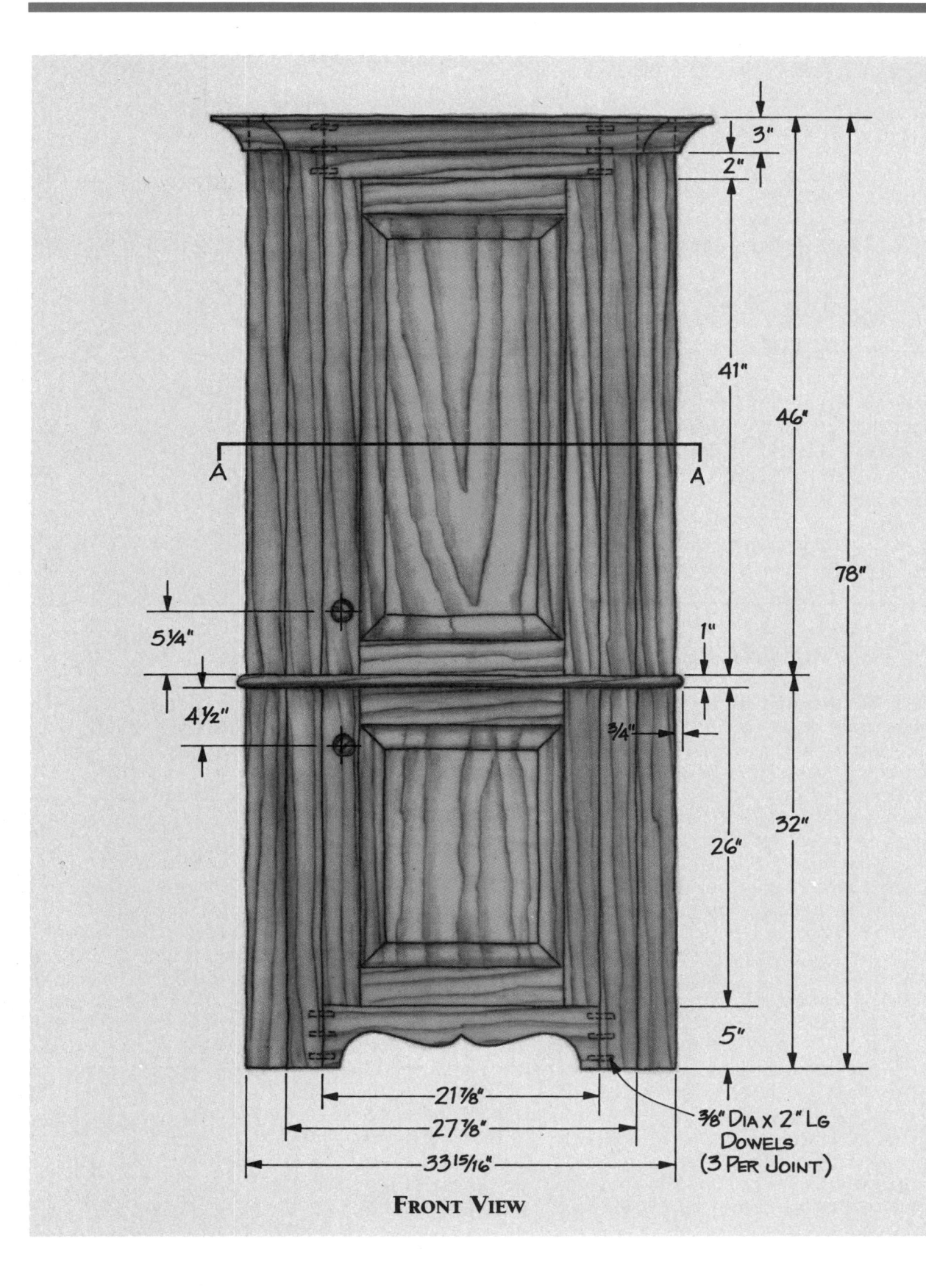

3"

2"

41"

46"

A   A

5¼"

1"

4½"

¾"

78"

32"

26"

5"

3⁄8" Dia x 2" Lg
Dowels
(3 Per Joint)

21⅞"

27⅞"

33¹⁵⁄₁₆"

FRONT VIEW

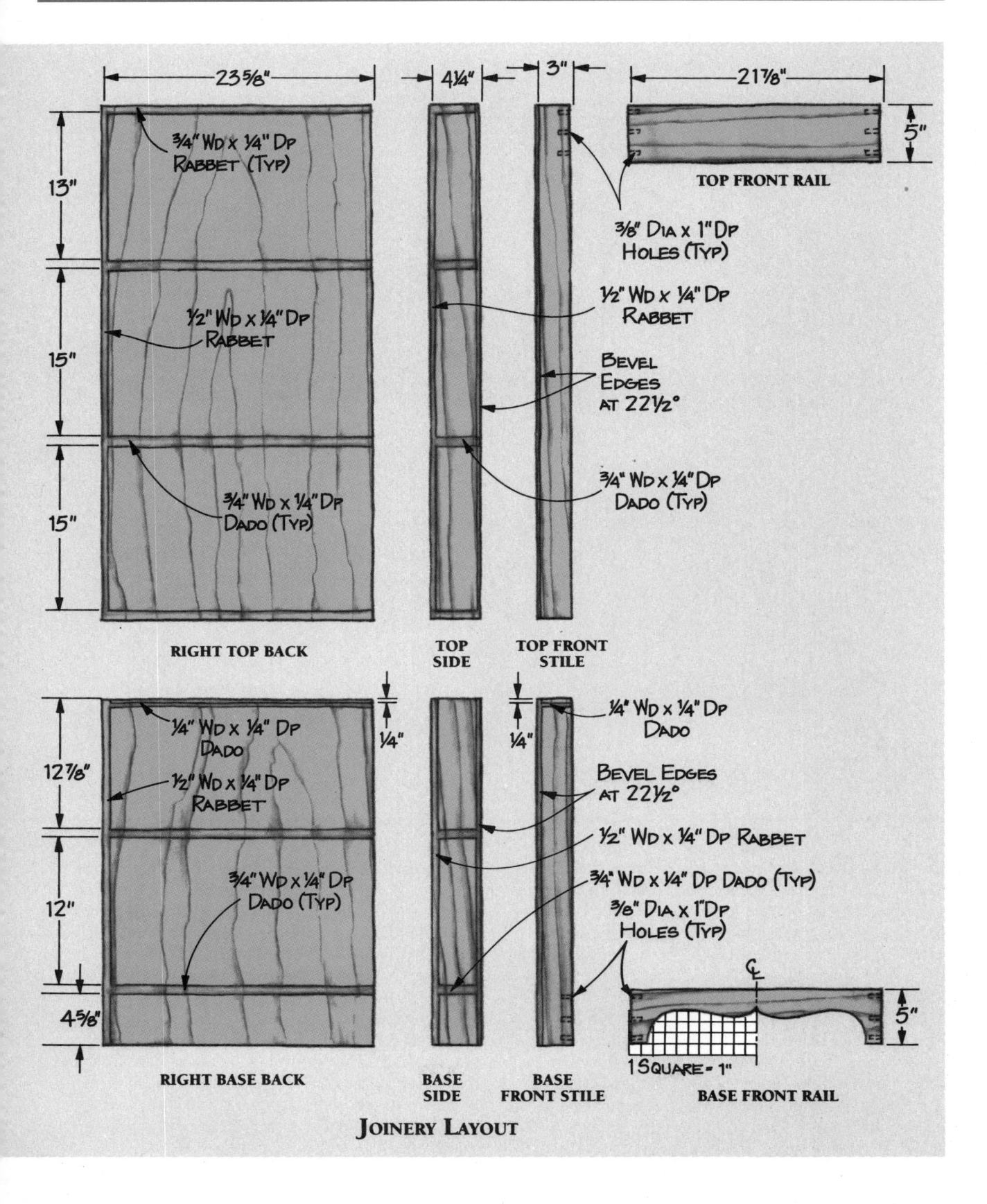

JOINERY LAYOUT

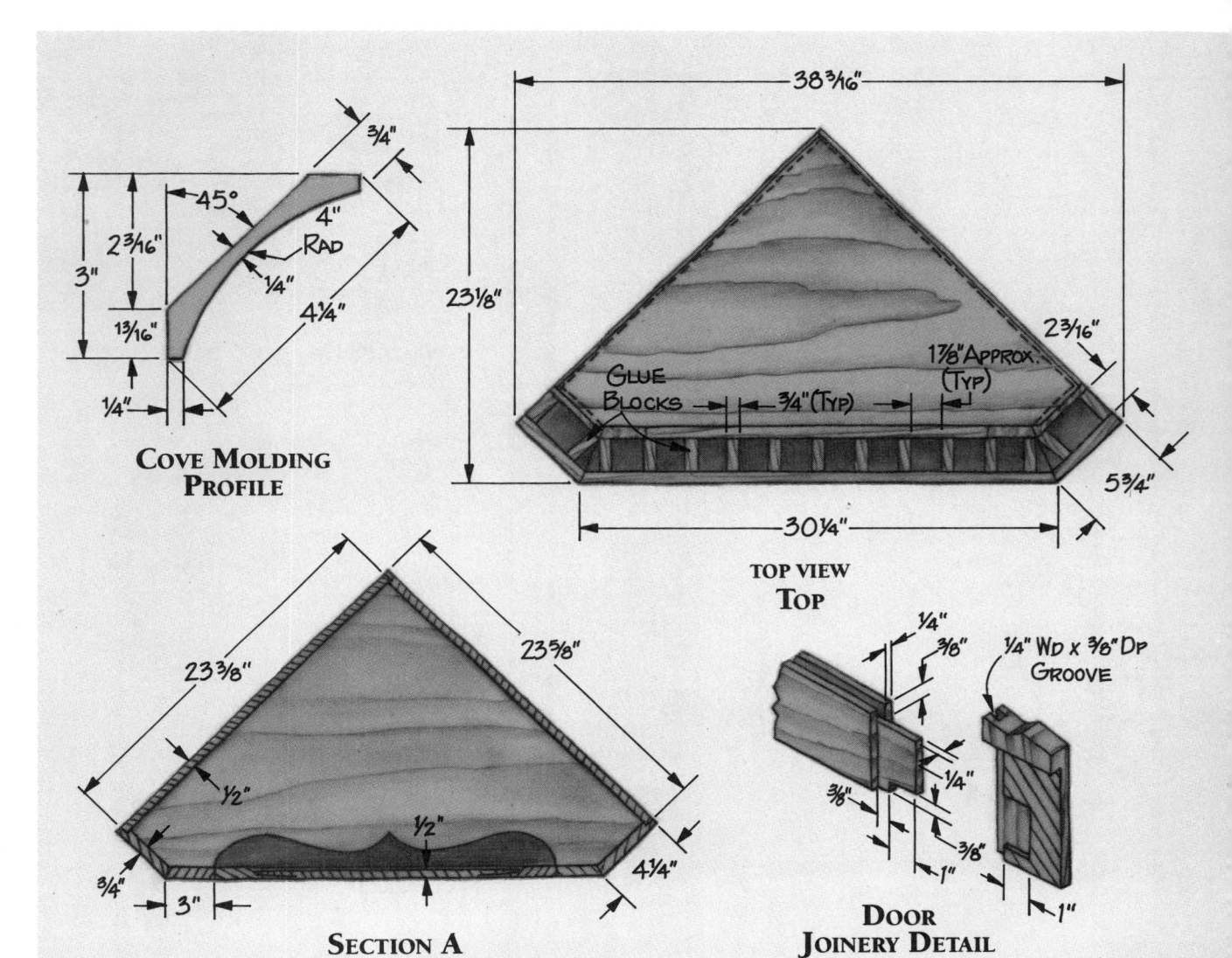

COVE MOLDING PROFILE

TOP VIEW TOP

SECTION A

DOOR JOINERY DETAIL

3 Make the dowel joints in the front stiles and rails. The front rails are joined to the front stiles with dowels. Lay out the locations of the dowel holes on the adjoining parts, then drill 3/8-inch-diameter, 1-inch-deep dowel holes. Use a commercial doweling jig to help guide the bit. **Note:** If you wish, you may substitute splines or biscuits for the dowels.

4 Cut the shelves and the base top. Carefully lay out the shapes of the shelves and the base top on the stock, as shown in the *Shelf Layout* and the *Base Top Layout.* To avoid a lot of waste, stagger the shelves on the long, wide board you glued up, leaving 1/2 to 1 inch of cutting space between them. (SEE FIGURE 7-1.)

Cut the shelves from the board with a circular saw, cutting wide of the lines. Trim *one* shelf to its final dimensions on the table saw. Using this completed shelf as a template, pattern saw the remaining shelves, following the procedure described in *Pattern Sawing* on page 83. Also cut the top to its final dimensions.

5 Cut the shapes of the top middle shelves and the base front rail. The front edges of the top middle shelves and the bottom edge of the base front rail are cut with decorative contours. Lay out these shapes as shown in the *Shelf Layout* and *Joinery Layout.* Cut them with a band saw or scroll saw, and sand the sawed edges.

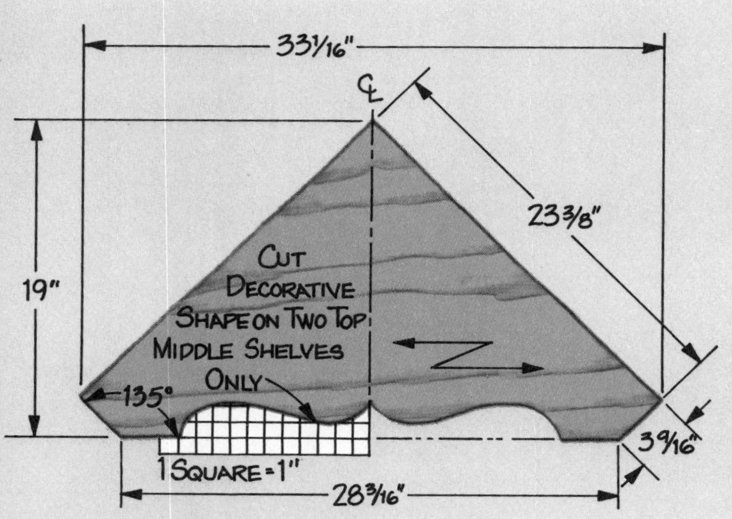

Shelf Layout

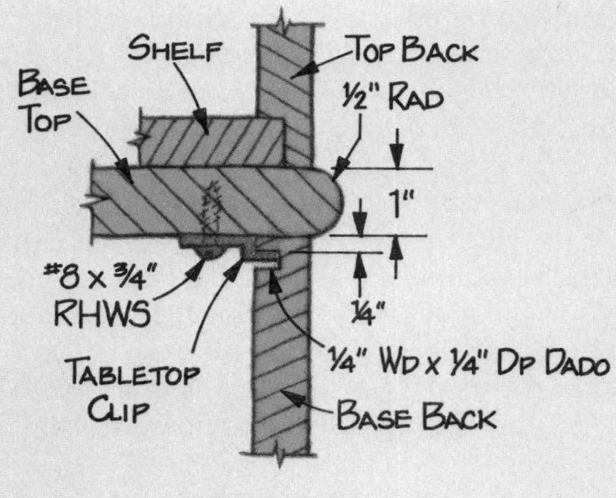

33¹/₁₆"

19"

23⅜"

CUT
DECORATIVE
SHAPE ON TWO TOP
MIDDLE SHELVES
ONLY

135°

1 SQUARE = 1"

3⁹/₁₆"

28³/₁₆"

SHELF LAYOUT

Base Top Joinery Detail

SHELF

BASE
TOP

TOP BACK

½" RAD

1"

#8 x ¾"
RHWS

TABLETOP
CLIP

¼"

¼" WD x ¼" DP DADO

BASE BACK

**BASE TOP
JOINERY DETAIL**

Door Knob Layout

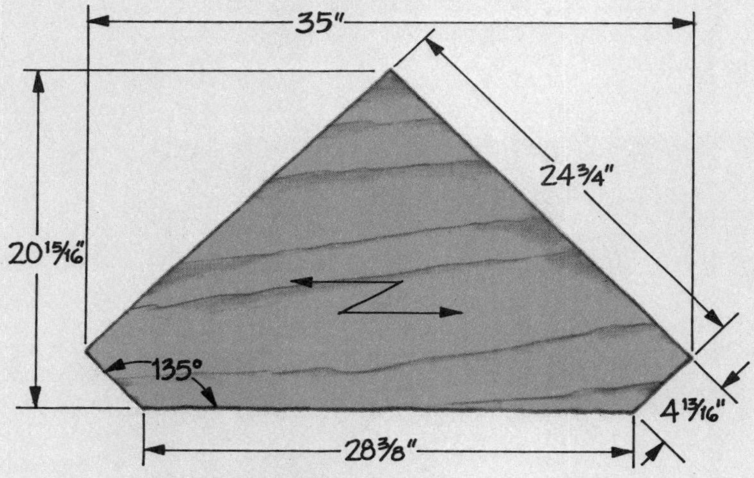

5/8" DIA
1" DIA   1" DIA
2" DIA   ¼" DIA
                HOLE THRU
      ½" DIA   ¼"

1/8"   1/8"   ¼"
7/16"
½"   1¹¹/₁₆"
      2¾"

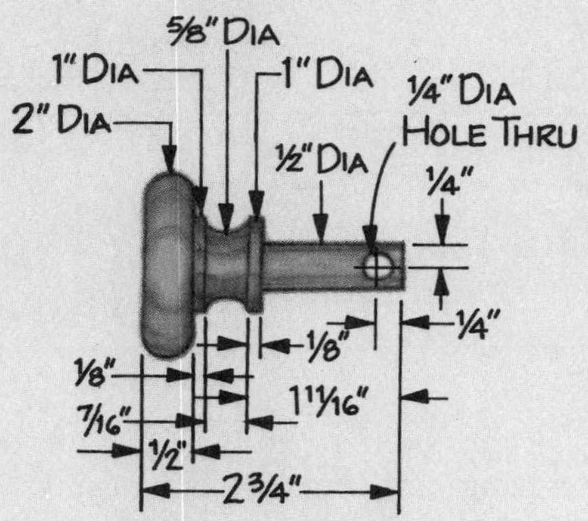

**DOOR KNOB
LAYOUT**

Base Top Layout

35"

24¾"

20¹⁵/₁₆"

135°

4¹³/₁₆"

28⅜"

BASE TOP LAYOUT

6 Mold the front and side edges of the base top.   The front and side edges of the base top are rounded, as shown in the *Base Top Joinery Detail*. Round these edges with a router, shaper, or molder, then sand them to remove the mill marks.

7 Assemble the base and top cases.   Finish sand all the parts of the base and top cases — backs, sides, front stiles, front rails, shelves, and base top. Assemble the backs and shelves with glue. Reinforce the glue joints with wire brads and finishing nails —

7-1 When you lay out the shelves on the stock, stagger them as shown. This will save a great deal of wood that might otherwise be wasted.

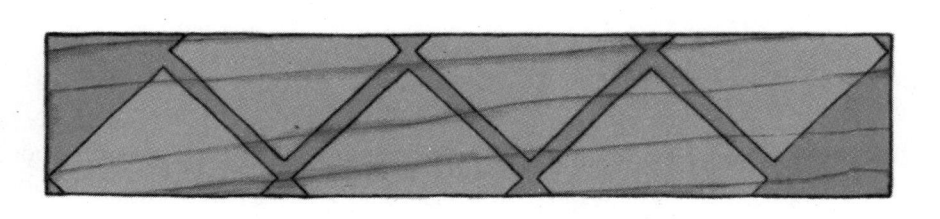

use wire brads when fastening one plywood part to another (the right backs to the left backs) and finishing nails when fastening a plywood part to a solid wood part (the backs to the shelves).

Glue the beveled edges of the sides to the front stiles. (SEE FIGURE 7-2.) Let the glue dry, and assemble the front rails and front stiles with dowels and glue. Before the glue on the dowel joints sets, glue the front/side assemblies to the shelf/back assemblies. Reinforce the glue joints with finishing nails and set the heads of the nails.

Fasten the base top to the base assembly with table-top clips and roundhead wood screws, as shown in the *Base Top Joinery Detail*.

8 Cut and install the cove molding. Using the table saw and an ordinary combination blade, cut the cove in the molding stock. (Refer to "Cutting Coves" on page 87.) Bevel the edges of the molding as shown in the *Cove Molding Profile*.

7-2 To clamp the sides and the front stiles together, make a simple jig from scraps of wood and plywood. Tack two long strips of wood to the face of a long piece of plywood, spacing the strips exactly 6¹¹/₁₆ inches apart. Place the sides and the front stiles in the clamping jig so the *square* edges rest against the strips and the *beveled* edges rest against one another. Apply glue to the beveled edges, then fasten the parts in the jig with band clamps.

TOP DOOR LAYOUT

Compound-miter the adjoining ends of the molding with the miter gauge angled at 74 degrees and the blade tilted to 16 degrees. (Refer to page 61 for additional instructions on making compound miters.) Affix glue blocks to the back face of the moldings, then glue the moldings and blocks to the top case, as shown in the *Top/Top View*. The top edge of the molding should be flush with the top edge of the case.

9 Cut the door joinery. The door frames are joined with haunched mortises and tenons, as shown in the *Door Joinery Detail*. You can make these joints with either a dado cutter or a table-mounted router.

First, cut ¼-inch-wide, ⅜-inch-deep grooves in all the *inside* edges of the rails and stiles. Rout or drill 1⅜-inch-deep mortises in the stiles, near the ends. Cut tenons in the ends of the rails to fit the mortises, then cut a notch in the top edge of each tenon to create a haunch.

10 Cut the raised door panels. The edges of the cupboard door panels are beveled at 15 degrees, as shown in *Section B*. Cut these bevels on the table

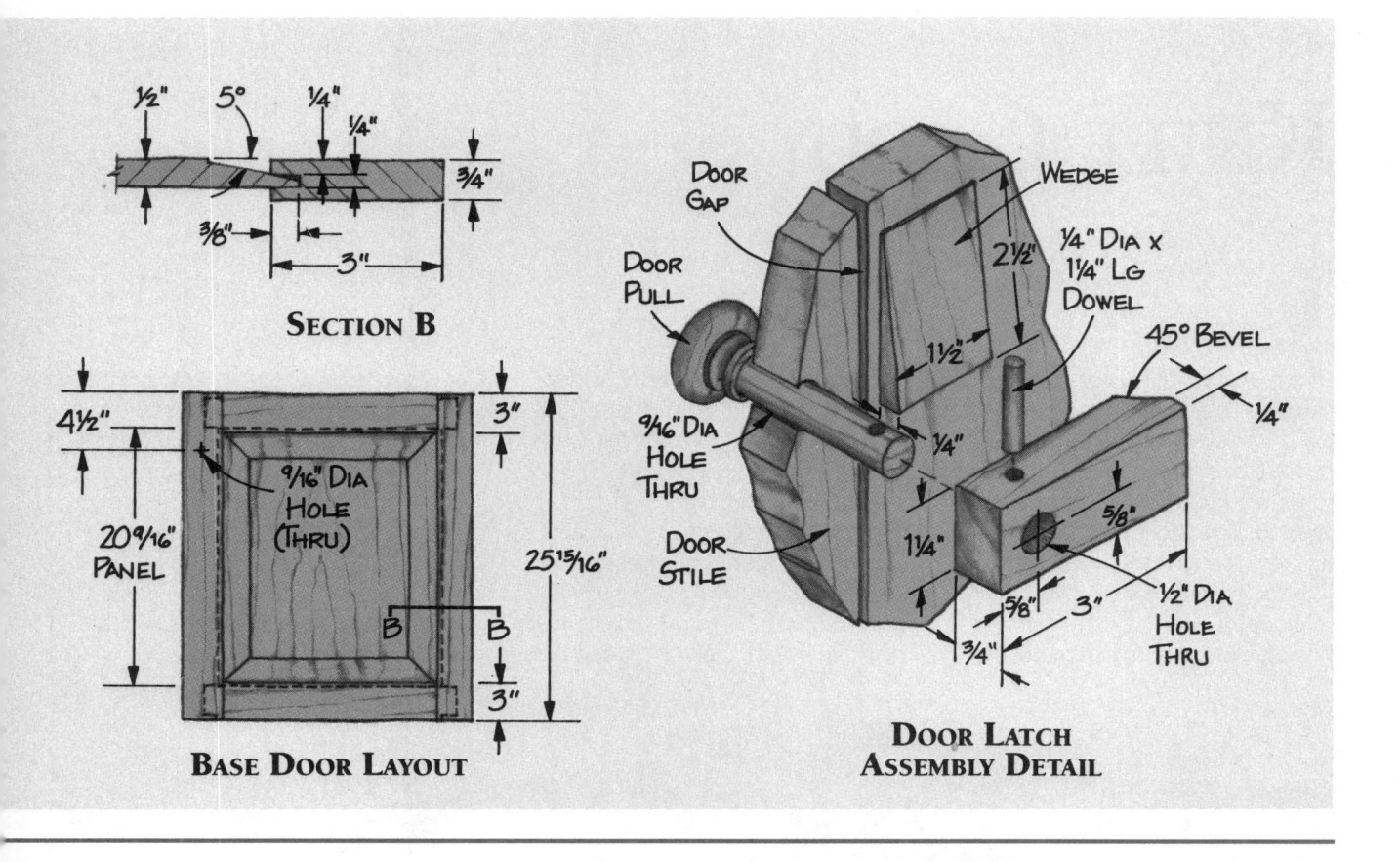

SECTION B

BASE DOOR LAYOUT

**DOOR LATCH
ASSEMBLY DETAIL**

saw, using a *Tall Fence Extension* (see page 52) to help steady the stock as you cut it. Refer to "Making Raised Panels" on page 78 for more information.

11 Turn the door knobs. Using a lathe, turn the door knobs to the shape shown in the *Door Knob Layout.* **Note:** If you don't have a lathe, you can make door knobs from ordinary wooden cabinet knobs. Purchase two cabinet knobs measuring 2 inches in diameter. Drill a ½-inch-diameter, ¾-inch-deep hole in the back of each knob and glue a ½-inch-diameter, 2⁵⁄₁₆-inch-long dowel in each hole.

12 Assemble and hang the doors. Drill ⁹⁄₁₆-inch-diameter holes through the left door stiles, as shown in the *Top Door Layout* and *Base Door Layout,* and ½-inch-diameter holes through the door latches as shown in the *Door Latch Assembly Detail.* Also bevel the ends of the door latches. Finish sand all the parts of the doors.

Glue the door rails and stiles together. As you do so, slide the panels into the grooves. Do *not* glue the panels in place; let them float in their grooves. Insert the knobs through the holes in the left door stiles and glue the latches to the inside ends of the knobs. Drill a ¼-inch-diameter hole through each latch where it joins its knob. Glue a small dowel in the hole, pinning the latch to the knob.

Mortise the right door stiles and right front stiles for hinges, then hang the doors on the cabinet. Glue the wedges to the inside faces of the left front stiles, just opposite the door knobs.

13 Finish the corner cupboard. Remove the doors from the cases and the hinges from the doors. Do any necessary touch-up sanding, then apply a finish to *all* wooden surfaces, inside and out. (If you do not finish the inside of the cupboard as well as the outside, the two surfaces will absorb and release moisture unevenly. The parts will warp or twist, and the resulting stress may distort the cabinet and pull it apart.) Rub out the finish, apply a coat of paste wax, and buff well. Replace the doors and stack the top case on the base case.

8

KNIFE CADDY

In every age, people have made carryalls to help them organize their lives. Today, we have briefcases, purses, backpacks, and duffel bags, to name a few. Two hundred years ago, our ancestors used saddlebags, baskets, pouches — and "caddies," like the one shown.

Wooden caddies were especially popular in early America. They were easy to make and wonderfully versatile. Caddies could be used to hold or carry tools, nails, sewing notions, foodstuffs, papers — the list is endless. The piece shown was inspired by an early nineteenth-century knife caddy, a carryall for eating utensils. The covers on the compartments kept the silverware clean between meals.

This project uses several simple joints, many of which can be cut on a table saw. The sides and ends are joined with compound miters, the divider is notched to fit over the ends, and the ledgers butt against the divider. To make the piece as strong as possible, some joints have been reinforced with splines, dowels, or screws.

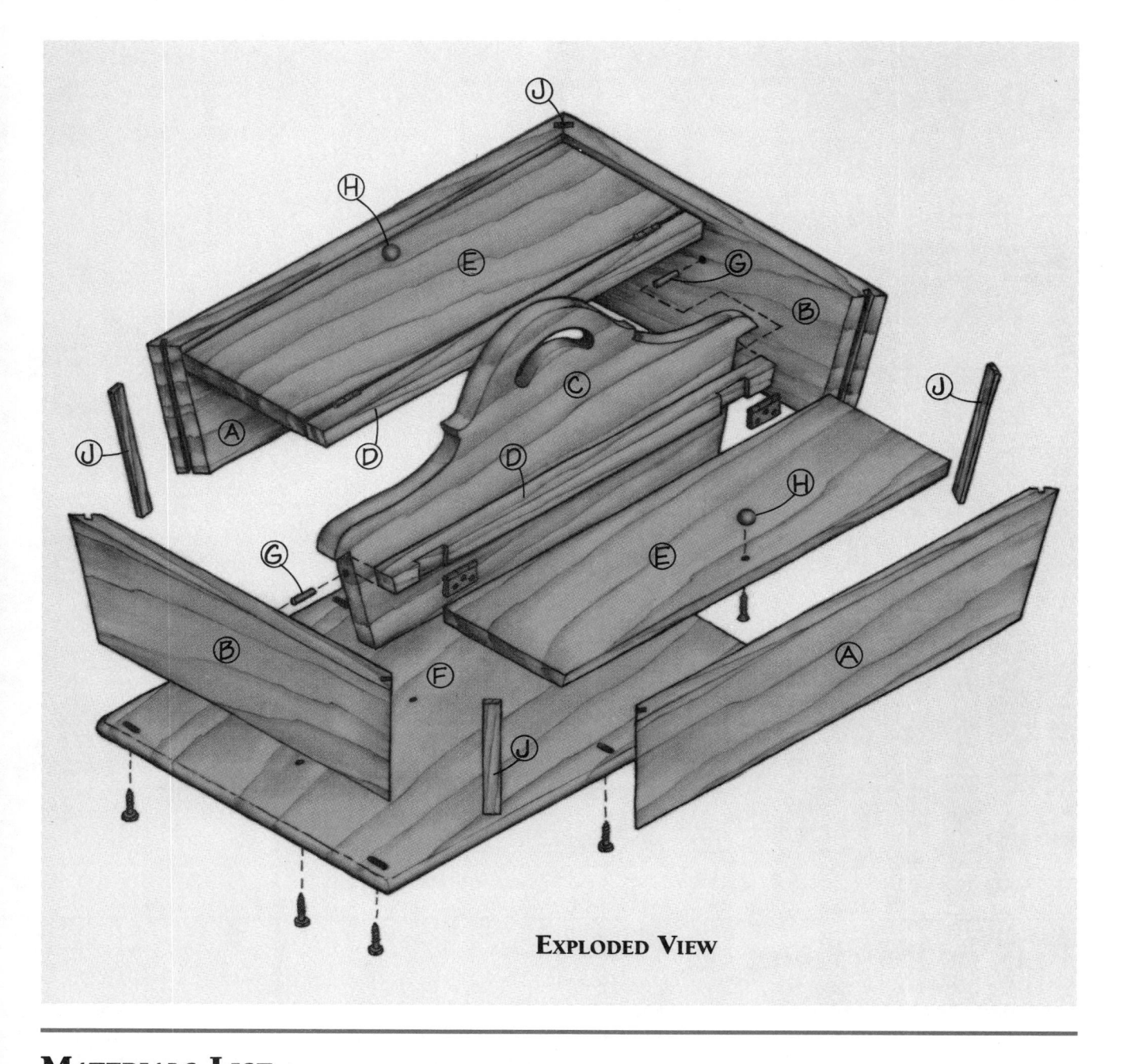

EXPLODED VIEW

MATERIALS LIST (FINISHED DIMENSIONS)

Parts

A.	Sides (2)	$1/2'' \times 4^{9}/_{32}'' \times 16''$
B.	Ends (2)	$1/2'' \times 4^{9}/_{32}'' \times 12''$
C.	Divider	$1/2'' \times 8'' \times 16''$
D.	Ledgers (2)	$1/2'' \times 1/2'' \times 14^{7}/_{8}''$
E.	Lids (2)	$1/2'' \times 4^{11}/_{16}'' \times 14^{7}/_{8}''$
F.	Bottom	$1/4'' \times 10^{3}/_{8}'' \times 14^{3}/_{8}''$
G.	Dowels (2)	$1/4''$ dia. x $1''$
H.	Pulls* (2)	$3/4''$ dia.
J.	Splines (4)	$1/8'' \times 1/2'' \times 4^{9}/_{32}''$

The pulls are round wooden balls, which can be purchased from most crafts stores and some mail-order woodworking suppliers.

Hardware

#6 x $3/4''$ Panhead screws (6)

#6 x $3/4''$ Flathead wood screws (4)

#6 x $1''$ Flathead wood screws (2)

$1'' \times 1^{1}/2''$ Brass butt hinges and mounting screws (4)

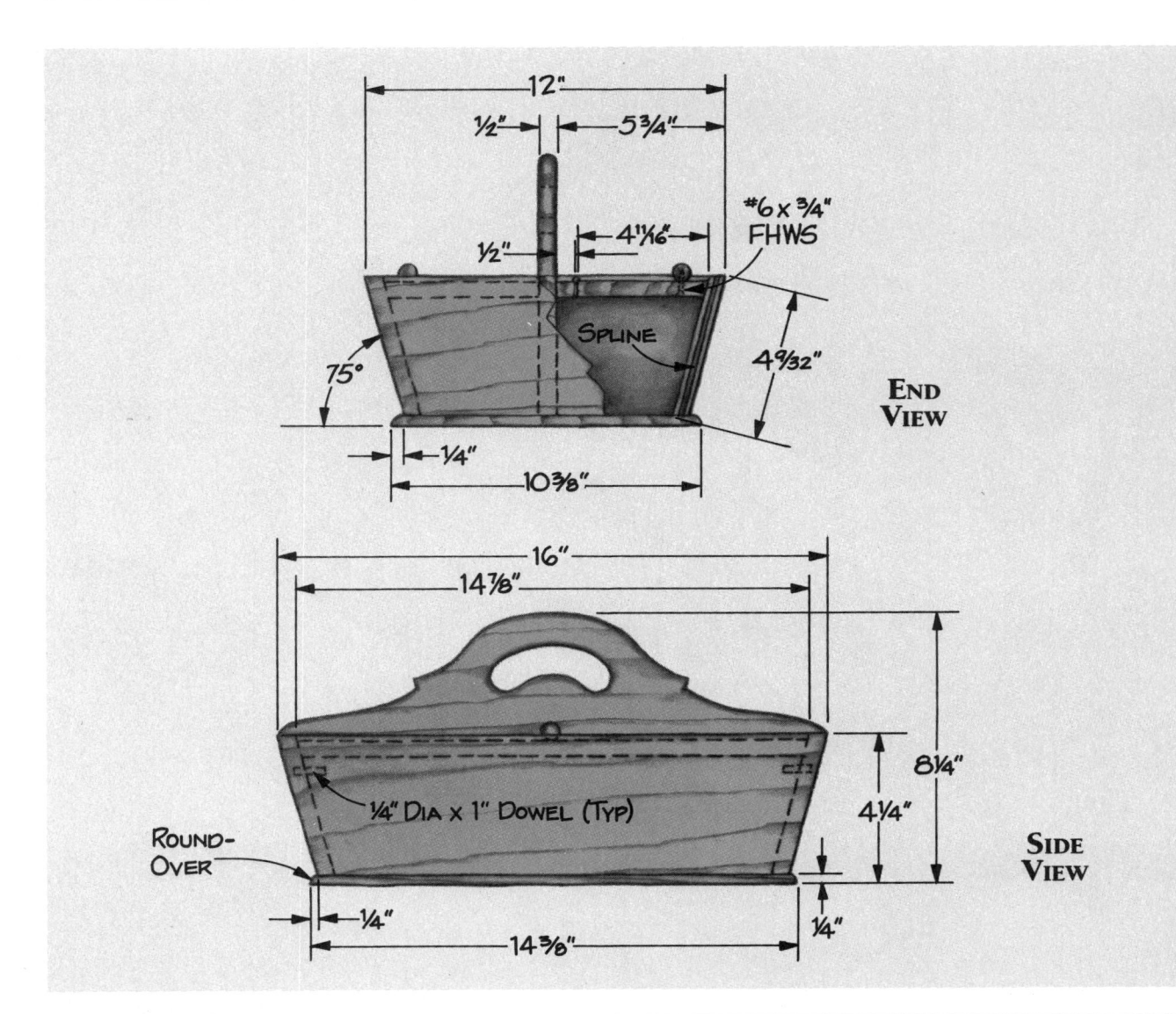

PLAN OF PROCEDURE

1 Select the stock and cut the parts to size. To make this project, you need about 6 board feet of 4/4 (four-quarters) lumber. The knife caddy shown is made from cherry, but you can use any cabinet-grade hardwood.

Plane the 4/4 lumber to ½ inch thick and cut the sides and ends to size. Cut the divider, ledgers, and lids about ½ inch wider and longer than needed. Cut several extra sides and ends to use as test pieces. Also cut ⅛-inch-thick strips to use as splines. Cut the splines so the grain runs the width of the spline. Plane the remaining stock to ¼ inch thick and cut the bottom to size.

2 Bevel and miter the sides and ends. With the table saw blade tilted to 15 degrees, bevel the top and bottom edges of the caddy sides and ends — *both* the good stock and the test pieces. The edges must be cut parallel to each other, as shown in the *End View/ Compound Miter Angles* drawing.

To make the compound miters that join the sides and ends, tilt the saw blade to 43¼ degrees and set the miter gauge to 78¼ degrees. Don't cut the good stock until you have tested these settings with scrap wood. The settings for this cut (or any other compound miter cuts — see the chart on page 62) only apply if your saw and saw blade are *perfectly* aligned

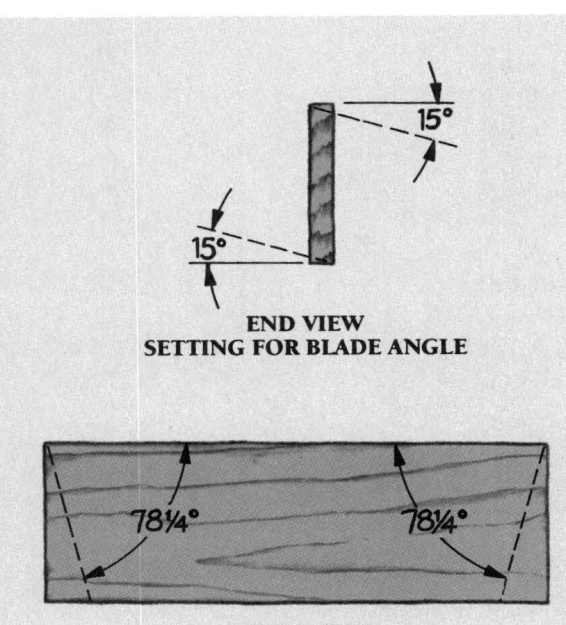

END VIEW
SETTING FOR BLADE ANGLE

15°
15°

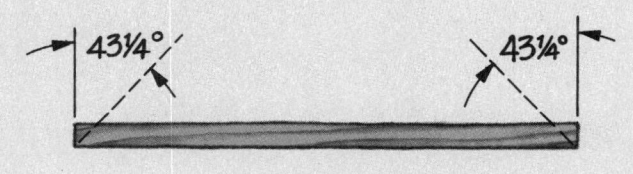

78¼°   78¼°

FACE VIEW
SETTING FOR MITER GAUGE ANGLE

43¼°   43¼°

EDGE VIEW
SETTING FOR BLADE ANGLE

COMPOUND
MITER ANGLES

3 Cut the spline grooves in the sides and ends.
The compound miters that join the sides and ends are reinforced with splines. To cut the grooves for these splines, leave the saw blade tilted to the same setting you used to cut the compound miters. Note the angle of the miter gauge, then adjust the quadrant on a tenoning jig to this same angle. (You can use the tenoning attachment for the "Sliding Table" shown on page 94.)

Place the jig against the fence of the table saw. Mount a side or an end in the jig so the mitered *arris* is flat on the work surface and the mitered *surface* is facing the blade. Adjust the position of the fence and the depth of cut, then cut a ⅛-inch-wide, ¼-inch-deep groove in the mitered surface of the board. (*See* FIGURE 8-1.) Repeat for all the compound-mitered ends.

8-1 To cut the spline grooves in the compound-mitered parts, hold the stock in a tenoning jig. With the blade tilted at 43¼ degrees and the quadrant at 78¼ degrees, the compound-mitered surface should be square to the saw blade. Cut the grooves in the right-facing miters with the quadrant tilted right, and those in the left-facing miters with the quadrant tilted left.

and adjusted. You may have to readjust the angles slightly to compensate for the idiosyncrasies of your machine.

Cut the scrap sides and ends with the angles set as shown. Dry assemble the scraps with masking tape, then check the corner joints and the slope of the sides. If there are any gaps in the joints or if the slope is off, readjust the blade setting and miter gauge setting a fraction of a degree, as described on page 61. Cut the scraps again, shaving about ¼ inch off each end of each board. Reassemble the test parts with tape and inspect the joints again. Repeat this process until you get a perfect fit. *Then* cut the good wood.

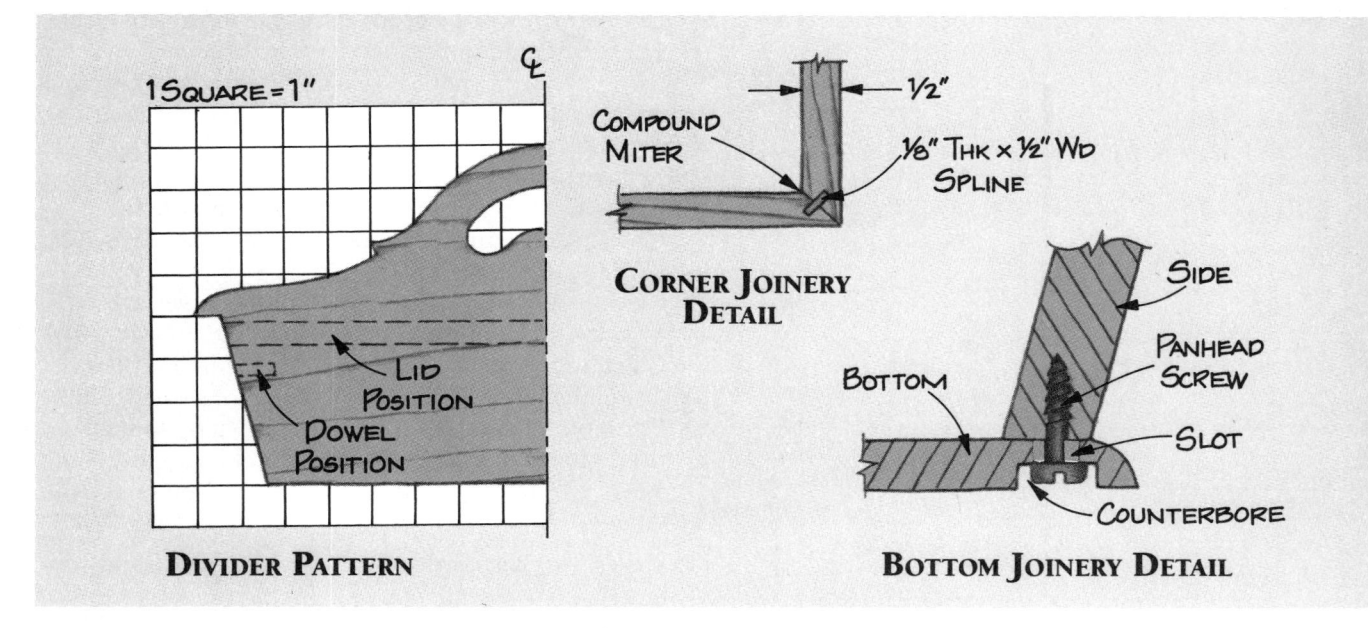

1 SQUARE = 1"

CORNER JOINERY DETAIL

½"

COMPOUND MITER

⅛" THK x ½" WD SPLINE

LID POSITION

DOWEL POSITION

DIVIDER PATTERN

BOTTOM

SIDE

PANHEAD SCREW

SLOT

COUNTERBORE

BOTTOM JOINERY DETAIL

4   Cut the divider to shape.   Dry assemble the sides and ends, holding them together at the corners with tape. Carefully measure the distance from end to end along one side. The *Side View* shows the distance to be 16 inches, but this may have changed slightly, depending on how you cut the compound miters.

Enlarge the *Divider Pattern* and trace it onto the stock. Adjust the dimensions, if necessary, to fit the assembled sides and ends. Cut the outside shape with a band saw, scroll saw, or saber saw.

To make the handle opening, drill two 1-inch-diameter holes in the divider, one at each end of the handle layout. Remove the waste between the holes with a saber saw or scroll saw.

5   Drill the dowel holes in the divider and ends.   The divider is joined to the caddy ends with dowels. To make the dowel holes, first draw a line on the ends of the divider where you want to drill them. The precise locations of these holes are not critical, but they should be about 1 inch below the top edge of the caddy ends when the caddy is assembled. Using a square, extend the lines so they are visible on both faces of the divider.

Dry assemble the sides, ends, and divider. With a pencil, transfer the lines on both faces of the divider to the caddy ends — there should be two marks on each end. Remove the divider and measure halfway between the marks to find the location of the dowel holes in the caddy ends. (*SEE FIGURE 8-2.*)

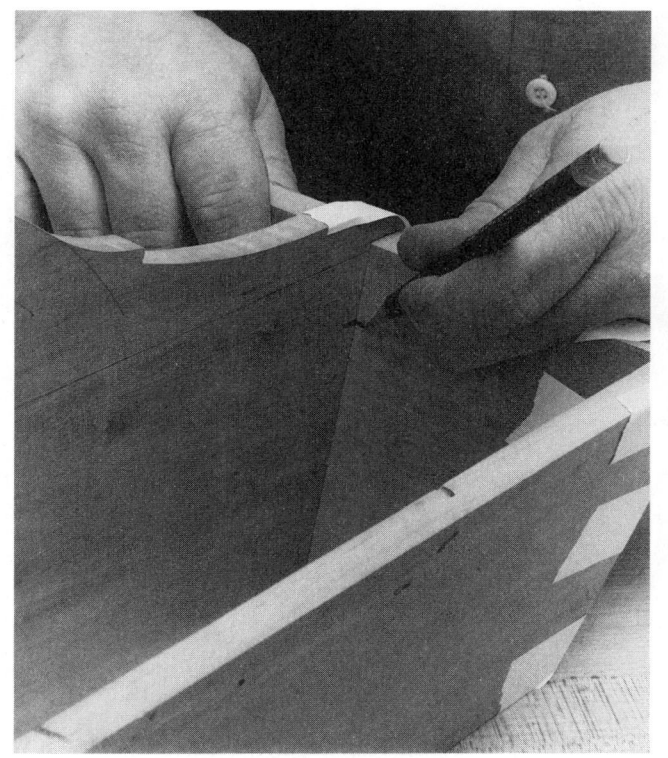

8-2   To locate the dowels that join the divider to the caddy ends, first mark their location on the ends of the divider. Dry assemble the parts and transfer these marks to the caddy ends.

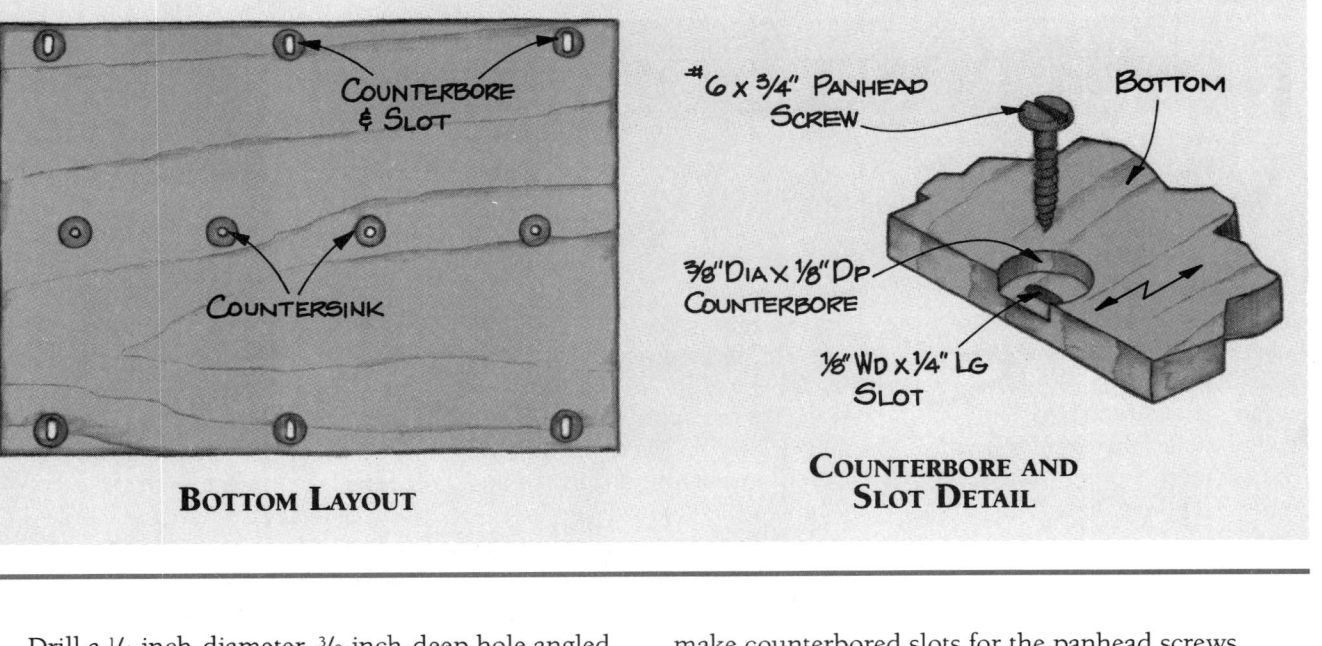

BOTTOM LAYOUT

COUNTERBORE AND SLOT DETAIL

Drill a ¼-inch-diameter, ⅜-inch-deep hole angled at 15 degrees in each caddy end. Then drill a ¼-inch-diameter, ⅝-inch-deep hole in each end of the divider. The dowel holes in the divider should be parallel to the bottom edge.

6 Round the ends and edges of the bottom.

Using a ¼-inch roundover bit and a router, round-over the ends and edges of the bottom. If you wish, you can also round-over the top edges of the divider and the inside edges of the handle cutout. Sand the routed surfaces smooth.

7 Assemble the sides, ends, divider, and bottom.

Finish sand all the parts you've made so far — sides, ends, divider, and bottom. Assemble the divider and ends with glue and dowels. Temporarily tape the parts to hold them in place. Before the glue sets, attach the sides to the ends with glue and splines. Again, use tape to hold the parts together. Wrap band clamps around the assembly and remove the tape. Let the glue dry, then sand the joints clean and flush.

Center the assembly on the bottom and mark the positions of the sides, ends, and divider. Using these guidelines, mark the positions of the screw holes in the bottom.

The bottom is attached to the divider with #6 x ¾-inch flathead wood screws, and to the sides with #6 x ¾-inch panhead screws. As shown on the *Bottom Layout* and the *Counterbore and Slot Detail,* you must

make counterbored slots for the panhead screws. These slots let the bottom expand and contract. To make the slots, first drill ⅜-inch-diameter, ⅛-inch-deep holes. Inside each of these stopped holes, drill two or three ⅛-inch-diameter overlapping holes in a straight line *across* the grain. Clean out the waste between these holes with a small file. Finally, drill and countersink pilot holes for the flathead screws.

Attach the bottom to the assembly with screws. You can glue the bottom to the divider if you wish, but do *not* glue it to the sides or ends.

8 Attach the ledgers and lids.

Carefully measure the distances from the divider to the sides. Then bevel the ends of the ledgers and lids and the *outside* edges of the lids at 15 degrees to match the slope of the sides.

Cut hinge mortises in the adjoining edges of the ledgers and lids. Finish sand the parts, then glue the ledgers to the divider. Let the glue dry.

Install pulls on the lids near the outside edges. Drive a #6 x 1-inch flathead wood screw up through each lid and into the wooden pull. Attach the lids to the ledgers with hinges.

9 Finish the caddy.

Remove the lids from the caddy and the hinges from the lids. Do any necessary touch-up sanding, then apply a finish to all wooden surfaces. The caddy shown is finished with two coats of Danish oil, then polished with paste wax.

9

Bow-Front Sofa Table

Bow-front furniture provides visual relief from conventional flat surfaces. The front surfaces are curved to project several inches out into the room. The tabletop and the front apron of this sofa table, for example, are gently arched so the middle of the piece is 3 inches deeper than the ends.

The bowed front apron on this sofa table was cut and bent with the aid of a table saw. The inside surface of the apron was kerfed to make it flexible, then glued to a curved brace to hold the bow. Although the kerfs weaken the apron slightly, when seen from the front, it appears to be as solid as the straight aprons.

The curved tabletop and front apron are supported by five tapered legs. These tapers were also cut with a table saw, as was most of the joinery that holds the aprons to the legs. In fact, with the exception of drilling a few holes and cutting a few curves, you can make this project almost entirely on the table saw.

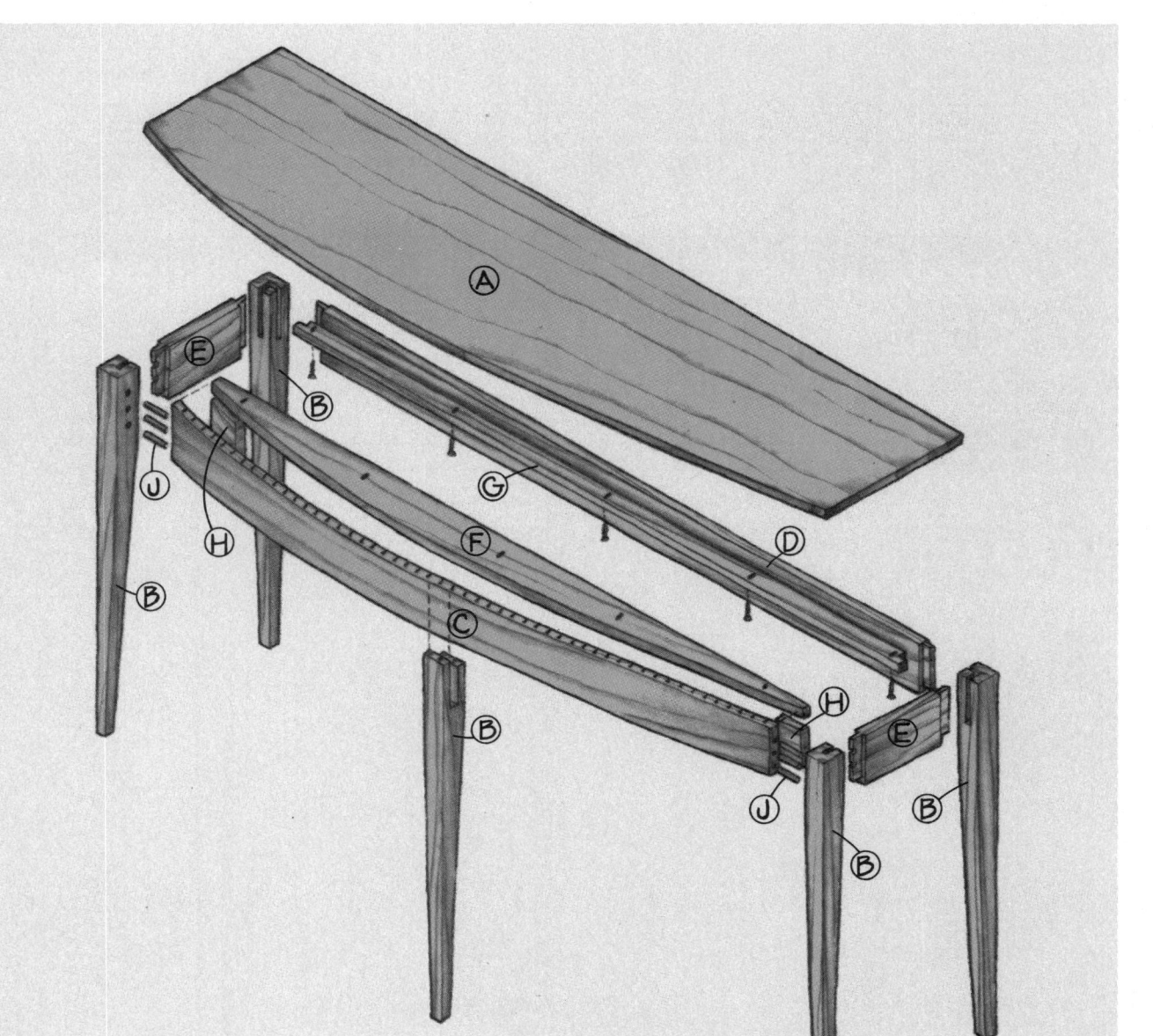

EXPLODED VIEW

MATERIALS LIST (FINISHED DIMENSIONS)

Parts

A. Tabletop   ³/₄″ x 15″ x 60″
B. Legs (5)   1³/₄″ x 1³/₄″ x 29¹/₄″
C. Front apron   ³/₄″ x 4″ x 53″
D. Back apron   ³/₄″ x 4″ x 54¹/₂″
E. Side aprons (2)   ³/₄″ x 4″ x 8¹/₂″

F. Front brace   ³/₄″ x 3″ x 52¹/₂″
G. Back brace   ³/₄″ x 1″ x 53¹/₂″
H. Glue blocks (2)   ³/₄″ x 2″ x 3¹/₄″
J. Dowels (6)   ³/₈″ dia. x 2″

Hardware

#10 x 1¹/₄″ Roundhead wood
  screws (10)
#10 Flat washers (10)

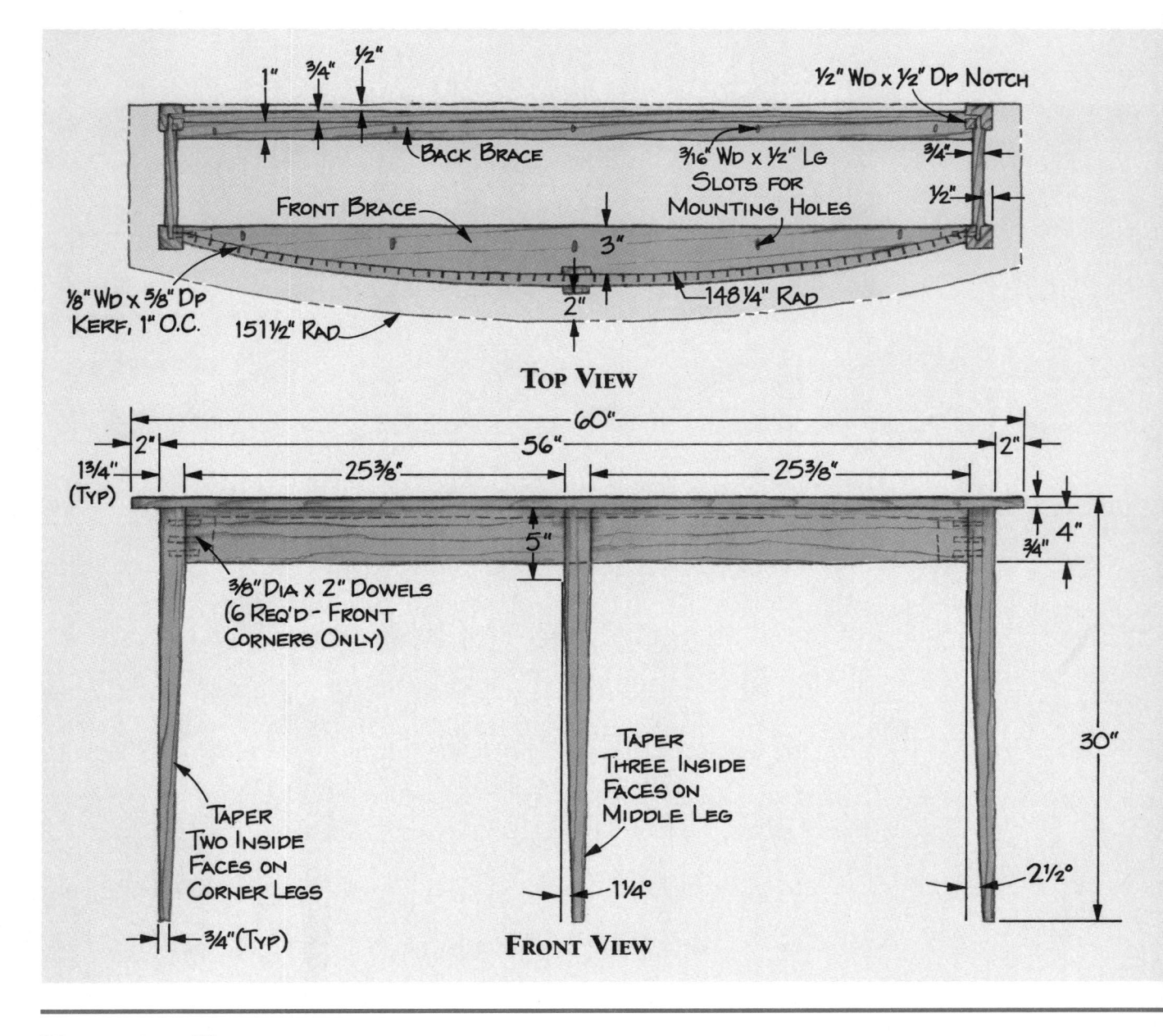

TOP VIEW

FRONT VIEW

PLAN OF PROCEDURE

1 Select the stock and cut the parts to size.
To make this project, you need about 14 board feet of 4/4 (four-quarters) stock, and 5 board feet of 8/4 (eight-quarters) stock. You can use almost any cabinet-grade wood; the sofa table shown is made from curly maple.

Plane the 4/4 stock to ³/4 inch thick and glue up the boards needed to make the tabletop. Plane the 8/4 stock to 1³/4 inches thick. Cut all the parts to the sizes shown in the Materials List *except* the front apron. Cut this about 2 inches longer than specified.

2 Cut the mortises in the legs. Using a dado cutter, cut ¹/4-inch-wide, 1-inch-deep, 3³/4-inch-long stopped grooves in the top ends of the legs. Center the grooves on the legs, as shown in the *Top View*. Adjust the dado to project 1 inch above the saw table and mark the "start point" on the rip fence. Clamp a stop block to the *outfeed* side of the rip fence, 3³/4 inches from the start point. (Refer to *FIGURES 4-17 AND 4-18* on pages 72-73.)

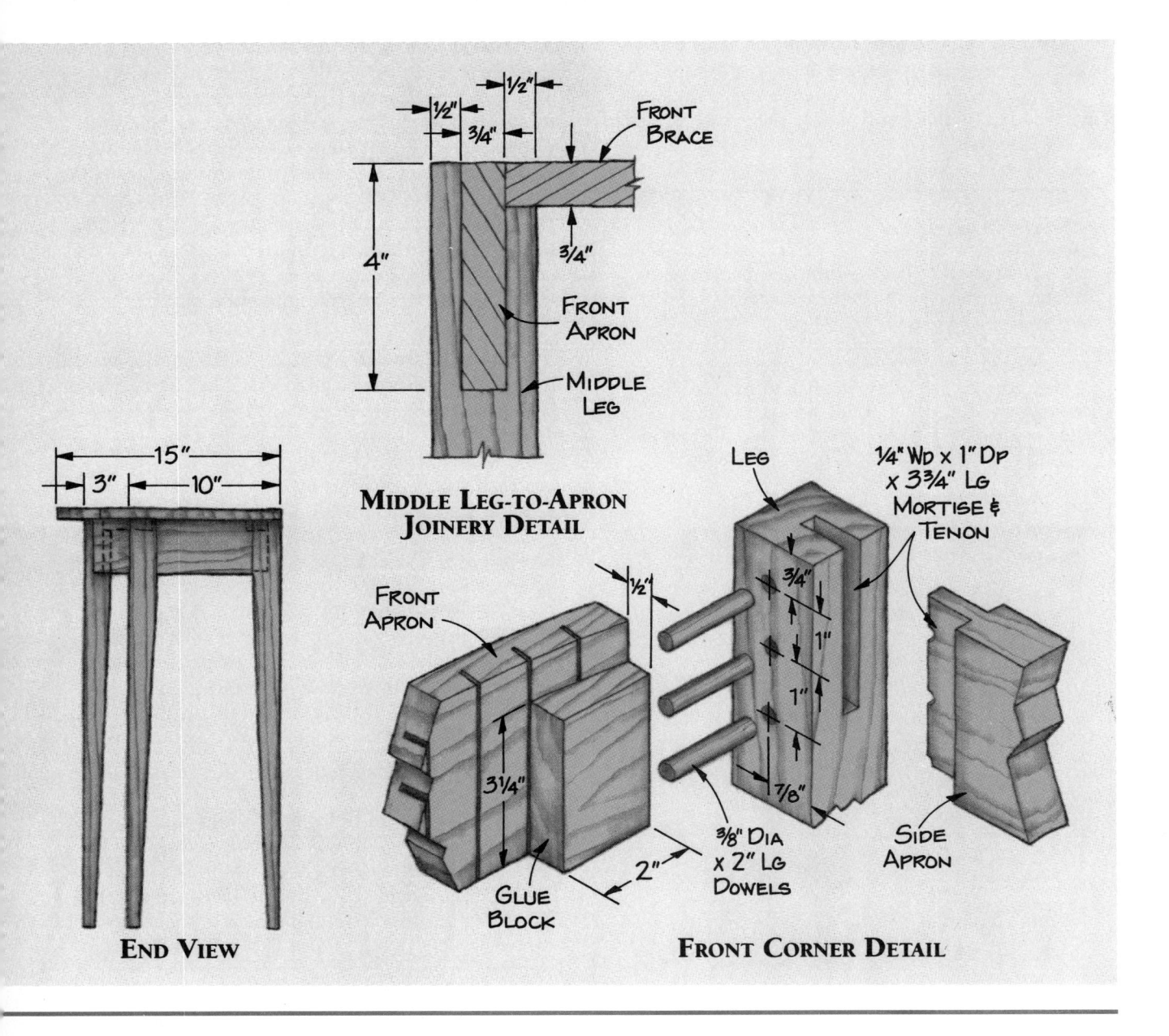

½" ½"
¾"
FRONT
BRACE
4"
¾"
FRONT
APRON
MIDDLE
LEG

**MIDDLE LEG-TO-APRON
JOINERY DETAIL**

15"
3" 10"

END VIEW

FRONT
APRON

½"
¾"
1"
1"
7/8"

3¼"

GLUE
BLOCK

2"

3/8" DIA
x 2" LG
DOWELS

LEG

¼" WD x 1" DP
x 3¾" LG
MORTISE &
TENON

SIDE
APRON

FRONT CORNER DETAIL

Cut *two* stopped grooves in each of the *back* legs (one in each adjacent inside face) and *one* groove in each of the *right* and *left front* legs (in the back inside face only). Square the ends of the grooves with a chisel.

Using a band saw or a coping saw, cut a ¾-inch-wide, 4-inch-long slot in the top end of the front middle leg, as shown in the *Middle-Leg-to-Apron Joinery Detail*. This will create two tenons. Shorten the *back* tenon by ¾ inch, making it just 3¼ inches long.

3 **Cut tenons in the back and side aprons.**
Using a dado cutter, make ¼-inch-thick, 3¾-inch-wide, 1-inch-long tenons on both ends of the back and side aprons. Carefully fit the tenons to the mortises — they should be snug, but not too tight. Cut ¼-inch steps on the *bottom* edges of the tenons; the top edges should remain flush with the top edges of the aprons.

4 **Cut the curved top, front brace, and back brace.** Using a large string compass, mark the 151½-inch-radius on the front edge of the tabletop. Cut the curve with a band saw or saber saw, and sand the sawed edges.

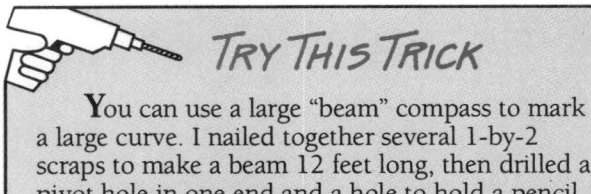

TRY THIS TRICK

You can use a large "beam" compass to mark a large curve. I nailed together several 1-by-2 scraps to make a beam 12 feet long, then drilled a pivot hole in one end and a hole to hold a pencil in the other. My pivot was just a finishing nail driven into a scrap of plywood, and the plywood was weighted down to the floor. I positioned the stock beneath the pencil, checked that the curve would begin and end at the proper point on the stock, then drew the curve.

Also mark the 148¼-inch-radius on the front edge of the front brace. How you cut this curve will depend on what tool you use. If you use a band saw, affix the glue blocks to the bottom face of the brace, flush with the back corners. Let the glue dry, then cut the radius in *both* the brace and the glue blocks. Sand the sawed edges.

If you use a saber saw, cut the radius in the brace, *then* glue the blocks to it. Shape the blocks with a hand plane, or sand the radius in them with a disk sander or belt sander.

Also cut the notches in the ends of the back brace, as shown in the *Top View*.

5 **Drill the slots in the braces.** The top is joined to the table assembly by driving screws through the front and back braces. These screws rest in ³⁄₁₆-inch-wide, ½-inch-long slots so the top can expand and contract. To make the slots, drill several overlapping ³⁄₁₆-inch-diameter holes, then smooth the edges with a small file. **Note:** The locations of these slots are not critical, but they should be evenly spaced every 8 to 12 inches along the length of the braces, as shown in the *Top View*. The long dimension of the slots should be *perpendicular* to the grain direction of the top.

6 **Make the bowed apron.** Using a table saw and either a crosscut or combination blade, cut a series of ⅛-inch-wide, ⅝-inch-deep kerfs in the back face of the front apron. Space the kerfs every 1 inch, as shown in the *Top View*. **Note:** Depending on the species of wood you're using, you may want to cut the kerfs a little shallower or a little deeper. Experiment with a scrap to find the kerf depth that will allow the wood to bend easily without breaking. (Refer to "Kerf Bending" on page 84.)

Test the kerfed apron by bending it along the curved edge of the brace. Do *not* glue it to the brace yet — just make a few test bends. When you are sure the apron will bend without breaking, glue it to the brace and blocks. Let the glue dry, then trim the ends of this assembly square to the back edge of the brace. (*SEE FIGURE 9-1.*)

7 **Drill the dowel holes in the legs and front apron.** The curved apron assembly is attached to the front legs with dowels, as shown in the *Front Corner Detail*. To make the dowel holes, temporarily slide the tenons of the side aprons into their mortises in the front legs. Mark and drill ³⁄₈-inch-diameter, 1-inch-deep dowel holes in the legs with the aprons in place, then remove the aprons.

Place dowel centers in the leg dowel holes and press the ends of the curved apron assembly against the legs. The dowel centers will leave small indentations showing where to drill matching dowel holes in the apron. (*SEE FIGURE 9-2.*) Drill the holes in the apron and test fit the apron to the legs.

8 **Taper the legs.** All the legs taper from 1¾ inches square at the top end to ¾ inch square at the bottom. The four outside legs are single tapered on the two adjacent inside faces. The middle leg is cut with a single taper *and* double taper. The back inside face is single tapered, while the right and left inside faces are double tapered. Each taper begins 5 inches from the top of the leg.

Adjust a *Tapering Jig* to cut a single taper with a run of 1 inch and a rise of 24¼ inches, as shown in "Making Taper Cuts" on page 80. Taper the inside faces of the four outside legs, and the back inside face of the middle leg.

Readjust the jig to make a double taper with a run of ½ inch and a rise of 24¼ inches, and cut a wedge-shaped spacer. Cut one side of the taper in either the left or right inside face of the middle leg. Turn the leg face for face, place the spacer between the leg and the jig, and cut the second side of the double taper. When you've finished, all the legs should be ¾ inch square at the bottom.

9 Assemble the table. Finish sand all the parts of the table, being careful not to round-over any adjoining ends or edges. Glue each of the side aprons to a front and a back leg. Also glue the back brace to the back apron. Let the glue set, then join the leg assemblies to the apron assemblies with glue and dowels. As you clamp the pieces together, make sure the side aprons are square to the back apron.

Let the glued-up dowel joints and mortise-and-tenon joints dry completely, then glue the middle leg to the front apron. Make sure this leg is square to the apron and centered between the front legs.

Once again, let the glue dry. Fasten the tabletop to the braces with roundhead wood screws and flat washers. Tighten the screws so they're snug, but not so tight that they will prevent the top from expanding and contracting.

10 Finish the table. Remove the tabletop and set the screws aside. Do any necessary touch-up sanding, then apply a finish to *all* wooden surfaces, inside and out, top and bottom. (If you neglect to finish the bottom surface of the top, the two sides will absorb and release moisture unevenly, and the top will cup.) Let the finish dry, rub it smooth, and apply a coat of paste wax. Replace the top on the table, being careful not to over-tighten the screws.

9-1 To trim the ends of the curved apron assembly, place it on the table saw with the *straight* edge of the brace resting on the saw table, and the *top* face of the brace against the miter gauge extension. Because this assembly is fairly long, you may want to support the opposite end with a roller stand. Turn on the saw and carefully feed the assembly past the blade, trimming the ends of the apron. When you've finished cutting, the ends of the apron, brace, and glue blocks should all be square to the back edge and top face of the brace.

9-2 Use dowel centers to help locate the dowel holes in the apron assembly. To do so, first lay out and mark the position of the front apron and the dowels on the front legs. Drill dowel holes in the legs and place the centers in them. Carefully position one end of the apron assembly next to a leg and align it with the layout marks. Press the two parts together firmly. The dowel centers will leave small indentations, showing where to drill matching holes in the apron. Repeat for the other end of the apron.

INDEX

Note: Page references in *italic* indicate photographs or illustrations.
Boldface references indicate charts or tables.

T

Table, *3*
  bow-front sofa, 116–121, *116*
  extensions, *3*
  insert, *3, 58, 65*
  rolling, *16,* 42
  size, 8
  sliding, *15, 42, 92*
  testing for flatness, *8*
Table saw
  accessories, 14–17
  choosing, 3–9
  invention of, 2
  maintenance, 37, *38*
  materials, 7
  miniature, 5
  parts, *3*
Tall fence extension, *50, 52,* 54, *79*
Tapering, *80, 81, 82,* 120, 121
  jig, *81, 82,* 83
Teeth, saw blade, 9, *10*
  bimetal, 10
  carbide, 10
  grind, 10, **13**
  number of, 14
  profile, 10, *11*
  set, *9,* 10, *11*
Template, pattern sawing, 83, *84*
Tenoning jig, *73*
Tenons, 72, *73,* 108, 119
Testing
  blade tilt, *25, 61*
  dado setup, *68*
  flatness of table, *8*
  miter gauge angle, *24, 25, 59, 61*
Thin-kerf blade, 12, **13**
Tilt, blade, 23, *24,* 60, 61
Tilt crank, *3*
Tilting-table saw, 5
Trimmers, *67*
Triple chip grind, 11, **13**
T-slots, *9*

U

Universal motor, 8

W

Wide dadoes, *71*
Wobble dado, *16, 67*

Z

Zero-clearance table insert, *32, 58, 65*

WOODWORKING GLOSSARY

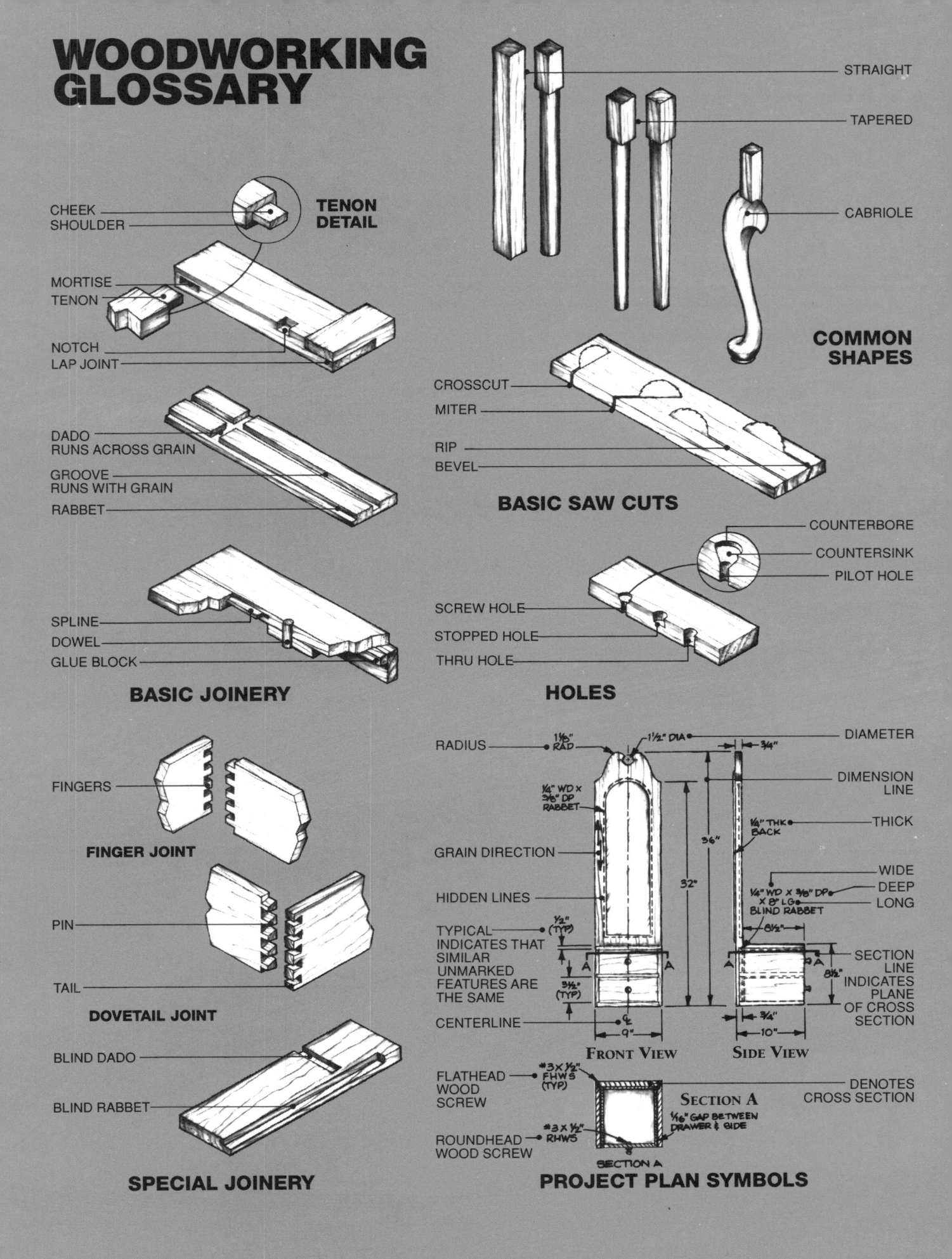

TENON DETAIL
- CHEEK
- SHOULDER

- MORTISE
- TENON

- NOTCH
- LAP JOINT

- DADO RUNS ACROSS GRAIN
- GROOVE RUNS WITH GRAIN
- RABBET

BASIC JOINERY
- SPLINE
- DOWEL
- GLUE BLOCK

FINGER JOINT
- FINGERS

DOVETAIL JOINT
- PIN
- TAIL

SPECIAL JOINERY
- BLIND DADO
- BLIND RABBET

COMMON SHAPES
- STRAIGHT
- TAPERED
- CABRIOLE

BASIC SAW CUTS
- CROSSCUT
- MITER
- RIP
- BEVEL

HOLES
- COUNTERBORE
- COUNTERSINK
- PILOT HOLE
- SCREW HOLE
- STOPPED HOLE
- THRU HOLE

- RADIUS
- 1⅛" RAD
- 1½" DIA
- ¾"
- DIAMETER
- ¼" WD X ³⁄₁₆" DP RABBET
- DIMENSION LINE
- ⅛" THK BACK
- THICK
- 36"
- 32"
- GRAIN DIRECTION
- ¼" WD X ³⁄₁₆" DP X 8" LG BLIND RABBET
- WIDE
- DEEP
- LONG
- HIDDEN LINES
- 8½"
- SECTION LINE INDICATES PLANE OF CROSS SECTION
- 8½"
- TYPICAL INDICATES THAT SIMILAR UNMARKED FEATURES ARE THE SAME
- ½" (TYP)
- 3½" (TYP)
- CENTERLINE
- 9"
- ¾"
- 10"

FRONT VIEW   **SIDE VIEW**

- FLATHEAD WOOD SCREW
- #3 X ½" FHWS (TYP)
- DENOTES CROSS SECTION
- **SECTION A**
- ¹⁄₁₆" GAP BETWEEN DRAWER & SIDE
- ROUNDHEAD WOOD SCREW
- #3 X ½" RHWS
- SECTION A

PROJECT PLAN SYMBOLS